Contents

*For those writers who have attempted to put into words
the true essence of hunting and fishing*

Foreword

This is no textbook on hunting and fishing. There are dozens of those. Essentially, this is a personal book about the most memorable of my own outdoor sporting experiences—in this country and over much of the world. For it has been my good fortune to travel to many of the best game and fish areas of the world, and to partake of the ultimate sporting experiences they offer. The only "how-to" parts of the book are the tips following the chapters and the appendix material. In these I have tried to list information which may be of help to the reader or sportsman who might wish to visit the same area and try for the same game or fish.

The reader will find little social commentary in this book. I have hunted since I was a small boy, and will continue to do so as long as I am able. The question of hunting is a moral one and can only be decided by the individual. It has been established beyond any question as a sport practiced by some 20 million Americans and uncounted millions in other parts of the world. It is a tradition as old as man; it is also a valuable wildlife management tool. I have no quarrel with the person who has intelligently thought out the issues and chooses not to hunt. I only ask that I not be judged morally by the emotional and uninformed.

Jack Samson

Preface

As so many of our generation who have come to write of the outdoors, Jack Samson and I were imprinted with a love of forest and lake, river, mountain, and sea, and all creatures therein by early experiences; and if we possessed some writing talent we could only dream, at first, of making a living by telling others of the glories we had seen and experienced. There were only a handful of major magazines (as there are today) and few big-circulation newspapers with space or inclination for such pursuits; and, realizing that little mouths had to be fed, we drifted into various callings as general reporters, editors, teachers, or public relations men. (Some of us also had a fling at a novel, a play, or poetry, but those fires, in most instances, were slowly extinguished by the cold drizzle of advancing years.)

Thus it was that we found ourselves, in our twenties, thirties, and forties, returning to our first love only on vacations and weekends.

Jack, with whom I have spent many happy days fishing and hunting across much of the globe, followed such a route. A reporter for two wire services and a foreign correspondent for one of them, a Nieman fellow, a flier for General Chennault in World War II, Jack continued to hunt and fish whenever he could, to do an occasional free-lance magazine piece, and, during one period, an outdoor column for the Associated Press.

During all these years, his writing skills and his knowledge of the natural world increased; and when he went to *Field & Stream,* first as managing editor, and shortly thereafter as editor, he was prepared for his role. And, equally important, he had mellowed, had reached a point where a giant blue marlin hooked and fought for several hours, then lost, was just as pleasing as one in the boat; where one Atlantic salmon gleaming on the wet stones along some great river was as good as two; where four black ducks flying out of range at sunset were as exciting as a brace in the blind.

The result of this happy mix of experience, maturity, and sensitivity shines brightly in *The Sportsman's World.* It is good, clean, hard, and oftentimes inspired writing.

There is no one I know who can capture the essence of big-game fishing as neatly as Jack Samson. In the striped marlin story out of Ecuador, one grows to know not only the fish, but the men who go after them. There is humor, empathy, excellent descriptions of the angling, and a sense of tradition and history—a splendid piece.

There are equally perceptive accounts from all over the world: Atlantic salmon in Quebec, Iceland, and Scotland; cape buffalo in Africa; antelope and elk in Wyoming and Montana; bass fishing in Japan; trout and salmon in Alaska. Of unusual value are the end-of-chapter notes which include names of outfitters, guides, transportation, accommodations, and local regulations.

The variety is compelling and the information solid, but variety and information alone would not be enough. What makes the book most special is the talent, insight, and discipline of the man. *The Sportsman's World* is a shining example of what "outdoor writing" can be at its best.

Nelson Bryant
Wood, Field and Stream
The New York Times

THE
SPORTSMAN'S
WORLD

He swung off the bicycle and began to push it slowly between two walls of tangled willows. An occasional frozen puddle shattered like crystal underfoot. In the tangled underbrush on both sides, the first faint, sleepy sounds of awakening birds began. It was becoming easier to make out the road ahead, and he sped up a little as he thought of the long walk to the special sandbar.

When the dirt track finally ended in a dense clump of matted willow, he wheeled the bicycle into the undergrowth and leaned it against the rough, silver-gray bark of a cottonwood. He carefully unwrapped the shotgun from its canvas covering and, trying to keep his fingers from shaking with excitement, fitted the barrel to the stock.

The wooden fore-grip snapped into place with a sharp sound that made him wince in the early-morning stillness. He fumbled in one pocket and brought out a shell. Making sure the hammer was forward, he dropped the shell into the breach and carefully closed the gun. Hefting its weight in both hands, he grinned and made his way to the faint path that wound toward the river.

The trail, little-known to most, wound through the backwater sloughs and tangled tule beds for perhaps a mile until it ended at a wooded peninsula jutting a few hundred feet into the river. The boy knew almost every foot of the trail. In spring it skirted hidden ponds, lush with duckweed and overhung with thick growths of cattails. Here he had searched for spring peepers, stalked painted turtles, glinting the summer sun from half-sunken logs, and had listened to the mutterings of nesting ducks deep in the weed beds. The still waters, that in spring broke to the V of a swimming muskrat, were frozen now, and the cattails, tan and brittle, bowed in the grip of fall.

A quarter-hour of trotting along the trail brought him to the peninsula and the tiny blind built on the outer end of the narrow sandbar.

During the last week he had lain on the wooded spit of land, scouting the best place to build a blind. After watching the ragged flights of mallards, the rocketing bunches of teal, and the formations of baldpates and pintails sweep around the bend of the muddy river, he had picked the sandbar. For the last two days, he had dug in the wet sand and had hauled limbs and reeds.

Now, as he lowered himself into the shelter, he was glad of the reed floor. His feet were already cold from the damp trail.

Sky, behind the silhouetted mountains to the east, showed rose-colored and gold as he knelt and carefully lined up his six extra shells in front of the blind. He leaned the gun against a limb support and hunched down in the blind, looking upriver to where he knew the first ducks would appear. On the other side of the slow-moving water, a great blue heron stalked down the bank, pausing every few steps to peer rigidly into the water ahead. Off to the right of the blind, several red-winged blackbirds fluttered among the dry cattails, their rusty-gate notes carrying clearly on the morning air. He hunched against the wall of the blind and tried to keep his teeth from chattering.

It was the dim sound of two shots, coming from a couple of miles upriver, that started his pulse pounding. He carefully eased the gun into the crook of his arm and watched the next bend of the river. Several minutes passed before the black specks came into view. There were half a dozen birds in the flight, their wing beats winking against the dark trees of the river's edge.

Mallards, he thought and began to feel himself tremble. He carefully eased the gun barrel beyond the edge of the blind and softly cocked the hammer as the flock began to swing in toward him as it cut short across the river bend. His right leg, bent under him, was shaking as the flight reached the edge of the sandbar and started to pass to his left.

They were about 40 yards away when he rose and pointed the long barrel at the big drake in the lead. The recoil slammed him back against the blind, the flock flared up and to the right, and no bird fell. Recovering his balance, he broke the gun open and grimly shoved another shell into the chamber. As he swung back toward the flock it was well out of range. For a second, he stared after the departing flight. His eyes watered as much from the recoil of the gun as from disappointment. Rubbing his shoulder thoughtfully, he again crouched in the blind. His heartbeat was still loud in his ears.

No more birds came downriver in the next half-hour. The first long fingers of morning sunlight reached across the river and touched the tops of the tallest trees.

His next chance at ducks came and went on the whistling wings of a flock of greenwinged teal. He heard the sound of wings overhead and was on his feet, but by the time he had spotted the flight, they were several hundred yards downriver and flashing high above the far bank.

The sun's rays had reached the blind and felt good on his cold hands. He spread them out and wriggled his fingers. The gun metal had been as cold as the axe blade when he chopped wood before breakfast on camping trips. It was very quiet, and he began to feel comfortable. A marsh hawk quartered across the river above him, skimming over the willows to his left. Its white rump-patch gleamed against the dark branches along the water's edge.

He never knew what made him turn and look downriver. Later he thought perhaps he had heard the rhythmical "whoosh, whoosh" of wings even then, or maybe it was simply instinct. All he knew for certain was that suddenly there was the sound of great wings above the blind. A dozen huge Canada geese had come silently upriver, only about 20 yards above the water. There was no sound except wings beating.

He grabbed the heavy gun and twisted in the blind. Several of the geese had already passed over him by the time he thrust the barrel upward, pointed squarely at a huge gander directly above him, and pulled the trigger. The bone buttplate cracked against the top of his shoulder, the giant bird dipped a wing, half-rolled, and went into a loose spiral over the blind. The boy heard a shout as the big honker slapped into the water 30 feet in front of him. It was several seconds before he realized that he had done the shouting.

He told the entire story. It wasn't until the end, when he got to the part about fishing the bird out of the river, that his words began to tumble over themselves. His father sat quietly and watched his face. When the story was finished there was a long silence. Then his father stood up. He gently laid the bird back in the basket and, turning, rumpled the boy's hair. His voice was gruff. "Let's get out of those wet clothes. You better get some hot breakfast in you. Can't go duck hunting tomorrow if you catch cold." He started up the steps, then paused. "Think I'll call Harry," he grinned.

The boy stood in the driveway a few seconds before entering the kitchen door. He looked again at the goose and scuffed his feet awkwardly. The high sun felt warm on his still-damp shirt. He suddenly grinned and wondered if there had ever before been such a beautiful morning.

1.
The Black Marlin of Hawaii

I had caught a couple of sailfish off Miami while stationed at 36th St. Airport during World War II. There were a number of us in my antisubmarine squadron who liked to fish, and the six-week celestial-navigation course the Army Air Corps insisted all air crews take did not use up all our time. Some of us managed to get out to the Tamiami Canal for bass on a fly rod and on other days chartered sportfishing boats to go out into the Gulf Stream. I don't remember being particularly impressed with catching sails then—perhaps because the excitement of being in the big war overshadowed everything else.

But I do remember the first marlin I caught, and it was a long way from Florida. A good many years later—after a stint as a wire-service reporter for United Press in the Korean War—I was en route to the States for a welcome leave. I had gotten a bellyful of the big Pan Am stratocruiser which seemed to drone on forever from Tokyo to Wake Island and then to Honolulu. It was during a forced stopover for repairs in Hawaii that I decided to tour the islands just savoring the hot sun and lush vegetation on the big island. I came to the town of Kailua-Kona and walked out to look at a fleet of charter boats. My plane wasn't going to leave until the next day.

It was about ten in the morning and most of the boats were out, but there was one old wooden Owens lashed to the pilings. The skipper had just come up from the open hatch with an oily rag and was wiping his hands. His Hawaiian mate was asleep in the shade of the battered canvas top. The skipper looked like a refugee from the *African Queen*—a real Bogart type.

"I don't suppose," he said, eyeing me as if I were a Coast Guard inspector, "that you might want to go out fishin'."

I looked at the old boat. It looked to be about 32 feet.

"How come you couldn't get a charter this morning?" I said.

"Engine got cranky. I needed a new head gasket. Took me a couple of hours to fix it."

I noticed the outriggers were in good shape, the battered fighting chair was rigged with a sturdy harness, and the boat generally looked as though it had been well cared for. A couple of stout rods held old but shiny Ocean City reels.

"What you charge for the day?" I asked.

The skipper looked at the bay for a moment. "Normally eighty bucks," he said, "but since you won't get a whole day, fifty."

I grunted and leaned against a post.

"What's the sea like?"

"This side of the island is always in the lee. It's only a few miles out."

"What we after?"

I noticed the mate had opened his eyes and was slowly getting up.

"Marlin," said the skipper. "Stripes, blacks, and blues. Might pick up some sails, maybe a wahoo. Plenty of big dolphin. Never can tell."

"When can you leave?" I asked.

By this time the mate was busily polishing the brass on the old compass.

"How's two minutes strike you?" said the skipper. "She's fueled up."

"Where's all your bait?"

"Aboard. You might pick up some beer if you've a thirst. There's ice aboard and enough canned stuff to make a lunch."

I glanced at the rental car parked near the end of the dock. "The car all right?"

"Nobody will bother it," said the skipper. "Hop aboard. Kioshi here will get a case of beer while we get the lines off. I got some old clothes in case you don't want to get those fancy slacks all covered with billfish blood." That did it.

By the time the Hawaiian-Japanese mate got back with a case of American canned beer, the skipper had the engine turning over and all lines cast but a stern and bow line looped over a piling. I had slipped on a pair of faded suntan pants and an old T-shirt from a forward locker. My feet slid a bit inside a pair of ragged old boat sneakers, but I couldn't have cared less. It took us very little time to get out of the harbor and into blue water. The mate was all over the boat—getting the outriggers out, rigging wire leaders, and putting beer on ice. By the time we hit the fishing area, he had made me a corned beef and mustard sandwich and handed me a cold beer. The seas were only about two feet in the lee of the big island, and the rugged coast to the east loomed mistily in the noon sunlight. I could see several boats north of us, all trolling.

The mate placed both big rods in the gunwale holders and checked the strike drags. The lines looked heavy, and I suspect now—since that long-past day—that they were braided linen. One was slightly smaller than the other, and I would guess that they were 24-thread and 39-thread lines—about equal to our modern 80-pound and 130-pound lines. The reason I say that is that the wire leaders were both 30 feet long and the International Game Fish Association required leaders that long for the big lines. Also you never know in Hawaiian waters when you will encounter a big marlin. It was considered smart to use the heavy tackle on all big-game fish. After all, it was far better to catch a 30-pound wahoo on 130-pound line than to lose a 600-pound blue marlin on 15-thread line—about equal to our present-day 50-pound-test lines.

Kioshi came out of the cabin with a couple of strange-looking plugs, about 12 or 15 inches long, and laid them on top of the ice chest.

"Teaser plugs?" I asked, remembering the teasers used off Miami and Mazatlán for sailfish.

"No sir," he said, handing me one. "We use these to catch the billfish here. Dead bait don't work too good off these islands."

I looked at the one he had handed me. It was heavy, and looked as though it had been made from a combination of wood and chrome. The face was flat and was made of the shiny metal, with a hole drilled through the entire length of both the metal and the wood. The body might have been made from a broomstick handle, and a length of cable leader ran through the entire thing. The cable looked like it might have a test strength of about 500 pounds. One end held a swivel to be fastened to the wire leader and the other held a hook of about 10/0 size. The tail end of the plug was festooned with a skirt made from lengths of red rubber. I later found out the skirt was made from an inner tube. The plug slid free on the leader, and the single hook was not fastened to the plug. The other plug was a little smaller and was rigged with a single hook of about 8/0 size and carried a skirt of both red and green rubber. Both plugs were painted—mine blue with a red and black eye and the smaller one white with a black and blue eye set well back on the wooden body.

The mate fastened both plugs to the wire lines and ran them out and back of the boat on the port and starboard outriggers—where they dived and churned in the slight chop of the blue sea. Each time they dived beneath the surface they left a trail of bubbles 15 or 20 feet long before they surfaced and gulped enough air in the slanted and curved face and hollow core of the body to make more bubbles. I watched them for about five minutes as we droned along the coast, idly wondering when the skipper was going to throttle back to trolling speed. Finally I nudged the mate, who was honing down the point of a large flying gaff.

"When do we start trolling?" I shouted over the rumble of the engine.

"We trolling now," he shouted back. "Not like States. Eight to ten knots here is trolling speed."

I thought back to the Florida and Mexico fishing. The speed must have been no faster than four or five knots.

"Isn't that too fast for billfish?" I asked.

"Maybe in States," the mate grinned. "Not here. Billfish here hit these because mad. Not hungry."

I settled back in the fighting chair. What the hell, I thought. When in Rome. Besides, all I would be out was fifty bucks, and just getting out on the ocean for half a day was worth that. Besides, maybe we would luck into a wahoo, which I knew would hit fast lures.

I was dozing in the warm sunlight an hour or so later when the captain came down from his bridge and turned the wheel over to the mate.

"Mind if I have one of your beers?" he asked, reaching into the chest.

I nodded. "I couldn't drink a case if I wanted to," I said. "What's this business of trolling at eight knots for billfish? They don't hit balao baits or rigged mackerel at this speed in the States."

The skipper swallowed half a can of beer and wiped his mouth with the back of a salt-encrusted hand.

"They also don't catch blue marlin in the thousand-pound class and blacks close to two thousand." He smiled. "These monsters ain't interested in tidbits. When they want to eat they pick up a yellowfin of a hundred pounds or better. Ever try to troll a hundred-pound tuna?"

I shook my head.

"Well," he said, finishing off the can and reaching for another, "they mostly only take trolled baits that either make them mad or make them curious. That's why we pull these gadgets. They will take trolled live bait sometimes—bonito and the like—but it's too much trouble catching the bait."

"What do you make them of?" I asked. "Or do you buy them?"

"Oh, I buy a couple from some other skippers who like to make them, but mostly I make my own. Kioshi here likes to make them, too. The metal heads come from all sorts of stuff—like chrome bathroom towelracks and that sort of thing."

I watched the starboard plug jump and splash about 30 feet astern and the other doing the same thing about 60 feet back.

"Why the eyes painted on it?" I asked.

He laughed. "Hell, I don't know. Half the captains have some theory or other about it—like how far back they should be placed. But I'll tell you one thing: it's damn seldom a billfish hits one of these plugs when it doesn't have eyes!"

I grunted and opened another cold beer.

Another hour passed, and the mate came down and hauled in the plugs. He switched one and put on a black plug with a silver head and large white eyes set far back on the body. Then he tossed it back to ride as the far-out port bait.

I was rubbing some suntan lotion on the bridge of my nose a few minutes later when the mate let out a yell that froze me upright in the chair.

"Aiieee!" he shouted. "Here he comes!"

I barely had time to wipe the lotion off my palms on the slacks when the line snapped from the outrigger clip on the starboard side and the plug disappeared in an explosion of spray. I grabbed the rod, and the mate shaded his eyes to look astern. I could already feel the fish taking out line, but being new at big-game fishing, I waited.

"Hit him! Dammit, hit him!" The captain screamed from the bridge. "He's hooked!" I leaned back and struck as hard as I could.

"Not that hard, goddammit!" the skipper shouted. "You want to break the rod?" I barely heard him because the water burst open astern and a multicolored, blunt-headed torpedo took off across the choppy surface in a dazzling series of jumps. "Mahimahi!" yelled Kioshi. "A big one! Aiieee, look at him go!"

It was a beautiful dolphin, I knew *that* much. But it was the first time I had ever heard it called mahimahi. It put up a fine fight but was no match for the big rod or heavy thread line. It took about ten minutes to subdue it, mostly because I wanted to savor the fun of fighting it. Kioshi finally gaffed it, and we guessed its weight at about 40 pounds.

"Make a good meal," he said as he slid it into the fish box. I smiled and sat back down in the chair. As far as I was concerned, the day was already a success.

"Sorry about that strike," I said to the skipper, who grimaced but didn't smile. "I guess I got a little excited."

"Well," he finally shouted down, "don't worry about it. Everybody gets excited. I didn't know what it was. You couldn't have broken that rod on a dolphin, at least not on *that* fish, but it might have been a big marlin and those damn rods are expensive. Break one and there goes my profit for the day. Kioshi!" He waved at the mate. "Take the wheel a minute."

He climbed down and took one of the rods from the holder. He jerked the line from the clip and held the rod parallel to the horizon and pointed straight back. He eased off the drag until the spool was turning slowly.

I dimly remember—through the pain of my arms and back—seeing the double line and big brass swivel come up several times and catching a glimpse of the wire leader. But each time the fighting fish would thrash across the surface, and the mate would have to let go of the line.

Finally there was the blur of a gaff, the sound of the skipper landing on the deck to help, and the shower of water over me as the marlin was gaffed again and held against the side of the hull. I didn't know enough to help tail-rope the fish and just sat in the chair, exhausted, as the two hauled the fish over the starboard gunwale. It landed with a slithering thump on the deck, and the mate whacked it several times on the forehead with a wooden club.

And after that everything was a melee of slaps on the back, handshakes, whoops, grins, shouts, and the headiest feeling I had ever felt, up to that day, in my entire life.

And there was suddenly a need to lean over the side—my stomach wrenching and the bitter taste of bile and beer in my mouth. When I stopped and slid back to the deck, the skipper slapped me on the back and poured a cold can of beer over my head.

"Don't worry about it, son," he shouted. "Nothing to be ashamed of. You whipped hell out of that fish, but there ain't anybody who whips a black marlin in this world that's won an easy fight!"

And a black marlin it was. Not a Pacific blue as were most of the ones caught off Kailua-Kona, nor a striped marlin. It wasn't a big fish, now that I know how much black marlin weigh. It was 378 pounds, the dockmaster said later. I couldn't have cared less.

My arms, legs, and back were sore for a week, and I couldn't get out of bed for days without groaning. But that fish did something to me, and I really am not sure yet whether I am blessed or cursed because of it.

It made me an incurable big-game fisherman, that magnificent black marlin. May God rest its fighting soul.

Tips on Fishing in Hawaii . . .

A cliche of Hawaiian tourism promotion is the seemingly mandatory photo of a grinning tourist, rod in hand, posed beside some marine behemoth he or she has presumably wrested from the Pacific's depths. Actually, such a photo represents fact more than it reflects a tourist hustle.

Big-game fishing in Hawaiian waters, particularly off the Kona coast on the western side of the island of Hawaii, is a productive enterprise. Anywhere from one to twenty or more miles off Kona, anglers stand a good chance of tying into blue and striped marlin, dolphin, skipjack, yellowfin tuna, and other big-game species, including black marlin.

Most of the fishing done off Kona is out of the Kailua, a port that serves as home base for an extensive fleet of charter sportfishing boats. There is a commercial airport nearby, so getting to Kailua presents no problem. Most of the boats are well equipped, with tackle and bait included in the charter price. Anglers are expected to provide their own chow, but arrangements can be made to have food and ice included in the overall price. Rates vary, depending upon the size of the boat and the luxuriousness of its accommodations, but you can figure on spending between $150 to $200-plus per day.

Because the Hawaiians themselves are great sportfishermen, and a good run of marlin, say, will find them scrambling with tourists for charter boat space, any arrangements will have to be made well in advance. Travel agents and airlines can help, but your best bet is to contact the sportfishing fleets directly.

Along the Kona coast, for example, there's an organization called the Kona Charter Skippers Association (P.O. Box 806, Kailua-Kona, Hawaii 96740), and a letter of request should bring you all the information you need. There are similar organizations in and around most of the other sportfishing ports. Also, a letter to Hawaii's Fish and Game Division (see Appendix B) can get you started in the right direction.

The fishing in Hawaiian waters is good almost all year, so don't feel you have to be locked into a certain season. There are days, however, when prevailing trade winds drive the seas pretty hard, making the going rough. This is a situation your charter boat skipper will play by ear and experience, so if he decides to scrub the run, don't complain; the following day there might not be a ripple on the water, and you'll have one of the great adventures of your life, even if you don't spot a fish. Since most marlin in these waters are jumped within a few miles of shore, a zero-fish day will still give you lots of opportunity to admire some of the most beautiful scenery on earth.

If your vacation schedule is flexible, and you've got marlin in mind, aim for some time between late June and November. This isn't absolutely necessary, as mentioned, but the odds at that time are probably a little more in your favor.

A big industry in Hawaii is tourism, so accommodations are not hard to come by if you make arrangements far enough in advance. The prices of certain foods (many of which have to be imported) may seem high, but if you are on a tight budget, you probably shouldn't be thinking about Hawaii in the first place. On the other hand, the possibility of battling it out with a 900-pound marlin may tempt you to chuck it all and become a beach bum. A man could do worse.

2.
Wyoming: The One-Shot Antelope

Winter comes early to the rolling tan prairies of Wyoming, and the winds are chilly after the sun sinks behind the Wind River Range to the west. The aspens and alders have already turned a flaming gold and red by mid-September along the twisting bed of the Sweetwater River, Beaver Creek, and Wind River near the small town of Lander in the west-central part of the state.

The same cutting winds shake telephone wires running along highways leading to places with historic Oregon Trail names such as South Pass, Bridger, Gros Ventre, Sheridan, Clark, Powder River, North Platte, Big Horn, Crazy Woman Creek, Saddlestring, and Dead Indian Peak.

And as they have done since before man first hunted the great country southeast of the Grand Tetons, the chief, medicine men, braves, women, and children of the Shoshone Indian nation gather around campfires for the ceremony of the hunt, praying that there will be no hunger in the lodges of their people in the approaching winter. But it is no longer just the Shoshone who hunt the swift pronghorn antelope in this starkly beautiful land. They are joined by the white men who came to Wyoming an instant ago in Shoshone time—a mere century and a half—hardly enough moons to make one a part of the land.

But these men come for the same reason the Indians once gathered around the campfires: to be blessed, for they will leave the next morning before dawn to stalk America's swiftest big-game animal.

Lander, Wyoming, has become the annual site of a unique hunt that is peculiarly American and yet known to sportsmen around the world—the One-Shot Antelope Hunt. The hunt, from a modest start more than three decades ago, has grown in reputation until today expert riflemen from every state in the United States and many foreign nations vie for an invitation to be a member of one of the six three-man teams competing. To win the coveted one-shot trophy the hunter must kill his pronghorn with one bullet blessed by the Shoshone chief and his medicine men. If he misses, he can never try again—although he automatically qualifies as a "past shooter," allowing him to return annually to target shoot and mix with the hunters. But he can never again enter the one-shot event.

I was fortunate enough to be chosen as a member of an outdoor editors' team. Heading the team was Nelson Bryant, outdoor editor of *The New York Times* and an excellent rifle shot. The other team member was also a fine shot with both rifle and shotgun, Roger Latham, outdoor editor of the *Pittsburgh Press.*

We were competing with some of the finest rifle shots in America, from teams representing Wyoming, Colorado, and Tennessee, to a team of three astronauts led by moonwalker Jim Lovell and composed of astronauts Joe Engle and Jack Swigart. The state teams were captained by the Governors of their respective states: Wyoming (the host team), by Governor Stan Hathaway; Colorado, by Governor John Love; and Tennessee, by Governor Winfield Dunn. The international team was captained by Baron de Beaufort, and the three other members (one alternate) were Paul Eissenvenn, general manager of KLM Royal Dutch Airlines; Martin Shroder; and Walli Mohamed, a professional big-game guide from Kenya.

The hunters who had come from so many far places were to hunt an animal that is unique. The pronghorn is the only North American big-game animal which has no relatives anywhere in the world.

Elk and deer are not only members of the same family in this country, but are also related to various members of the deer family found in other countries. The bighorn sheep is not only related to the Dall sheep of Canada and Alaska, but to domestic sheep as well.

However, the American pronghorn has no relatives. Although it is called an antelope, it doesn't fit into that family and has no relationship to antelope of other countries.

Once, many thousands of years ago, the pronghorn family was big and varied. Many kinds of pronghorns lived in the western part of North America. Today's pronghorn is the family's only survivor. Why the pronghorn's cousins all died remains a mystery. Perhaps they were unable to survive the changes nature made in their surroundings—changes in climate and food supplies.

Today the pronghorn antelope lives in parts of fourteen Western states, in the southern tip of two Canadian provinces, and in northern Mexico. Wyoming probably has more antelope than any other Western state.

Nature has equipped the pronghorn for a life on burning deserts and frigid plateaus. The hairs on its coat are hollow. By flexing certain muscles, the pronghorn can hold its hairs at different angles—flat and overlapping to keep out the cold, or erect to allow circulation of the air when it is hot.

The pronghorn is the animal kingdom's second fastest runner. They have been clocked at 60 mph, even 70 for short, brief spurts. A speed of 50 mph is not uncommon, and 30 to 40 mph is not in the least unusual for this animal.

The pronghorn's vision is extremely keen and its hearing good. Standing on a

prairie knoll, the pronghorn can spot an object, particularly one that's moving, miles away.

In Wyoming, the pronghorn's life begins in May or June. Twins are common from the second time a doe gives birth. On the first day of its life, the 4- or 5-pound fawn is wobbly on its legs, but development is rapid. By the second day, it can run awkwardly. By the third, it is hard to catch, and on the fourth day, the fawn can outrun a man. By the fifth day, signs of a synchronized gait are obvious. By the sixth day, the pronghorn can run smoothly.

And so it was that, after a day of touring the spectacular country around Lander; after another day of watching the past shooters compete for trophies at targets, both still and moving; of sighting in our rifles on a range; of being made a blood brother of the Shoshone tribe; of being given a special antelope-skin medicine pouch for luck; and of having one of my 100-grain .257 magnum softpoint shells passed through the hands of Shoshone Chief Darwin St. Clair and his medicine men and handed solemnly back to me, blessed with luck, I found myself sitting on a log gazing into a roaring fire and listening to the beat of a Shoshone drum.

Other shooters sat near me, and as I looked at them, the pitch blackness of the night behind them, a chilling wind knifing through their clothing, and the light from the fire playing on their faces, I suspected they felt much the same as I did. Earlier, when the blood brother ceremony was performed by drawing a sharp obsidian spear point across the palm of my hand, leaving a line of Mercurochrome used to represent real blood, I had felt a bit awkward. Perhaps it might have been the feeling that the ceremony was a bit too contrived or that we were really all too old to be playing little boys' games. But now, with the voice beyond the fire telling of the origins of the hunt dance, of the customs of the ancient Shoshone, of the reason for the good luck charms, and of the blessing of arrows, spear points, and, later, guns and bullets, I no longer had that disappointed feeling.

In its place had come a sensation that I had been here before. Nelson Bryant later confessed to the same feelings. There was a gradual, almost hypnotic, identification with the hunters who had been on these frigid and wind-swept plateaus for uncounted thousands of years. The slow shuffling of the old men, the dipping and swirling of the younger braves, the side-step dance of the women, and the shy, mincing steps of tiny Shoshone children, all dressed in the soft leather, feathers, and colorful dyes and beads of the Plains Indians of ancient days, took me back over 200 years of American history. Jim Bridger and other mountain men must have sat by the fires with the Shoshone and planned a hunt. I had seen the wheel ruts on the plains, still visible in the late afternoon and just after sunrise, left by the legion of wagons going west to Oregon so long ago. I am sure cavalry troopers on those chilly fall nights must also have sat by Shoshone fires, sharing the age-old comradeship of hunters. And the rhythmic, hypnotic beat of the drum, accompanied by a rising and falling nasal chant—the chant for success on the stalk—took me to another time and another place, visited by all too few in this busy modern world.

We were awakened at 3:30 A.M. by our guides and ate a skimpy few mouthfuls of food, washed down by hot coffee or tea. The food, however, failed to calm stomachs churned into contorted knots by days of mounting pressure. Teams were split up to hunt with Governor Stan Hathaway of Wyoming, and our guides were Angus Campbell (Pee Wee) McDougall, the diminutive sheriff from Lander, and another Lander resident, Frank Hill. Also with us in a four-wheel-drive vehicle was Harold Mares, a past shooter and chief judge of the hunt. My confidence was anything but bolstered by all their stories of how they had missed their one-shot chance years ago; by their tales of great shooters and international celebrities who had missed, for no apparent reason, unbelievably short shots at standing pronghorns; by the success rate that was less than 40 percent in thirty years; and by the wind outside that was blowing at about 25 to 30 knots. The temperature was hovering somewhere around the 45-degree mark, but I knew what that wind was going to do not only to my tiny high-velocity bullet but also to the chill factor. I had been on many an antelope hunt in years past (but with a full clip of shells) and, knowing the ways of pronghorns, had turned down the offer of a brightly colored, warm quilted jacket, preferring the freedom of movement and camouflage of a light linen coat.

We jolted along a narrow, winding ranch road as the eastern sky changed from violet to a lighter blue to an orange. Finally the sun was just on the edge of the horizon. I carried binoculars, as did Pee Wee, and I saw some antelope about half a mile away at the base of a small foothill. The light was getting better rapidly, and I thought I saw a buck in the herd.

Pee Wee stopped the vehicle and looked at the animals.

"Nope," he said. "All does." We started moving forward again in first gear.

"What's legal shooting time?" I asked.

"Sunrise," the sheriff said "Six-thirty-five."

I looked at my watch. It was 6:42. I took the rubber caps off the 3-9X variable scope, placed them on the dash, and opened the bolt of the .257 magnum. I placed it between my knees and held the single, slim cartridge in the palm of my right hand.

"Antelope," Pee Wee said suddenly, pointing ahead. I saw three pronghorns running west to east about 300 yards ahead of us. He stopped the vehicle and raised the glasses.

"One of them at least is a buck," he said. "If they turn they may parallel us. It's not really good light yet. Now don't take just any shot. Remember, you've only got one chance in a lifetime."

I felt my pulse go up about thirty beats a minute.

"Let me out," I said. "They seem to be circling. Something must have spooked them. They're running full out."

"Okay," the sheriff said, "it's your decision, but remember what I said."

"If they seem too far out or if you're not sure about them being bucks or does," Harold said, "don't try it. We have all day."

I nodded and stepped out.

"I'll keep this rig moving," Pee Wee said, hoarsely. "Maybe they will keep watching me. They are swinging around now, and it looks like they are going to pass us to the east."

I nodded. Everything seemed to have become uncomplicated suddenly. If I got a shot, I was going to hit the animal or I was not. My heartbeat slowed down to something approaching normal, so I raised the rifle and looked at the pronghorns running against the orange skyline about 200 yards northeast of me. It was too hard to keep them in view with the scope set at its highest magnification, so I turned the ring to position 4 to give me more of a field of vision. The antelope swung closer to me and were almost in line with me when I decided against an offhand shot. I compromised with a sitting position, resting my left elbow on my left knee.

And suddenly there they were—three bucks speeding beautifully in front of me. It was not the bounding sprint of the mule or whitetail deer or the lurching gait of an elk, but an incredibly level and fluid running motion. For some reason I shall never know, they suddenly slowed from the streaking run and began to mill in a circle, watching the vehicle as it slowly moved down the rutted road. I picked up one buck, lost him as he circled, picked up a second, and started the slow squeeze just as he jumped and began to run to my right. The third buck was nervous and ready for an instantaneous dash, but his curiosity kept him milling in that peculiar circle, his head up and dust blowing downwind from beneath dancing hooves. The crosshairs settled on his shoulder, and the muzzle of the barrel moved in a circle as I tried to stay on him as the slow, steady trigger squeeze began.

The muzzle blast caught me by surprise, as it should. I clearly heard the *whack* of the high-velocity bullet, then the pronghorn went down in a cloud of dust. The gun had grouped 1 inch high at 150 yards on the range. If it had not been changed by impact, temperature, or a half dozen other factors that haunt rifle shooters, it should have been a good killing shot. I rose to my feet, flipped the bolt back, and picked up the spent shell. I was looking at it when 6-foot 3-inch Harold Mares picked me up as though I was a child and swung me around like a rag doll. After that it was MacDougall, Frank Hill, and Stan Hathaway pounding me on the back.

Harold walked off the distance after the jubilation eventually subsided. My hands were shaking so much from the release of tension that I couldn't hold a cup of scalding tea. The range was 157 yards. The bullet had severed the spine.

After that, all was fun, but anticlimactic. We didn't win, the astronauts beat us, but that made little difference to me. I look at the single-cartridge trophy on my desk today and know what was really the climax of the hunt—just as the Shoshone hunter must have known when he drew back his bowstring and the mountain man when he cocked the hammer of his muzzle-loader in a bygone time I somehow had been privileged to relive.

Tips on Hunting Antelope in Wyoming . . .

Any hunter of North American big game—that is, any hunter who is serious about it—either has taken or aspires to take a pronghorned antelope. It's an animal whose very existence can drift in and out of a hunter's imagination for a lifetime. Part of the pronghorn's hold on the imagination is undoubtedly the variety and vastness of the terrain over which it must be hunted. The antelope, while it is often encountered in high country, is pretty much a herd animal and tends to stick to the areas in which it can find the best grazing—the plains and foothills. It is a creature of wide open spaces,

and a man would have to be a dolt not to appreciate and respond to the splendors of the backdrop against which the drama of the hunt and its denouement is played.

For beauty, for tranquility, for a feeling of oneness with the earth and its rhythms, few locales can equal the solitude and grandeur of Wyoming's wilderness areas. From its western mountains to its broad eastern plains, Wyoming affords the contemplative hunter all he could ask for in the way of harmony with the outdoors.

In a recent year, Wyoming sold about 65,000

antelope licenses, which indicates the rapidly expanding state of the herds throughout the state. When you consider that in the same period the state sold less than 20,000 elk permits and less than 2,000 licenses for moose, it becomes clear that Wyoming offers outstanding antelope hunting.

Nonresident big-game licenses are issued on a lottery basis. Names are pulled out of a hat early in the year, and winners are notified in plenty of time to make arrangements. Details of the scheme are available through the Wyoming Game and Fish Department (see Appendix B).

Should you be lucky enough to win a license, there are several good outfitters to handle arrangements for any and all game. A good contact, for example, is Bob Jacob of Timber Top Outfitters (Box 89, Lander, Wyoming 82520). Jacob can not only outfit you and set up accommodations, but he can also bird-dog specific game in specific locales.

The best Wyoming private hunting is exemplified by the K Bar Z Ranch. Working out of the ranch itself, or out of two well-situated hunting camps, K Bar Z guests have access to an assigned region within the heart of the Absaroka Wilderness Area, in the western part of the state. The ranch provides guides, horses, and wranglers, and all the equipment and facilities you'll need and want.

Should you go to the K Bar Z, for example, there are a couple of things you'll want to take along—warm clothing, for one; even in summer it can get pretty cold in the mountains, particularly at night. You'll want comfortable, well-broken-in boots, too, and appropriate rain gear. You may find yourself camping out now and then, and you'll probably want your own sleeping bag and air mattress.

Granted, K Bar Z's ten-day hunting packages are on the luxury side, costing between $1,000 and $1,300, depending upon the game you're after, but the $100-per-day breakdown is fairly common. Getting by for much less is going to be economy all the way, so save your money until you can go first class. After all, you'll be going after first-class game in first-class country.

3.
The Rockies: Timberline Trout

The slight wind which had blown all afternoon, rippling the surface of the tiny, high-country lake, died just as the brass-colored sun sank behind a ridge of ponderosa pines a mile to the west.

With the stillness came the first tentative rises as trout began their evening feeding. Standing waist-deep in the icy water, I stripped out lengths of the weight-forward floating line from the reel and kept the Woolly Worm in the air. The soft swishing sound of the airborne line competed only with the chattering of an irritated red squirrel that was perched on the dead limb of a blue spruce down the bank to my right.

Most of the rises were either slight dimples on the surface or quick splashes, indicating small trout taking one of the tiny flies of a hatch that must have started only moments before. There were literally thousands of the small blue-gray flies skimming just a few inches above the mirrored surface.

Suddenly, about 20 feet out, the water swirled and I caught a glimpse of a broad back and a dorsal fin. I made two false casts, then dropped the black Woolly Worm about 2 feet past where the water still moved from the rise. Letting the wet fly sink a few feet, I mentally counted to five before I raised the tip of the 7-foot fly rod and gently brought the fly toward me in a series of slow movements.

On about the fourth pull, the surface bulged as the big trout took the fly without breaking water. Watching the white floating line at the spot where it was joined to the 9-foot tapered leader, I saw it snap out straight and set the hook by reflex. There is no mistaking most of the really big trout of the high timberline lakes. When hooked, they first make a straight run, not wasting time with frantic jumps, as do the smaller rainbows. They either head for the safety of a weedy bottom or for some sunken tree where they have broken off leaders before. This one was no exception. I kept the rod tip high over my head as the big fish bore down in about 30 feet of clear, frigid water, which was almost black in color. Long ago I had worked out a system of handling big rainbows in these high-altitude lakes, so when the 30 feet of fly line had disappeared from the reel, there was still another 50 yards of 8-pound monofilament backing to give the fish plenty of time to tire itself out.

This trout took another 30 yards of that, almost reaching the middle of the lake before it stopped. Realizing the punishment it was taking from the rod and the more than 35 to 40 yards of line, it then thrashed its way up to the surface where it began a series of jumps that tore the smooth surface into a jagged scar of white water. Tiring of that, it decided to head for a sunken pine about 50 yards down the shore to my right. I had to apply all the pressure the light mono could take in order to turn the trout away from that shelter. Far from whipped, the fish began a steady fight in the depths, giving and then taking line when it chose. It was a long battle and my right arm was starting to feel the constant strain by the time the big fish surfaced near me and began to swim in ever smaller circles. The stillness was broken only by the

occasional splashes of the big trout's tail. The red squirrel had stopped its almost mechanical chatter—like some child's toy which had finally run down. Perhaps it was fascinated by the battle between the two antagonists, man and fish.

When the trout finally gave up and floated beside me on its side, I slid the net under it, lifted it from the water, and made my way to the grassy bank. Holding it aloft in the late afternoon light, I turned it slowly, admiring the silver coloration, speckled with black spots, and the broad, burnt-orange stripe that ran down the center of the sides. Hooking a pocket scales to the jaw, I hefted it again. The trout weighed just over $4^3/4$ pounds; heavy bodied and small headed, it showed the fast growth rate of fish in the high lakes.

I like big flies for big trout in the timberline lakes, which lie at an average altitude of between 9,000 and 10,000 feet above sea level. This is not to say I have not taken some very nice fish on small flies, however. On many an evening rise, I have hooked big trout using No. 18 and No. 20 dry flies on long leaders tapered down to 5X and 6X, but most of the strikes on these flies have been by smaller fish. Also, I have enjoyed taking a number of sizable rainbows and a few big cutthroats using small nymphs, such as a No. 20 black or red ant, fished slowly and about a foot below the surface.

But my most enjoyable success over the years has been achieved by using the big wet flies—particularly Woolly Worms tied on No. 12 to 14 hooks. I find the black Woolly Worm with a red tail a constant winner. I have had excellent luck with a black-and-green combination and a black-and-gray combination, and occasionally I hit using a golden-bodied Woolly with gray hackle. But generally, it is the old reliable black that produces the most strikes in this particular type of lake. I found this to be true in lakes ranging from Yellowstone Park down to some of my favorite, tiny timberline lakes in southern Colorado and northern New Mexico. Most of the lakes I fish are too high to reach by vehicles, but some can be appoached to within a few miles before foot power becomes mandatory. I was introduced to these small lakes a number of years ago when the late Harold Walters of Santa Fe, New Mexico—one of the most avid mountain climbers and backpackers of the Southwest—used to explore the high country to the east of Taos. While Harold was busy setting up his battered 4×5 plate camera and tripod for the magnificent scenic shots he took of his beloved peaks, I would fish for trout in such icy jewels as Heart Lake and others, nestled at the foot of mountains such as Truchas Peak and Wheeler Peak. They were mostly dainty native trout—scrappy and beautifully marked—which we cooked and ate with gusto after a long day on the trails.

They were small because I used small dry flies almost exclusively in those days. It wasn't until later—upon exploring such northern New Mexico waters as the Latir Lakes, the chain of Canjillon Lakes, and high lakes in the country near Chama, New Mexico, and across the Colorado border, that I discovered the effectiveness of the larger Woolly Worm wet flies. After that it was a challenge to take the big ones on the big flies.

I was fishing in one of the little, nameless lakes on the New Mexico-Colorado border when I caught the rainbow that tipped the scales at 4³/₄ pounds. After weighing that fish, I placed it in the holding pocket of my fishing vest and waded back into the cold water to wait for another rise at which to spot cast. I use only 30 or so feet of weight-forward floating or sinking fly line—tied to the 8-pound monofilament backing with a blood knot—as a shooting head. It is not a new system and many other fly fishermen have developed their own methods of using shooting heads on fly lines by cutting off sections of tapered line. I find 30 feet plenty long, and the line and leader can be cast 60 feet on a calm day, as the 8-pound mono runs easily through the guides. It is also easier to store on the small, battered reel I have used for more years than I care to admit. I hold on to this reel because it balances well with the 3³/₈-ounce split bamboo rod I cherish for both small and fairly large trout.

Again I began stripping line off the small reel until it floated in big loops on the calm water beside me. Trout were rising all over the lake by now—some breaking water only a few yards from me—but I was watching for that special rise. It is somewhat hard to explain, but a big trout takes a surface fly or even a subsurface fly in a different manner than smaller fish do. It doesn't smash at it, try to beat competing fish to it, or swirl, exactly. It takes it much as an Atlantic salmon does. The top of the back just in front of the dorsal fin is usually the first thing one sees. This generally means that the fish has already taken the fly and is submerging. But because it is done so effortlessly and quickly, the angler's reaction is to strike after this "roll" when the dorsal fin appears, then sinks. On this type of strike the slight delay seems to make no difference, since the fish fully intends to devour the fly—unlike Atlantic salmon, which will hit a fly out of annoyance or pure reflex on their spawning run and will spit it out if not struck quickly.

I have noticed that big trout in the high lakes feed with a fairly even rhythm, moving about the shore. If a big fish rises down the shore from me, I gauge the distance and start counting. The chances are good that the fish will rise within half a minute again—either farther down the shore or closer to me. Each rise is also approximately the same distance apart, much the same as a person alone will take regular, unhurried mouthfuls. The small trout seem to feed at random—as do children—grabbing food whenever and wherever it is available, as if there would never be a tomorrow. Apparently, like adult humans, the big trout realizes there will be plenty of tomorrows—and many more meals.

There was a slurping sound to my right, a sure sign of a big fish rising, and I began counting to myself as the circles slowly widened from the spot about 25 yards away. At the count of eighteen, the fish rose slightly farther out in the lake and about 10 yards closer to me. I put the fly in the air and began counting again. I had reached twenty-seven and was beginning to wonder if it had been spooked by the big fly when the trout gently rose only a few yards from where it had risen the second time. It was a fairly long cast for the light rod, and the fly landed about 5 feet short of where I would have liked it. Nevertheless, I let it sink for about 5 seconds and then began the slow retrieve. I was resigned to the fact that the short cast had not caught the trout's attention and had the fly not more than 10 feet from the rod tip when the water swirled. I saw a wide flash of silver beneath the surface, and my rod tip slapped down sharply. Caught completely off guard, I tried to set the hook with the rod held almost horizontally and the fish diving for the bottom. Even with the light, limber rod, the sudden tension was too much and the tippet parted close to the hook. My muttered comment in the stillness was acknowledged by a black-and-white Canada jay on a charred ponderosa stump, which cocked its head quizzically at me.

I tied on another black Woolly Worm with an improved clinch knot. The other knot had not pulled out; the break was a clean one with no curled ends. Like most trout fishermen who have lived through the transition from gut to monofilament leaders, I have learned the value of knots. There was a time when, after soaking gut to make it pliable, I would have been absolutely certain that a simple fisherman's knot would hold most trout. The slippery but durable mono has changed all that, and many of us have had to become knot experts. For those of us who require reading glasses, tying blood knots and improved clinch knots in 4X or 5X tippets in the gathering dusk has become one of the less entertaining challenges of the game.

I took two smaller rainbows in the next quarter hour, not so much because there were no big ones around, but because there were so many trout feeding that the temptation to cast a good rise was irresistible. They ran less than 2 pounds each, but put up a heart-warming battle.

I am convinced that big trout in these small, high lakes do not remain in a favorite cove or under the shelter of a rock or fallen tree during feeding periods. I am certain they circle a lake slowly, feeding fairly close to the shoreline. During the periods when the sun is high, I believe that they retire to the shelter of sunken trees, weed beds, or deep channels made by streams leading into such lakes. On certain occasions, when the logs are available, I have fashioned crude rafts and paddled them to the deeper water. There I have found that by using a sinking fly line and Woolly Worms, and letting the raft drift with a slight breeze, I can pick up good, big trout even in the middle of the day. A slight jigging movement of the fly seems to help. Fishing the deep dropoff along a weed bed far out in a lake will produce strikes even when no fish are feeding on the surface.

Also, by keeping a notebook over the years, I have discovered that my best success on timberline lakes—particularly for lunker trout—comes early in the spring when the water is very cold following the runoff or when the ice has just melted. The next best time is in the fall when the aspens of the high country have turned a flaming gold and the temperature takes a bone-chilling dive as the sun goes down. The warmer months of July and August—although there are periods of good feeding on the part of small fish—have not proven as productive for the big ones. On several occasions, I have taken large rainbows and some bulky cutthroats with Woolly Worms in open water between snow-laden shore and ice still on the major part of the lake. Sometimes this open water may be only 5 or 10 feet wide, but the fish are

voracious after the long winter months and the big flies must look like a nine-course dinner to them, judging by the force of the strikes.

I have never found the fast retrieve to be of any value in fishing Woolly Worms. A slow, gentle movement appears to be the best method, although I have had a number of big trout take the fly the instant it hit the surface. Apparently in that clear, cold water a feeding trout—with its lightning-like reflexes—can not only spot an incoming fly, but can be there to intercept it when it lands.

This was almost the case on my last big fish of the evening. There was a good rise off to my left, and I dropped the fly within a few feet of the spot. The big trout must have literally doubled on itself as it took the Woolly Worm before it had time to sink. I managed to set the hook well this time without popping the light tippet, and the fish decided to jump rather than dive. There is not a true fly fisherman alive who doesn't feel his heart pounding in his chest and temples as a big rainbow starts a series of twisting, tail-lashing jumps across the surface of a still body of water. This one was well into the 8-pound monofilament when it turned and started another series of jumps quartering to my right and slightly toward me—causing me to strip in line through my left hand as fast as I could. It was a good fish and put up as tough an underwater battle as it did on the surface. I almost lost it when, as I reached for the net, it decided to make one last spurt for freedom. It was almost identical to the first rainbow—perhaps a few ounces lighter. I didn't bother to weigh it. This one was a female—more silvery and without the orange stripe and slight jut to the jaw characterizing the male.

A great horned owl passed silently over my head as I slid the fish into the pocket. I saw the huge bird's reflection in the water as it headed for the far shore, where it swooped up into the branches of a gnarled juniper to wait for dusk and the slightest movement of rodents in the grass bordering the lake.

With the two good fish stowed, I disassembled my rod and slid it into its aluminum case. It was almost dusk, and I had about an hour's walk down the mountain to the car. The air, even for early May, was turning cold as I picked up a lightweight jacket from a lichen-covered boulder near the head of the trail and slung my chest waders across one shoulder. Before starting down, I turned to look at the lake again. The feeding had slowed, and only a few small rises dimpled the water. No wind creased the glassy surface that mirrored the green slope slanting up to the bare ridge to the east of the lake. The great horned owl sounded its five-note hoot, and the call echoed and bounced from the dark fringe of spruces and the sides of the hollow bowl surrounding the quiet lake. I could smell the dank, black earth of the lake bank and the odor of freshly caught trout on my hands and jacket. The scent of wet canvas waders was mixed with that of spruce needles—all breathed in with the unbelievably clear air of the high country as I started down the narrow trail. The world below me may have become a complex place, but up on the timberline it is still the few and simple things that bring one happiness.

Tips on Trout Fishing in Northern New Mexico . . .

The idea may seem a bit farfetched—most outsiders tend to think of the Southwest as hot and dry, almost desert—but the trout enthusiast who overlooks New Mexico is turning his back on some of the best fishing available in the United States. The streams and lakes of the Jemez Mountains southwest of Santa Fe are the source of more than one tall trout tale. There a trout fancier will find outstanding fishing for stocked rainbows and native cutthroats and browns.

The prospects for rainbows and browns are best

in the Jemez River, Rio Las Vacas, Cebolla Creek, San Antonio, and the East Fork of the Jemez. Although their cutthroats are fewer in number, prospects are excellent in the Nambe River, the upper Cebolla, the Pinos Negras, Rio Frijoles, and Clear Creek, which flows through San Gregorio Lake, itself good cutthroat water.

Above Highway 64, up near the Colorado border, is Navajo Reservoir, a somewhat unique body of water in that it supports both warm and cold water species. In addition to rainbows and browns, coho and kokanee salmon, fishermen will find largemouth and smallmouth bass, crappie, bluegill, catfish, and northern pike.

Another good spot in the northwest part of the state, particularly for brown trout, is the Cimarron River. The Cimarron was devastated a few years ago by an oil spill, but now seems on the road to full recovery.

Both rainbows and browns can be taken in the west and middle forks of the Gila River, as well as in the waters of Iron Creek.

Penasco River, below Mayhill in the southern part of the state, is good brown trout water, as is Carrizo Creek, near Ruidoso.

New Mexico's trout season pretty much parallels every other state's—that is, from early spring to early fall, with the dates tending to be keyed to spawning runs of cutthroat in the spring, brown trout in the fall. Details and exact dates as well as a schedule of license fees can be obtained from the New Mexico Department of Game and Fish (see Appendix B).

"Sportsman's paradise" is a phrase that applies to a lot of New Mexico; therefore accommodations geared to fishermen are reasonably plentiful, ranging from plush private preserves to roadside cabins. As is true anywhere, an inquiring mind and an alert ear are your best means of lining up something you can afford and in which you'll be comfortable. Published guides of one kind or another (for example, the Mobil Guide) can save you a lot of wear and tear, to say nothing of grief.

Bring sunglasses, anti-sunburn lotion, a sweater and a light jacket (it can get chilly at night in those mountains, even in August's dog days), and—if only for peace of mind—a snakebite kit.

4.
The Teal of Taiwan

There are those who say it never gets very cold in Taiwan, but they are the ones who are there in the warm weather. Take it from me: it gets cold; it gets cold and it gets wet and when it gets both, that's the time to get on the warm clothes because the duck hunting is fine.

In the north, near the capital city of Taipei, the hunting is especially good during January and February. Then the winds sweep across the rice paddies and the valley of the Tamsui River seems to be one huge lake. The Tamsui is a wide, muddy river that winds to the sea, and when the driving wind and rains come, it whips the water's surface into whitecaps.

Over the valley flash the teal flights, greenwings and cinnamons. With the wind, they sweep down the main channel of the winding river and light on the long sandbars. There they mix with the flocks of domesticated ducks that are constantly watched by Chinese boys with long slender sticks, who guide them from the shore. It is hard to hunt them in the driving rain, but it is harder to hunt them on the clear days. The teal are wise, and it's a lucky man who gets within 100 yards of them in good weather. The only way to get close is to go out when the visibility is poor and try a sneak in a small boat. Even then, it is tough. A 50-yard shot is the closest, and it is downwind shooting with the wind and the rain behind the hunter's back—and at the back of those fast-flying ducks, too.

The last time I hunted there was the best. It was during the first week in February, and the weather was at its foulest. Everybody on the island was fed up with the weather—everybody but Gene and me, that is. We had been waiting for seven weeks for the dreary rains to come. The year before, I had been in Japan when the bad weather arrived in Taiwan, and Gene had spent all summer telling me what I had missed. Even during the pheasant shooting days earlier in the winter he had continued to talk about the teal and the rain in the north. Gene is the kind of hunter who will tell you of the magnificent angle-shot he made on a mallard last year while he is making a hard double on a pheasant at that moment. The trouble with him is that he is usually telling the truth.

Making our way on the Tamsui was tough. Hiring a Chinese boatman to row was no solution as the wind was downstream all day and the current was swift. Going down for the hunt was fine, but it took hours getting back home in the evening. By that time we would be soaked and the trip just wasn't worth it. Our solution this year was a 5½-hp outboard. Gene had built a light-plywood, 12-foot skiff and, as it turned out, it was just the answer. The boat had so little water and wind resistance that we were able to make good time.

The wind was hitting about 25 knots when we nosed through the slanting rain downstream. The top of Green Mountain was lost in the haze, and visibility was only good for about 200 yards on either side of us. I sat in the bow while Gene tried to keep the small boat in the center of the backwater stream to give us shots at either bank. There were lots of jacksnipe on the shore plus sandpipers, willet, and killdeer, but we were after ducks and decided not to risk tipping our hand.

The water had already seeped down my neck underneath the army jacket by the time we reached the main channel. I tried to hold the barrels of my favorite double low to keep the water out. Gene was shooting his rusty 12-gauge pump which he claimed would outshoot a .30/06 for distance. I was inclined to agree after seeing some of his hits.

Farmers on both sides of the river were ploughing the rice paddies in the downpour. In their wide coolie hats and bark capes, they slogged behind their oxen, knee-deep in the gelatinous mud of the fields. It was easy to sit in the bow of the tiny boat, looking into the haze, and imagine people doing this thousands of years before. There had been the same river, oxen, men, rain, wind, and rice paddies when western civilization was unborn. There had also been the same ducks. The only thing really new was the foreigners with their outboard motor and modern guns.

A sharp "pssst" came from Gene, and he swung the bow toward the far bank. There were several hundred large ducks gabbling under the shelter of the high bank. The Chinese call them "walkie walkies" as they are barnyard ducks and can't fly. They are domesticated mallards and white ducks that have been raised by Taiwanese since the beginning of time. The usual small boy was huddled on the bank with his ever-present long stick dangled over the flock. The tame ducks acted as magnificent decoys for wild mallards and teal. For some reason, the boy never seemed to bother the wild ducks; perhaps they figured all flocks came equipped with a small boy and long stick. We both squatted down in the boat while trying to get upwind of the flock. A hundred yards above them Gene throttled down the small motor to a purr, and we drifted toward them.

"Look for the small, black spots among the walkie walkies," Gene hissed. I nodded and slipped off the safety. We were about 50 yards away when two small specks swam from the downstream edge of the flock and began paddling furiously

along the bank. They were followed by four other specks. We were gaining on them when the boy began waving to us and pointing toward the teal. Chinese youngsters love to watch guns go off and this one was no exception. The teal were making good time, but we were gaining on them. The first two took off when we were still almost 50 yards above them, and we held our fire as the last four kept swimming, glancing nervously over their backs as they rode the muddy current.

At 40 yards the first of the four leaped straight into the air and was followed by the other three. Gene's gun blasted in my right ear just before I fired. We had both aimed at the lead teal, and he dropped back into water from a height of about 6 feet. Gene fired again as the other three banked into a sharp climbing turn, and I held my fire figuring if he couldn't reach them with that full-choked 12 there was little sense in my wasting shells. The trailing hen wavered as his gun blasted and flew behind the flight to head for the middle of the river. Gene dropped to the seat and swung the boat toward her as she hit and skidded along the muddy surface about 100 yards from us in the center of the stream. I was looking back at him when I heard the familiar whistle and caught the flash of wings out of the corner of my eye. I swung over my left shoulder and pulled ahead of the leader as the first pair of teal crossed the boat and headed upriver against the wind. It was sheer luck, but as I fired the leader folded and dropped to the water about a dozen yards to our right.

Gene was too busy with the motor to try for the second one, and we swerved to pick up my duck before the current carried it past us. It was a fine green-wing drake and it was stone-dead when we reached it. After retrieving the hen from down the river and the first hen close to the bank, we waved to the boy and headed downstream. The rain was coming down in solid sheets by then, and we hunched against it as the current added to our speed down the muddy channel. Our shots had stirred up other teal and twice we were caught unaware as small flocks flashed out of the rain and whistled over our heads. The visibility was down to about 50 yards, and by the time we had raised the guns, the ducks were misty shapes disappearing in the rain. They were all coming downriver with the wind and must have been traveling close to 60 miles an hour as they passed us. After the third flight had swished past, I turned and faced aft. Gene grinned at me from the stern.

"Shoot all you want," he said, "but just remember this is my favorite hunting cap and I don't want to lose it . . . along with my head."

In the next half hour, I got in some of the finest wing-shooting of my life. For some reason, the teal kept coming down that river in the rain, slashing out of the grayness right in front of my face and either flaring up and over the boat or dropping suddenly to skim the surface on either side. Gene steered the boat with one arm and spotted the fallen ducks when they dropped ahead of the skiff. There was no way of telling from what angle they would come next. There were doubles and sometimes a flight of a dozen, dipping or flaring in perfect unison.

It was a three-ring circus—a day that will live as long as I do. There was only the rain and the freezing wind, the flashing teal and the smell of cordite; twin barrels glistening with tiny beads of moisture and hot to the touch; the faint outline of the grey mud banks sliding by on both sides and Gene's Comanche-like yell whenever a streaking teal pinwheeled from the flock and skittered across the water.

It was an interlude when the world seemed to be moving in slow motion. There were no boundaries and nothing penetrated. There was only the shot of the moment and the thrill of a hit or the brief annoyance at a miss when you know the reason why. I felt neither the cold rain nor the cutting wind as I fired and reloaded, the empty shells flipping over my shoulder and landing with faint plops in the swirling water.

A flight of three teal came boring out of the haze astern and dipped into a sharp bank as they saw the boat. I fired the right barrel almost without thinking, and the lead teal took the charge dead center. There was a burst of feathers, and I instinctively ducked as the bird hurtled past my head and bounced off the gunwale in the bow. The other two veered and were lost in the rain before I could get my balance. Gene whooped and doubled over with laughter.

"Enough is enough," he gasped, straightening up. "How about letting me get a few shots before you rid the world of ducks!"

After fishing the shattered cinnamon teal drake from the water, we changed places, and Gene squinted into the wind upriver. I had gotten six teal and had missed four in the time that had seemed but a few minutes. Gene's pump boomed now as the small ducks continued to streak by us. I got a wrenched neck trying to watch for sandbars ahead, ducks coming from behind and where they fell when the loads of No. 6 shot spun them from the flights.

The visibility was down to almost nothing before we realized it was getting dark. On hunting and fishing trips, I have noticed it always gets darker twice as fast as during any other day of the year and it gets dark in a hurry when the February rains sweep Taiwan. By then, we had fifteen teal and had not missed enough to take the edge off the shooting. In the wind and rain, we were lucky to have hit any! It was cold and it was wet and even the new outboard sounded wheezy as we headed the light boat back upriver.

Gene, who is one of nature's noblemen even under the worst of conditions, fished a flask from one of his jacket pockets and tossed it to me in the bow. I swear it's the only reason we made the dock that night. It took us almost two hours to make it back against the headwind and current. I've seen prettier sights than that dock boy waiting for us with the headlights of the jeep shining across the water as a beacon, but at the moment, I'd have to think a long time to remember what they were.

I had to leave for Hongkong the next week, and I haven't hunted either the rivers or the cane fields of Taiwan since, but if I ever get a chance to go back, especially when the bitter rains hit the island, I've got another date with those rocketing teal.

Tips on Duck Hunting in Taiwan . . .

For most of us, the only duck that comes to mind when we think of the Orient is Peking duck and its pressed variations listed on the menus in Chinese restaurants throughout the world. Yet reason should tell us that Orientals—the Chinese in particular—must have had something from which the original dishes were prepared. And slightly deeper reasoning should tell us that domesticated waterfowl must have been preceded by wild varieties. Ergo, there must have been—at least at one time—duck hunting in the Orient.

All very inscrutable, of course, but not only was there at one time duck hunting in the Orient, there still is, and it can afford a dedicated waterfowler the shooting experience of a lifetime.

In the non-Communist Republic of China (Taiwan), duck hunting becomes something far removed from the experience familiar on American inland lakes and rivers and the tidelands of American coastal waters. It's hard to pin down just why this is so. After all, water is water and marshland is marshland the world over, and hunting methods, while they vary from place to place, are not all that different. Maybe it's the position of the sun in a new sky. It might be the boats a hunter comes across in the course of a day's hunt. More than likely, it's the unfamiliarity—at least in most Occidental eyes—of an Oriental face pressed against the stock of a shotgun.

Anyway, it's different—and delightful. Not only is the locale exotic, but the hunting is excellent.

Taiwan's climate is more or less subtropical. In the north, annual temperatures average around 70 degrees. It's warmer in the south, where temperatures average about 75 degrees. You'll find summerweight clothing comfortable from April through November. From December through March, however, you'll need a sweater or two and a light topcoat. And all through the year, you'll need some form of rainwear; why the Taiwanese don't have webbed feet is something that baffles everyone except residents of Seattle.

Waterfowlers thinking about a trip to Taiwan can count on accommodations ranging from opulent to minimal. The same is true of food; meals can be elaborate affairs designed and prepared to soothe an emperor's wrath—truly gourmet fare—or they can be on a par with a peasant's bowl of rice. Some of the larger hotels offer a Western-style menu, complete with steaks to delight a cattleman.

You'll find that Uncle Sam's battered and at times maligned dollar gets pretty good mileage in Taiwan. What's more, it and its bearers are genuinely welcome. One Yankee dollar will get you about 38 Taiwanese dollars, and 60 or so of those can, for example, buy you a meal guaranteed *not* to leave you hungry again in a half-hour. And the smile that goes with the service is built-in—not necessarily an extension of an outstretched palm.

Hunters should be advised that seasons vary from locale to locale, and that there is no one prime time for waterfowl. Hence, it's a good idea to get the very latest information available before you venture forth. Information about seasons, fees, game availability, travel arrangements, and so on can be obtained by writing to China Air Lines (Chung Shan Road North, Taipei, Taiwan) or Adventures Unlimited (Abercrombie & Fitch, 19 East 45th Street, New York, New York 10017; telephone 212–682–3600).

5.
Ecuador:
Striped Marlin—
the Great
Jumpers

In the spring, the days get hotter on the calm sea, and the outline of Puntita Santa
Helena shimmers in the bluish haze that cloaks the surface of the Pacific about twelve
miles off the Ecuadorian fishing port of Salinas. And with the hot days, the great
jumpers—*Picu Rayado,* as the native skippers and mates call them—cruise on the
surface, their dorsal and tail fins out of the water as they search for food pushed up by
the cold waters of the Humboldt Current. Along with the striped marlin, the Pacific
sailfish, *Pez Vela,* come up behind the baits—their huge sails tearing the surface as
they slash at the rigged balao and mackerel skipping behind the old diesel-powered
wood boats of the big-game fleet. The beautiful dorado, or dolphin, are
everywhere—slicing inward at the baits until the mates grow tired of gaffing them
and rerigging flat lines and outrigger lines.

But they do not throw back the dolphin, and they keep the striped
marlin—as well as every fish taken in these teeming waters, from the big-eye tuna
and black marlin taken by the boats with the big rods to the myriad of bottom fish
hauled up on handlines by native fishermen in the sailing canoes. The land is dry and
poor on the west coast of Ecuador, in the area near Guayaquil, and the people of the
small coastal villages live off the sea. There is almost no rainfall, and the barren,
cactus-studded, sandy land is barely able to provide enough growth to feed the
scattered herds of gaunt burros and foraging goats. So it is to the sea that the natives
turn for food—venturing out each day from the fishing village on a heading of 240
degrees until the fleet reaches the spot where the mushrooming effect of the cold
water bulges from the depths, bringing up plankton and small fish and drawing the
big predator fish in from the cold current to feed on the baitfish.

Jose Gomez is fifty-one years old and has been fishing this sea off his home
since the time when he stood all day in a hollowed-out log and fished with a handline,
as native fishermen were doing now on the horizon to our port side. They are dropped
off each morning by the big sailing canoes and picked up late in the day before the
canoes sail gracefully back to Salinas—the setting sun at their sterns.

But there are times, Jose admitted, when the fishermen are not picked up.
There are the sudden storms and the log canoes capsize easily. The big canoes

sometimes find the hollowed-out logs floating in the sea, empty. *"Tiburon* (shark)? *Quien sabe?"* shrugs Jose. But now Jose is the skipper of the 38-foot wooden plank boat *Haridor,* outrigged and powered by two ancient diesel engines he knows as well as he does the faces of his wife and children. With him are two young mates who are learning the business of rigging baits, running outrigger and flat lines, handling wire leaders, and gaffing the big fish that bring big-game fishermen from all over the world to this best of all striped marlin grounds.

It is the hope of the two mates that they will run their own boats some day, but such a boat, however old, costs a great deal of money. Jose and his fellow skippers—like veteran German Bazan—were mates for decades before being assigned boats by Knud Holst, the Danish-born boss of the fishing fleet.

Good skippers like Jose are the backbone of the fishing fleet and very valuable to Holst and the people who run the big, plush hotel at Punta Carnero, jutting into the sea from a rocky point six miles from Salinas. It is here the big-game anglers from Spain and Buenos Aires, Miami and San Francisco, New York and Houston stay when they come to catch the billfish. Successful hookups are important to the international airlines such as Braniff, which count on the good fishing for those smitten by the incurable fever of big-game angling. Also, the skippers are respected men of Salinas and wealthy by the standards of the fishing village. It is the tourists with the big rods and shiny reels carried in canvas cases who bring money to the fishing ports of Ecuador, as they do to the other great big-game fishing places of South America—places such as Cabo Blanco in Peru once was. But the Humboldt Current moved inexplicably far off from where it flowed close to shore at Cabo Blanco in the 1950s. In those days, men with the big-fish fever roamed the waters off the cape—where the water dropped from a depth of 35 fathoms to as much as 2,000 fathoms just a few miles offshore. It was here that such anglers as Kip Farrington, Stokes, Seeley, Mike Lerner, Woodward, Ernest Hemingway, Bill Carpenter, and Al Glassell sought the black marlin, *Picu Negro,* and took many in the 1,000-pound-plus class. Glassell's monster 1,560-pound black, taken off Cabo Blanco on August 4, 1953, still holds the world's record.

But it was another place and another time, and Gil Drake, Jr., Caribbean editor of *Field & Stream,* New Yorker Constantine Kazanas, and I were after striped marlin—not for world records, but for action color photographs of jumping billfish. For in the cold water off Salinas, it is not unusual to see thirty to fifty striped marlin on the surface in a day, and Jose and his fellow skippers average three fish boated each time out. Many days as many as six are taken. They are not released here because the townspeople eat marlin, and it forms the staple of their diet. Though most of us who follow the big fish release and tag our catches if they are not hurt and bleeding from a hook, this keeping of fish does not seem wasteful. As long as they are utilized it seems proper. It is only in areas such as the west coast of Mexico, the Bahamas, the West Indies, and Florida—where many times fish are killed simply to be photographed at the dock, then either buried or thrown away—that keeping them has no appeal for sportsmen.

"*Pesca!*" Jose called, pointing off to the starboard. I stood up from the seat beneath the cabin roof where I had been sitting out of the hot sun and stared in the direction he was pointing. The fish was on the surface—as the rest had been—swimming slowly in quest of food. At the same time, I heard the two mates say something from atop the cabin roof as they obviously spotted the fish shortly after Jose. Gil was topside with them, his two cameras fitted with Polaroid filters strung about his neck. Six billfish had risen to the baits already, and we had taken three—one of them hooked in the side as it took a quick swipe at the bait. Connie had battled that one stubbornly until it finally came alongside, never jumping because of the placement of the hook. His other one was a fine jumper, as was mine, and we had gotten what we hoped were some excellent action shots with the long zoom telephoto lenses.

Jose eased the throttles ahead as he swung the boat in an arc so that the skipping baits would pass in front of the cruising fish. As we had done before, we all moved to the side of the boat toward the fish as it finned lazily ahead. We were alongside it and not more than 30 feet away when it saw the hull or felt the vibration of the screws and went down. This was nothing new; most of the marlin dove when the boat and bait came close. The eyesight of a billfish is very good, and it can spot bait from an incredible distance. I glanced up and nodded at Gil, who was standing up and shading his eyes with his hand. He was wearing polarized glasses and, more than any big-game fisherman I know, has eyes that can easily spot billfish beneath or behind the baits.

"Want to try this one?" I asked Connie, who was leaning on the starboard gunwale, trying to spot the fish. There was a brief, understandable pause before he answered.

"No, it's your turn," he said. "I got the last one."

We both knew this, but the two marlin Connie had taken were his first. He was still jubilant with excitement, even though it had been more than an hour since he'd caught his second fish. Some big-game fishermen say the first marlin is always the best. I am not sure that is true. For me, each marlin is the best.

"O.K.," I said. "If he's hungry and comes up."

I moved to the port rod holder which held the special 50-pound-class rod and reel I had brought along. The other three rods out were boat rods—two carrying 80-pound monofilament and one flat line with 50-pound mono. My wide-spool reel held about 750 yards of braided, small-diameter 50-pound line. It was a beautifully balanced combination of rod, line, and reel, and I had hoped to test it later in the week on the bigger black marlin if we could get a charter to go a greater distance offshore where the current flowed, approximately 70 miles out.

"Port rigger!" Gil shouted from above me, and I instinctively rested a hand on the reel drag lever. The tip of a dorsal fin surfaced behind the skittering mackerel, and my heart pounded as it always does at the sight of billfish. The fin suddenly went down, and I swung to watch the other outrigger bait.

"Flat line, flat line!" Gil shouted, and there was the fish again—its lavender stripes aglow, the way the great fish have of "lighting up" when excited or hungry. This time I thought it was going to take the rigged balao bait, and I started to reach for the other 50-pound rod. The fish simply stayed behind the bait—its dorsal fin weaving from side to side as it inspected the bait from all angles.

"Take it, take it!" Connie shouted from where he stood at the transom. "Nope," Gil called from the cabin top. "He's going to the left rigger this time, watch it!"

I shaded my eyes and moved to a position close to the 80-pound rig as the fin came up again. I had no sooner braced my feet when the fish went down again. There was a pause as we all looked at the boat wake. A number of times during the day marlin had come up, inspected the baits for as long as five minutes, then—either because something about the baits bothered them or perhaps because they were just not hungry enough—had sounded and not returned. It is not uncommon in big-game fishing to have fish do this all day, or for a number of days.

I was walking away from the big rod and had decided to move back into the shade until the fish made up its mind, when apparently it did. Without coming up behind the bait first, it suddenly struck the port rigger bait with no warning.

"Blind strike," I heard Gil yell. "Right rigger!"

The geyser of white spray had not yet settled by the time I picked up my favorite rod and lowered the tip. Feeling the weight immediately, I set the hook twice and then raised the tip and fitted the metal butt section into the socket of a belt harness I was wearing. Fighting small billfish from a belt harness is more enjoyable than from a chair. It gives me a chance to move about the cockpit more easily, and it is simpler to face the direction of the fish than having to wait for someone to swing a fighting chair toward the fish.

The surface of the sea erupted in the center of the wake about 50 feet behind the boat, and the marlin climbed high into the air in a writhing, twisting jump that carried it a dozen feet above the water.

Connie let out a shout of excitement as the fish continued to thrash in midair—hanging there as if in slow motion. The jolt passing up the rod to the upper arm and shoulder muscles always catches one by surprise, even when the angler knows it is coming. There is such unbelievable power and speed in even the smallest of billfish that it is difficult to believe fishermen have succeeded in defeating so many.

The fish came down flat on its side and almost immediately came out again in a jump fully as spectacular as the first.

Gil slid off the roof and landed on his feet with a thumping sound behind me. "Beautiful!" he said, focusing the camera again. "I think I got that first jump. The angle is too much from there. I think this will be better."

The marlin came out again, and we were facing in just the right direction for photographs. The sun was ahead of the moving boat and at an angle—giving the sea a royal blue color in the late afternoon. The camera shutter clicked, and I heard Gil grunt with satisfaction.

The reel was screaming a highpitched note as the line ripped off it and the shocks of fighting fish came up through my extended left arm. The right, gloved hand was only needed to keep the reel upright and steady. It would be some time before this fish slowed enough to get back any line. It was more than 100 yards out now and going into its fourth jump, bursting from the sea in rage and whipping its bill from side to side as it hurled itself into the air.

Both mates were standing on the cabin roof, giving them a better view of the leaping marlin. The fish turned a complete cartwheel this time before crashing back to the surface, only to appear again going straight up. It seemed to climb until it was difficult to believe it could go higher—twisting and literally churning its length in the air until it must have been at least 20 feet high.

The camera clicked next to me, and Gil yelled jubilantly.

"My God," he said, "did you ever see a fish jump like that! I think I got that picture. It went higher than that boat near it!"

I hadn't noticed until then, but a small boat was close to us and trolling across to our port side. The fishermen on the boat were facing us and must have had a startling view of that marlin as it came out near them.

"Six!" Connie shouted as the fish came down and went up again. The fish was not greyhounding, as most billfish will do when going away at full speed— making rapid, short and low jumps by quickly churning the tail just below the surface. This striped marlin was making each new jump—after going under completely from the previous one—and using all its strength each time it came out. I have never seen a marlin jump as that one did and I doubt if Gil has. We have both seen a lot of jumping marlin.

"Seven . . . eight . . . nine . . .!" Connie continued to shout as the incredible fish stripped out line far to the rear of the small boat it had just passed.

The marlin made seventeen towering jumps on that first run. Following that it made a greyhounding run of twenty-seven streaking jumps before sounding and giving me a chance to get back a little of the 500 yards or so it had taken out without slowing down.

When it went several hundred yards straight down and refused to move, I had Jose move the boat forward slowly at a speed of about two knots—until the angle of the line changed enough to lift the head of the fish and convince it that diving was not the answer. When it came up, it came up with a rush, and getting the long, curved billow of slack back straight took some fast reeling. The first jump after the dive was almost as high as the record jump near the small boat. The direction of the battle had changed now, and the fish was leaping between us and the late afternoon sun—changing the light settings for Gil and reducing the color values considerably.

"These are going to show up more like silhouettes," Gil grunted as the camera clicked away.

The fish, after another unbelievable series of jumps, finally began to show signs of tiring. Connie was getting hoarse from shouting, and one of the mates reached for a gaff as the marlin began a head-shaking battle on the surface about 50 yards from the stern. My back, arm, and leg muscles felt good, but the fingers of my left hand were cramped from the constant strain of the jumps.

Gil waved the mate back from the gaff and sat down in one of the chairs to don his snorkel, mask, and flippers. The young mate finally nodded after Jose carefully explained in Spanish that Gil was going to take some underwater pictures when the marlin came close to the boat. The mate looked dubious, however, as Gil slid over the side when the marlin was about 30 feet away. The hook was in the side of the mouth and there was no blood to attract sharks. We had made certain of that

before Gil left the boat. However, the mate probably had grave doubts as to Gil's sanity. Sharks are not a problem in the waters off Ecuador—as they are in the warmer waters of the Caribbean and the Gulf Stream.

The fish, fighting every foot of the way, finally came to gaff after 45 minutes of one of the finest battles any billfish ever waged. Gil got some photographs from the water, and the mates finally slid the marlin aboard.

The fingers of my left hand finally unclenched enough to accept a cold can of the fine, light, locally brewed beer. Connie, hoarse and grinning like a youngster, was as soaked with sweat as I was in the suffocating Ecuadorian heat.

The mates rigged the baits, Gil put away his diving gear and retired to the shade of the cabin, and Connie went forward to get a beer for himself. Jose, from behind the wheel, looked at me for a brief moment as I took a swallow of the beer and rested a hand on the side of the marlin—lashed to the top of the transom. He smiled slowly and nodded toward the still-wet marlin—its magnificent purple stripes and silver sides fading to black in the throes of death.

"Muy fuerte," he said simply. *Strong* is as good a word as any I would have chosen for such a fish.

Tips on Game Fishing in Ecuador . . .

Less than 200 miles below the Equator, off the point at Salinas, Ecuador, a strange—and for sport fishermen, a singularly fruitful—phenomenon takes place. Here the Humboldt Current of cold water sweeping up from the south meets the Panama (or Counter Equatorial) Current of warm water flowing down from the north. The currents meet, turn west, and parallel each other as they flow out into the broad expanse of the Pacific.

As it flows southward before meeting the Humboldt, the Panama Current carries with it numerous species of bait fish, which feed on plankton and other nutrients that bloom as the cooler waters flow into warmer climates. Sweeping north with the Humboldt are striped marlin and other game fish bound for what they know are easy pickin's. The result is a game angler's paradise.

Although there can be off-days, as is true anywhere, it is not unusual to spot up to one hundred marlin zapping along on the surface. What's more, a good percentage of them can be induced to charge a skipping balao or other bait fish.

During the few off-days each month when striped marlin are not as prevalent (usually a period when the Humboldt swings farther offshore), it is possible to encounter huge black marlin and large Pacific sailfish. And whatever the marlin fishing, these waters also offer Pacific big-eye tuna and, throughout the year, a plentiful supply of dolphin, plus a few swordfish. Closer to shore, there are plenty of big jacks, roosterfish, and amberjacks.

Although the fishing is good all year long, any season for striped marlin would have to be from November through April. Again, however, outstanding fishing for stripes is by no means confined to these months. April through June is the peak time for black marlin.

Bring along lightweight fishing clothes (suntans are fine), a lightweight windbreaker-type jacket, a sweater or two (just in case), appropriate boating footwear, and a rainsuit. Since there are times, out on the water, when sudden, unexpected rain comes down in buckets, the rainsuit is a must.

It's always a good idea to figure on using your own tackle. You can borrow or rent good 50- to 80-pound trolling gear, but you'll be a lot more comfortable utilizing tackle with which you are familiar. If you are a casting buff, by all means bring along your own tackle: a hefty spinning rod laced with 15-pound line is just about right for dolphin in these waters. Whether or not you want to bring along a heavy duty fly rod depends upon how adventurous and dedicated you are.

Overlooking the Pacific and several miles of open beach—to say nothing of some of the world's best fishing waters—is the Hotel Punta Carnero. A luxury hotel, the Punta Carnero is nevertheless relaxed and informal; a sport shirt and slacks, for example, are fine for dinner. The hotel is about a two-hour's drive out of Guayaquil and well worth the trip. A nearby fishing fleet operated by Pesca Tours is at the disposal of the hotel's guests.

It ain't cheap. Not counting airfare, five days of offshore fishing and six nights at the Hotel Punta Carnero will come to about $600 per head (double occupancy). Included are transportation to and from the airport at Guayaquil, meals, room, boat and crew, bait, and—if you wish—tackle.

A number of special fishing packages are available, but your best bet would be to contact Adventures Unlimited or Adventure Associates (150 S. E. Second Avenue, Miami, Florida 33131; telephone, toll free, 800–327–5781) or the Hotel Punta Carnero (P.O. Box 5589, Guayaquil, Ecuador), or Lou Garcia, Vice-President Public Relations, Braniff International (135 East 42nd Street, New York, New York 10017; telephone 212–972–4292).

6.
Quebec: Salmon of the Mighty George

The huge, rolling George River—running black and deep northward toward the frigid waters of Ungava Bay in extreme northern Quebec—is one of the most difficult of the salmon rivers to fish.

Its waters, even in August, are frighteningly cold and in many places run 100 yards or more wide, and most of the mammoth pools have never been measured for depth.

The giant river has its beginning near the border of Labrador, several hundred miles to the south in the rugged mountain highlands near Resolution Lake. By the time it nears the sea, or passes Helen Falls Camp, where we stayed, one can land a float plane on many of its long pools. It is the only river I have ever fished that frightens me. Even with a belt cinched up tight around the waist of chest waders, the thought of slipping and falling into that rushing torrent and being swept down the chutes and over some of those awesome falls is enough to keep one constantly testing his footing with felt soles on the glassy-smooth glacial rocks.

That is not the only inconvenience on the George. Even in late August, the mosquitoes are a menace. While the stoic Eskimos seemed never to notice them—and indeed the insects seldom stay long on the skin of their faces and hands—they literally covered us. Because of the insect repellent, they did not stay long enough to bite, but the fact that they were there made seeing and breathing a problem. It was only when the wind blew, and thank God the wind blew in gusts almost constantly, that they would leave long enough for an angler to concentrate on the salmon.

And it is cold. It is cold in July and it is cold in August; and by the first part of September, the snows come and there is no more fishing for salmon. But then the herds of caribou float across the spectacular land, and it is time for the Eskimos and the white hunters to pursue these great game animals for winter meat—along with the flocks of ptarmigan and geese covering the lichen-spotted ridges and lowland marshes of the region.

But none of the great salmon rivers affords a sensation such as the one a fisherman first feels when he sees the George. It seems incredible that the river would not be filled with 30- to 50-pound fish. Its mere size and power seem incapable of allowing anything smaller to pass upstream. True, there are 30-pound-plus salmon galore in the George, but there are a great many 8- to 20-pound fish also—which is just as well—as big salmon don't hit that often and fishing the George would be frustrating if it held only big fish.

This was my first trip to the George. I had been invited by Willard F. Rockwell, Jr., chairman of the board of Rockwell International, a man I had never met. But I had heard he was an ardent hunter and fisherman. One of his people had called me and asked if I wanted to fish the George. It did not take long to decide. The farthest north I had fished for Atlantic salmon had been the Miramichi River in eastern New Brunswick, and the thought of fishing 500 miles or so south of the Arctic Circle was enough to make me cancel two other appointments.

I took a taxi from my Washington, D.C., hotel, where I had been attending a conservation meeting, and arrived at Dulles International Airport at 9 A.M. on the day we were to leave. There were eight or nine people making the flight—aboard a sleek, twin-engined, turboprop plane. There were also a couple of Rockwell International people on board sort of as tour directors, but not the host, whom we were told had been called to a last-minute meeting and would join us at camp the next day.

The flight from Washington to Montreal, our port of entry, was pleasant and most guests played gin or read. From Montreal—over some truly magnificent, lake-studded country—the plane droned on until we landed at the Eskimo community of Fort Chimo late in the afternoon. From there, we unloaded the gear into two planes—both float-equipped. One was a twin-engine Beechcraft and the other a single-engine Norseman—workhorses of the Arctic bush pilots. It was only a short flight to Helen Falls Camp, but it will be a long time before I forget that first sight of the big river. We landed with me flying in the co-pilot seat, after the young Eskimo bush pilot discovered I held a private pilot's license. Because of the wind, we came in downriver on a big pool below camp. The river was more than 100 yards wide here and, as we swung about to taxi back upriver to where the tent camp perched on a ledge about 50 feet above the river, I estimated this one pool to be at least a quarter of a mile long.

It was almost dark before we unloaded all the gear. The mosquitoes seemed to be trying to eat us alive as we passed the equipment and supplies up the bank to the campsite. There were six sleeping tents, able to accommodate at least three cots each. They had board floors and each came equipped with a small centrally-located metal stove. It reminded me of the press tents we had set up at Munsan in Korea, from where we covered the end of the war and the peace talks at Pan Mun Jom—except that these tents were white, not olive-drab.

The big mess tent was run by Eskimo women cooks, with young boys and girls doing everything from cutting and hauling wood and water to washing dishes and waiting on tables. With the coming of darkness, the temperature took a sudden dive and passing from tent to tent required a heavy down jacket. After drinks and a huge dinner of broiled brook trout and char fresh from the river, steaks, sourdough biscuits, green vegetables, and even freshly-baked cherry pie, I turned in—leaving a few die-hard gin players in the cook tent, along with a couple of salmon fishermen too excited by the river to sleep.

After a big breakfast, veteran guide Bill Littleford tested all my leader knots and the nail knot connecting the leader to the fly line.

"Looks good," he pronounced finally, hefting the 9-foot rod in his huge, gnarled hands. "Here," he said, picking a fly from his stained hatband, "try this fly. It works better than almost anything else—this and the silver rat."

"What is it?" I asked, inspecting the nicely-tied but uninspired-looking salmon fly.

"Just called The Rat," Bill said.

"That's good enough for me," I said, tying on the fly. It had a bronze peacock herl body with a fine golden tinsel tag, and the wing was mixed black-and-white calf tail hair. Several turns of badger hair had been put over the wings.

The big cargo canoes—each equipped with a 40 hp outboard motor—carried three fishermen and two Eskimo guides upriver to where the series of fishing pools began. As we skirted the gigantic falls and whirlpool just above camp, I leaned over to Littleford.

"That's a monster of a pool," I shouted over the sound of the motor. "How deep do you think it is?"

"No idea," he shouted back. "We ran a sealed fifty-gallon oil drum over it a few years back. It didn't surface for two hours. When it did, it was three hundred yards downstream and so battered you wouldn't recognize it!"

I shook my head—imagining what would happen to a cargo canoe full of guides, fishermen, and gear that got caught in it.

By the time we beached the big canoes a mile upriver, dry snow was spitting in the wind—keeping the mosquitoes off us a bit. The temperature must have been in the mid-50s and most of us were wearing down underwear beneath waders, heavy shirts, down jackets, and, in some cases, parkas. My hands stayed cold all the time. I cannot fish with gloves on and decided to settle for cold and cramped fingers.

The big pools were dramatic salmon fishing spots—classic in their shape and huge reproductions of those found on such rivers as the Restigouche and the Miramichi. There were salmon in all the holding areas. The Eskimos—who have the most incredible eyes for spotting resting salmon I have ever seen—would wave one of us over and point to a slick just above a chute or a falls.

Finally, after peering into the swiftly-running, dark water where the guide kept pointing, I could make out the long shapes of salmon—resting in the relatively quiet water, just the slow motion of the tails giving away their presence as they gained strength for the next assault on the chutes and falls above.

But they—like their cousins the world over—were not hungry and were not in this river to feed. The spawning urge was strong and only now and then would one make a casual rise to inspect a fly—and even then it was the instinctive movement of a fish which dimly remembered feeding on such a fly in this same river in the years before it went to sea.

The fishing was difficult in the cold wind; the gusts made an accurate cast tricky, and the rock-strewn shore behind provided a perfect place in which to break off the barb of a hook on the back cast. I have seldom fished so hard for salmon in my life—whether on Iceland's frigid streams or Scotland's heavily-fished rivers. I got a half-hearted rise in the middle of the morning, but the big fish never took the fly—simply rolled close to it. By lunchtime—when the Eskimos built a fire at the base of a cliff and made hot tea to go with our sandwiches—my right arm was dead from continuous casting.

The afternoon was not much better. One member of the party, an attorney from Pittsburgh, Pennsylvania, Bill Meyer, caught a nice 14-pound salmon after a spectacular aerial battle that lasted twenty minutes before the fish was subdued. It was bright silver and fresh from the sea—which was about 75 miles downstream at the mouth of the George at Ungava Bay.

Fishing a long chute above some falls, I experimented with letting a streamer fly drift under a huge rock ledge 30 yards below me. My heart almost stopped when a dark shape whipped out into the current, smashed the fly, and headed downstream. It was a strong fish and it fought a long, stubborn underwater battle before we finally led it into the shallows and an Eskimo guide netted it. I knew it was no salmon from the start because it did not jump or fight like one, but I was not prepared for what it was—a 17-pound lake trout. I had expected a big brook trout or Arctic char. Littleford said there were a lot of lakers in the river—staying their entire lives. We kept it for food.

By the time the party was ready to return to camp in the late afternoon, I was nursing a very tired casting arm, legs that were rubbery from climbing over jumbled rocks, and hands and lips chapped from the cold wind. Most of the party hit the sleeping bags right after dinner. There were very few card players that night!

The next day started out the same—cold, blustery, and devoid of salmon which showed any interest in a fly. In the middle of the morning, I leaned my heavy fly rod against a bush and assembled a light seven-foot fly rod to break the monotony of casting a big rod into the ever-present wind. I wanted to catch a mess of trout for the evening meal. I have seldom experienced such magnificent trout fishing! I fished only one pool, using a small red-and-white wet fly, and in an hour's time caught and released more than fifty beautiful brookies and char. The bigger brookies averaged 4 pounds apiece. I kept a dozen before putting away the small rod and getting back to the salmon fishing.

About 2 P.M., after casting to the same stretch of water at least a thousand times—moving downstream one sidewise step at a time after a series of casts in order to cover each square foot of the water—the wet fly stopped below me in mid-current. Knowing it could be caught on a submerged rock, I raised the rod tip and gently set the hook anyway—just in case. It was a wise move. A big salmon started up the center of the slick like an express train—gaining speed rapidly until it felt the pressure of the rod and the whirling reel, took to the air in one mind-boggling leap, threw the fly, crashed back to the surface, and disappeared.

After a day and a half of no strikes, I stood in the cold wind and stared at the spot where the fish had fallen back to the water. Only another salmon fisherman could appreciate my feeling at that moment! After slowly reeling in the line and inspecting the fly—which was intact—I began fishing again, this time resolving not to be caught off guard and allowing the next fish any slack line.

The weather grew worse instead of better. I worked my way upstream to a series of shallow pools and was joined by Bill Littleford. He showed me a few good holding spots and retired to the shelter of a large rock behind me to get out of the wind. An occasional spatter of cold rain fell, and the sky upstream was almost black with an approaching squall. Another fisherman was patiently casting about 100 yards downstream from me. I did not know who he was nor could I tell. He wore an olive-drab parka with a hood sheltering him against the wind and rain.

I had cast to the same stretch of water for what seemed like several hours. My arm had long since ceased to feel any tiredness, which is the way it is when I fish for salmon. The hope of the rise or take on the next cast erases fatigue. It is almost the only fishing sport I know where an angler will put up with extreme physical discomfort for hours or days just to get that one rise. Big-game saltwater anglers will put up with all sorts of physical discomforts, too, but that is *after* the strike—such as in fishing for the big bluefin tuna and large marlin.

And suddenly, there it was. It was no spectacular rise, just the casual lifting of the head, the sudden engulfing of the fly, and the black, glistening shape of the dorsal fin and back showing as the fish sank back to its position in the current. It is then that the reflexes take over. I am convinced my wrist set that hook before I realized a salmon had taken that fly.

The line came taut and the rod bowed as I raised the rod tip, but the fish had not yet realized it was hooked and remained steady in the water. My heart began pounding as I realized the hook had been set and quickly shifted my feet so that I would be set when the fish began its run. Then it began to move—slowly at first, then gradually gaining speed until it was taking line off the reel at an incredible rate. I cupped the whirling reel handle as gently as I could with my left hand—being careful not to interrupt the smooth revolutions of the reel and break the leader.

The salmon's first leap was literally breathtaking—one of those where the fish thrashes in the air, almost touching its nose to its tail several times, before falling back to the river. The fly remained set this time. My shout must have carried downstream as well as back to the base of the hill where Bill Littleford was resting, because I suddenly heard pounding feet from both behind me and from downstream.

"A beauty," Littleford yelled. "Watch him!"

The salmon came out of the water again and repeated almost the same jump.

By now things had started going into that slow-motion action that happens whenever I have a big, active game fish on.

"Keep the rod tip up," I heard a different voice shout from over my left shoulder. "He's going to keep right on going!"

I grunted and nodded my head. It was no time to return comment.

The salmon, after another series of jumps, which took it more than 100 yards into the linen backing on the fly reel, turned in the center of the current and began streaking downstream. There were three huge rocks in the way. I began moving to my left, trying for higher ground so that I could keep the line and leader out of water as the fish approached the exposed tips of submerged rocks.

"Down this way," the man on my left said, pointing to a large, flat rock which stood several feet above the rest. I scrambled to the top of the rock, holding the rod as high as I could with both hands. The fish whipped by on the other side of the first two rocks and then, fortunately, cut between the last two. I could not have kept the leader clear of that remaining big rock.

"Good," said Bill, moving down to the shallow water below me, the long-handled, aluminum landing net grasped in his hands. "Now keep the pressure on him. He's got a lot of fighting to do yet!"

And a lot of fighting the salmon did. There was one run that almost carried it down to the mouth of a chute below, and it was only by running and stumbling down the shore that I was able to steer it clear of rocks and stop its run short of the head of the chute. As it was, the fish made three more long runs upriver—complete with several spectacular series of jumps—before settling down to an underwater battle in the middle of the current below, where it remained deep behind a large rock, shaking its head now and then. After such a battle, I am always cautious about putting too much pressure on a salmon. Following such runs and jumps, the hook is likely to have worked a hole in the fish's jaw and is more apt to pull out. However, there comes a time—especially with a strong fish like this one—when you have to start putting pressure on, or it will simply not give up. One doesn't want to give a strong, sea-fresh fish too much chance to regain strength. They are so incredibly strong that any help they get can cause them to summon that last burst of energy needed to get away.

"I think it's going to start coming in," said the voice behind me. I nodded as the fish began moving slowly from the center of the current toward us—ever so slowly—as I leaned into the 9-foot rod and wound the reel slowly.

"Good, good," said Littleford as he waded knee-deep into the stream—the long-handled net held close to the surface of the water ahead of him.

When the fish was about 10 feet from the guide, it spotted his legs, or the shiny net, and streaked off on another upstream run that whipped off nearly 75 feet of line before it slowed and stopped in the current.

"Damn!" said the man beside me. It was all that was needed said. I had fully expected the hook to pull out on that run. I began the slow retrieve again and this time the big fish was tired. It came, weaving in the current and turning on its side, until it rode the surface above Bill. As it floated by, Littleford quickly reached out with a smooth sweeping motion and plunged the net under the tired fish.

"Aaayaaah!" I heard the man grunt with satisfaction beside me, and I felt a sudden slap on the left shoulder.

Littleford swung the big net toward the bank and stumbled through the shallow water, the salmon thrashing in the nylon netting. I turned to the fisherman beside me. He was grinning widely.

"Nice fight," he said, shaking my hand. "Hell of a fish!"

I couldn't say anything. I felt too elated.

Bill laid the fish and net down on the sand and slowly extricated the fish's head from the mesh.

"Whew!" he breathed, pointing to where the black fly dangled in the side of the lower jaw. "That thing was just about to work out. One more run like that last one . . .!" He shook his head, removed the fly from the fish's jaw, took his short "priest" from his parka pocket, and solidly rapped the still-twisting salmon at the base of the skull. The big, silvery fish stiffened, quivered, and lay still. Littleford held it up by the gills, grinning at me. "Hen fish, probably was in the ocean a day or so ago." He gazed at the salmon. "Beautiful!" he said softly, "as many as I have seen, I still can't get over them."

"What will she weigh, Bill?" the man asked.

"Can't tell exactly," Bill said, "didn't bring a pocket scale. Seventeen— maybe eighteen. Nice fish." He glanced upstream as a gust of rain hit us suddenly.

"Hey!" he shouted. "Let's get under that big ledge!" He scrambled up the bank with the fish. "We are going to catch hell from this one!"

The other man and I, after a startled look at the wall of rain coming rapidly downstream, headed for shelter.

We no sooner reached the protective ledge than the deluge struck. Wind whipped the rain around us, and we inched as far back as we could against the slanted rock wall. Bill slid the salmon into a pocket of moss to his left and dug inside the deep pouch of his stained parka. He came up with a half-full bottle of bourbon.

"Anybody want some of this?" he grinned, holding it aloft.

The fisherman beside me nodded and took the bottle, upended it and, after a long swallow, wiped the neck with a hand and offered it to me. The whiskey warmed my throat and stomach as it went down, and I grinned as Littleford tilted the bottle up to his lips.

"Ahhh," he said, as he replaced the cap, "that hits the spot. Jesus, look at that downpour . . . oh, sorry, you guys don't know each other." He pointed at me. "Al," he said, "Jack Samson." We shook hands, hunched up against the rain and wind. "Jack, this here's Al Rockwell."

I nodded and shoved both cold hands inside my parka and smiled happily at the storm—thinking about the salmon.

It wasn't until a couple of minutes passed that I realized Rockwell was my host on the trip. I hadn't even known he was called Al.

I have hunted and fished with him in a number of places since, and I don't remember hearing any of his friends call him anything else. Also, I can't think of a nicer way to meet a guy.

Tips on Fishing the George . . .

Few sportsmen haven't, at one time or another, pictured themselves calmly working a pool of some remote Canadian river, deftly flicking out a fly at which a big, hungry, savage Atlantic salmon is almost honor-bound to strike. Enough people have done it to give the dream credence, and many of them have done it in and along the banks of the George River in northern Quebec. The George offers not only Atlantic salmon, but also outstanding prospects to take both brook trout and Arctic char.

The rub, however, is that the season is comparatively short. It opens early in July and runs until September, with the peak period—for salmon, anyway—being August and early September. The locale is, after all, pretty far north (above the 56th parallel) and one would have to be a glutton for punishment to want to flog a stream either prior to or after the close of the George River season.

Obviously, if you go, you will need warm clothing, even in August. And you will need a rainsuit, one that really does its job (there are days on the George when you will feel you must be in Rangoon during the monsoon season). You will also need an ample supply of insect repellent. The wee beasties can be voracious, and failure to deal with them can ruin a trip. Make sure, then, that your fishing clothing can be made snug at the neck and wrists. Bring along a headnet, too. You'll need felt-soled waders and a pair of stout, comfortable walking boots. Make sure you pack a pair of sunglasses; there *are* times when the sun shines. Really.

Your primary weapon should be a fly rod in the 8½- to 9-foot category, rigged with a salmon reel and at least 150 yards of backing. Bring along a couple of smaller, lighter rods for the trout and char.

The customary salmon flies—Silver Doctor, Gray Ghost, Jock Scott, Blue Charm, or Black Rat, tied on size 4, 6, and 8 hooks—apply on the George. Smaller flies—tied on 8, 10, and 12 hooks—will do nicely for brook trout, as will bucktails and streamers, a few of the latter tied on larger hooks.

A good place to stay is the George River Lodge, which offers comfortable heated cabins and good, hearty food in plentiful amounts. There is one guide for every two fishermen at the Lodge, and his services are included in the overall cost (as is the use of outboard-powered canoes). Fishing and hunting (for caribou in the early fall) permits are obtainable at the Lodge but are not included in the price.

Rates at the Lodge vary from week to week, depending upon the number of salmon in the river, but you can plan on spending between $750 and $1,200 per week, plus airfare.

Out of Montreal, Quebecair services Schefferville, from which you'll have to charter an aircraft to fly you to the Lodge. Adventures Unlimited can fill in all the details, or you can write to Bill Littleford (Nemacolin Inn, Farmington, Pennsylvania 15437). Bill is the outfitter for Helen Falls Camp, mentioned in the previous story.

7.

South Africa: The Cape Buffalo

"The buffalo stands proudly. He looks man in the eye with deliberate confidence, and whether he decides to run or fight, his decison is quick and clear. His flight is effective, his attack terrifying. It is almost impossible for a man with a rifle to stop the charge of an old bull. Anyone who says he can do so with certainty has not faced many charges, for charging buffalo come on as relentlessly as time. Their life may be destroyed within them but shattered legs carry them on; blind eyes seek out their enemy as they hold their own death at bay. All things eventually come to an end, but the end of a buffalo charge may come a lot later than a man might wish.

"When a buffalo is wounded he will plan his revenge with a cunning and determination that is beyond belief. He will run off, and then circle carefully downwind and take up a well-concealed ambush where his charge will have the best chance of success. However carefully the hunter moves, the buffalo's nose will tell him when to charge. If the hunter passes too far off, the buffalo will wait. He will stake his life only on a certainty. He does not know the meaning of the word 'bluff.' The death or savage gorings of ten professional hunters in twenty years are an indication of how the odds run. The score for the others of the Big Five is three each for the elephant and the rhino and five each for the lion and leopard."—Tony Dyer, professional hunter and former president of the East African Professional Hunters Association, in *Classic African Animals* (illustrated by Bob Kuhn).

The sun had just risen above the eastern horizon and was directly in our faces as the Land-Rover jolted slowly through the dense and tangled undergrowth of the Botswana bush. I was standing up in the back of the vehicle with the bushman tracker and gunbearer, holding onto the welded steel bars that serve to support canvas in the rainy season. But there was little chance of rain this morning. Although May by stateside calendar count, it was late fall in southern Africa and cold enough to require down jackets at this time of the day and when the sun went down.

We had already passed impala feeding in the thick cover, their dainty heads swinging to regard us as we ground by slowly in the sandy ruts. Near a water hole a mile back there had been a cloud of dust hanging in the shafts of early sunlight and a glimpse of several zebra as the main body of the herd thundered away into the tangled undergrowth. Giraffes ambled off in their curious slow-motion gait as we approached, but we had no thought of hunting anything but buffalo—nor had we for days.

The tracker suddenly grunted, shaded his eyes, and reached down through the opening in the roof of the cab to tap professional hunter Mike Bartlett on the head.

"*M'bogo,*" he whispered and pointed ahead.

I looked carefully and saw nothing—in spite of polarized glasses and a wide-brimmed hat keeping the glare of the rising sun from my eyes. Native trackers have eyes that are beyond belief. The hunting car jolted to a stop, and the engine coughed into silence as Mike turned off the key. He rose and stood on the seat, his glasses sweeping the brush where the tracker pointed. He finally nodded and slowly lowered the glasses. Without saying a word, he slid back down to the seat, slowly opened the

door, and beckoned to Ed Zern. As Ed quietly got out, the gunbearer beside me handed the heavy .378 bolt-action rifle down and swung a leg over the side of the vehicle to join the two men. Mike raised a hand to the tracker and me and motioned toward the brush. We nodded and remained quiet as the three moved into the heavy cover at a crouch.

I swung the 7×35mm glasses up and searched the bush ahead of them as they began the stalk. It was too thick to see anything from my position, and I kept the glasses on the three men as they moved ahead of us: Mike in the lead; Ed following, carrying the bolt-action rifle; and the bearer close behind with the .375 H&H double rifle.

The stalk took at least 20 minutes, and during that time not a sound came from the direction of the buffalo. I watched the men until they finally disappeared from view at least 100 yards ahead and slightly to my right. After that, it was simply a matter of waiting, while the sun climbed slowly above the horizon and my hands gradually warmed in the dry and brittle air.

The crash of the shot caused both the tracker and me to start. I swung the glasses to where I had last seen the three men, but saw nothing. Then, carrying clearly in the quiet morning air, came the noise of breaking limbs, the pounding of huge hoofs against the dry earth, and a bellowing sound. And after that—nothing. Off to our right there was the coughing bark of a zebra, startled by the blast of the shot and its echoes across the stillness. I looked at the tracker and he shrugged. One shot seemed strange with a buffalo in the thick brush, unless it had dropped dead at the impact, which wasn't likely. Still, the crashing of brush and the sound of hooves could have been other buffalo leaving the scene. We waited. Remembering the habit of a wounded buffalo of circling back to wait for his pursuers, I unsheathed the .416 Rigby, put two shells in the magazine, and laid it across the top of the cab in front of me.

Fifteen minutes passed and I was beginning to wonder about the safety of all three men when the tracker suddenly tapped me on the shoulder and pointed to our right. Mike was trotting toward us across an area of low brush, carrying the double rifle. He slowed down as he approached the car and finally leaned the rifle against the right fender.

"We may have something of a problem," he said as he filled his pipe from the tobacco pouch. I said nothing.

"It's possible it may be gut-shot. I don't know."

"Great," I said.

"Ummm," he nodded. "Couldn't be helped. There were two bulls. We got fairly close, perhaps sixty yards. The one on the right was bigger and I told Ed to take him." He paused to light the pipe.

"Just as he was squeezing off, the damned smaller bull winded us and spooked. The bigger one spun about and I'd just started to say 'Don't shoot' when the gun went off. They both ran into the thick brush and stopped. We have been waiting for some sign that either the smaller one left or the bigger one is dead, but—" he sighed—"nothing."

I nodded. "I'll take the .416 and we can move in slowly."

Mike shook his head. "No," he said, "thanks very much but that's what I am getting paid for. I appreciate it, but if he comes out of there I want to be very sure of where you two are. I'm not being paid to kill clients by accident."

I nodded and said no more.

Mike climbed into the vehicle.

"Might as well get up as close as we can with this," he said as he started the motor. The tracker and I grasped the bars as we jolted over the soft sand in the four-wheel-drive.

Ed and the gunbearer were standing beside a tree as the Land-Rover pulled up. Ed looked glum as Mike turned off the engine and opened the door. Mike motioned the tracker down and handed the gunbearer the .378 while he checked his cartridge belt for shells for the double rifle.

"Look," Ed said, "I'm going in with you. It will be easier with more than one gun."

Mike smiled apologetically.

"Please, Ed," he said, "I've already told Jack. It's too dangerous. If that buff comes out of hiding, God knows from what direction he will come. I must be absolutely certain there is nothing to distract me. If you or Jack are there, it will just make things very much more chancy. I would appreciate it very much—"

Ed nodded slowly.

Mike, the tracker, and the gunbearer began to move slowly into the brush. Ed leaned against the tree and ran a hand over his forehead.

"If that kid gets hurt—" he said. "He can't be more than thirty years old—"

I looked at him.

"Ed," I said. "He's right."

He watched the backs of the three men as they moved slowly into the thicket.

"I know, I know," he said quietly.

He climbed up with me in order to watch the white hunter, the tracker, and the gunbearer as they inched ever so slowly into the dense cover. No sounds broke the morning stillness and the men moved in slow motion. I recalled hearing Fred earlier in the week saying that a wounded buffalo could conceal itself in a patch of cover so small it would seem impossible that it could hide its immense size. The same is true of lion and leopard.

The approach took at least half an hour—all of it agonizing. Mike and the tracker at times remained on tiptoe as they gazed intently at something we could not see, only to crouch and move forward again and again. I was able to watch them all the way through the glasses. Finally I saw Mike raise the double rifle and aim at something. He held the rifle at his shoulder for what seemed like minutes before slowly lowering it. I then saw the tracker reach down, pick up something, and hurl it

into the bush ahead of him. The rifle came up again, remained, and finally came down slowly. Mike turned about and waved an arm over his head at us. I waved back. He motioned us to come in.

Ed shook his head slowly in relief as I reached out and slapped him on the shoulder. "Thank God," was all he said as we jumped to the ground and climbed into the car.

We drove the car through thick bushes until we were only a few yards from the huge buffalo. Mike was standing beneath a tree, a grin on his face, and he shook Ed's hand as we walked up. Both the tracker and gunbearer were also smiling.

"Everything worked out," Mike said. "Apparently just as you shot he was wheeling to his right. The bullet ranged up through the lungs and came out on the right side of his neck. The other bull spooked when we first moved the car toward him."

We walked around the huge bulk admiring the thickness of boss. Ed was beginning to smile. It was a very heavy head.

"It's a good thing the stalk took as long as it did," Mike said softly, puffing on his pipe. "He might have waited us out."

Ed nodded slowly as the skinners went to work on the carcass, the razor-sharp skinning knives opening gleaming white canyons in the 3/4-inch-thick gray hide.

In thirty minutes, the skinner had taken the hide off, removed the massive head and had loaded four quarters of meat atop green boughs they had placed on the floor of the Land-Rover.

"Enough meat to feed a village for a month," Mike said, watching the knives skillfully separate the meat from the spinal area. "This will all be dried as jerky in a few days."

"Look," I said, pointing up into the sky. Where half an hour ago there had been nothing in the clear blue above us, now there were dozens of vultures slowly circling, gradually dropping in altitude. About 100 yards away several of them perched atop an acacia tree.

"How do they know so fast?" Ed asked.

"White color," Mike said. "As soon as an animal dies—whether from a hunter or a carnivore—there is the color of white, white fat when the skin comes off. They have incredible eyes. One sees the white and starts to circle and another sees the first one begin circling, perhaps from miles away, and so forth."

"How much meat will the skinners leave?" Ed asked.

"Very little. Some around the neck and back area and the hide, ribs, and the stomach and most of its contents. There will be precious little left by nightfall when they get through with it." He waved at the circling scavengers.

He moved over to help the skinners lift the heavy head and cape into the back of the hunting car, where it lay, the eyes still staring balefully at nothing.

"Well," Mike said, dusting his hands on his bush jacket, "Piece of cake."
Like hell, I thought. *Like hell.*

"That's when he handles man-killing with all the ardor of a weasel at work in a henhouse. Unlike the 'toro' of the Spanish bullring, a Cape buffalo attacks with head up and baleful red-rimmed eyes glued solidly on his target. Any matador stupid enough to try a veronica on this outsize wild ox would find himself shish-kebab'd in two shakes. For variety, in the middle of his mayhem, he likes to crush a man beneath his big, splayed hooves and sometimes, maddened by the odor of salty human perspiration, he'll use a raspy tongue to lick a helpless hunter's flesh clear to the bone. I have had to stop a charging buffalo at 12 yards and it is not my personal idea of a picnic."—Russell Barnett Aitken, in *Great Game Animals of the World.*

And the days merged into each other, mornings clear and cold with the sun rising an incredible pinkish-orange to the northeast over the marshes of the Cuando River. Hot tea woke us up at 4:30, and a breakfast of eggs and ham, wolfed down in the frigid dining hut of Chobe Camp, fueled the body long enough to keep circulation moving in fingers until the rising sun warmed them into life on the rutted, sandy roads of the bush. Down jackets could be discarded by about 8 A.M. and by 9 the tsetse flies would awaken from the cold and begin to buzz about the hunting car whenever it stopped in the shade of an acacia tree or heavy termenalia bush. Insect lotion smeared on hands and face discouraged direct attack by the flies, but one always found a spot to rivet through a light shirt.

There were greater kudu, but none big enough, gray ghosts in the grayish-green thorn brush.

There were the herds of impala, an occasional eland, waterbuck, zebra in droves, swamps full of dainty lechwe, scattered groups of wildebeest in the brush, and giraffe everywhere. Ostriches streaked across open sandy spots just when the last thing we wanted to see was an ostrich. Scurrying mongoose crossed the road in front of the hunting car, and flocks of guinea fowl and francolin ran ahead of the vehicle in the narrow ruts of sand. But still there were no buffalo.

Harry finally got the sitatunga antelope he had been hoping for for three years. The great bateleur eagles swung in circles high over the swamps and brush, and the ringing call of the fish eagle wafted from the dead limbs on which the regal bird perched near water, while the tiny, incredibly colored malachite kingfisher perched in the sunlight along the winding river like an impossible jewel in a sea of green swamp grass. Elephants moved casually through the brush, paying little heed to the hunting car—except for one enraged cow that charged full speed and was outrun in deep sand by the Land-Rover. "Probably had a calf in the thick bush," Mike casually remarked after leaving the trumpeting animal behind. *Or perhaps it didn't like cars,* I thought. But still few buffalo, and those all cows and young bulls.

The down jacket went back on as the sun set each evening in a northwestern sky of orange, rose, and lavender—a color captured by no camera, few artists, and almost impossible to describe, except to those who have seen an African sunset. A shower is torture in the nighttime chill, yet necessary after 20 or 30 miles per day in the hot, dry, dusty bush. Clean clothing is a luxury earned by the agony of the run from the shower to the tent. The burning acacia logs of the campfire smell a bit like mesquite, and no beer in the world tastes better around a hunting fire than South African Windhoek or Castle pilsner. And the talk, before a meal of impala steak, guinea fowl, or sitatunga, was of the day, the frustrations and the triumphs, the accidents and the laughs that make up any hunt, whether it be for elk in Colorado, whitetail bucks in Pennsylvania, or gemsbok in Kenya. There was John Lawrence, the hunter/artist, now a dean of white hunters—moustached, craggy-faced, and bronzed from decades in the bush—with his tales of lion charges, white hunters flattened by elephant, and buffalo mauled by lions and ripped by streaking leopards. Over dying coals we talked of the days of the long-ago war when Lawrence was a major in the British Army in Burma, and of names all but a few of us who were there have forgotten—Lashio, Lungling, and Myikyina. And there were the names of men who believed that long war would stop wars—Chennault, Stilwell, Merrill, and others long dead. After the coals died down and the blankets felt good, the lion came into camp and hauled off a quarter of buffalo as though it were a pork chop. The skinners, cooks, and trackers kept a big fire going all night and talked until dawn in the large thatched-roofed hut. During the darkness the hoarse, coughing grunts of a hyena echoed across the swamp as the animal circled the camp and, just before dawn, the night was split with blood-chilling shrieks as a leopard systematically began killing baboons perched high in a grove of trees.

The morning had been the same as a dozen others—giraffes spooking everything close by with their seemingly awkward lunge into the heavy cover, and impala bounding in unbelievable leaps over low brush. One lone roan antelope near a waterhole had watched us idly as we moved past. Warthogs had run, stiff-tailed, into thorn brush and, at one sunbaked wallow, a satin-smooth black mamba eased its sinewy length across the gray earth as the tracker and gunbearer nervously watched its progress.

"No need to kill it," John said, casually. "Bloody deadly if they strike, but it's part of everything."

I was on the outside of the front seat, while Ed sat in the middle and John drove. The sun was high and we had turned about to head back to camp for lunch. The .300 Colt Sauer between my knees was in case of a good greater kudu, but had not been fired in four days.

Suddenly the tracker reached down and punched, not tapped, John on the shoulder. The Land-Rover braked to a sudden stop, and John turned off the engine. He leaned forward and raised his tiny single-lens glass. After a moment, he said a few whispered words in bushman. There was a hushed reply from above. John slowly waved me to the door, cautioning silence with his hand as he did so. Ed took the .300 and I eased from the door. John stepped from the driver's door and reached up for the rifle. I came around the front of the hunting car and stood beside him. He handed me the .416 Rigby.

"Big buff," he said. "Chamber a round."

The 9-pound-plus rifle had no weight as the huge cartridge with its full-jacketed bullet slid into the breech. It was a matter of closing the bolt and making sure the safety was off. John, already in a crouch, started moving off to the right, beckoning me to follow. One must remember to keep eyes to the ground to avoid any dry limbs. My heart hammered in my chest and temples, and at the time, it did not seem strange that John carried no backup gun. Suddenly he was waving slowly and pointing ahead—ahead to where a huge black shape moved at a leisurely walk through the brush, which reached as high as its shoulders, perhaps 100 yards from us.

"See him?" John whispered. There was little need to ask.

"Hit him," John said.

The heavy rifle came up as though in a slow-motion movie. The crosshairs finally found him in the maze of tree limbs and branches. There were only the faint, insistent voices—always there on important shots: *Hold it steady on the shoulder, a bit back and not too low. Move it with the motion of the game and squeeze, squeeze. Don't jerk the trigger, hold it on—*

The crash of the shot surprised—as it should—but I felt no recoil.

The buffalo seemed to stumble a bit, then broke into a lumbering, incredibly fast run, circling to our right, head up and eyes searching for us. Another bulky shell slammed into the chamber.

"Hit him again!" John's voice was low, clear, and insistent.

The huge animal, dust spurting from around his churning legs, swung toward us, and the blast of the big rifle slammed back against the shoulder, yet again there was no sense of recoil.

The buffalo tore down several medium-sized trees in its path and leveled a number of bushes as it swerved to our left, head high and still searching—then it suddenly folded in midstride and crashed to the earth in a cloud of dust. It tried to get to its feet, thrashing about and bellowing, huge horns hooking at the air, and bits of limbs and earth flying upward.

"Hold it," John said. "Hold it. He may be down for good."

Minutes seemed like hours as the big bull continued to roar and thrash about, finally grunting less and less, until only the massive head and horns were moving.

"Let's go," John said, moving toward the animal, about 30 yards away. We stopped nearby, making sure the big bull was now immobile.

"Finish him off," John said softly.

The 410-grain slug went home and this time the big gun kicked —noticeably.

A few tick birds flew off into the brush as we cautiously approached the huge bull. Air was still escaping from the lungs and several ticks moved about on the surface of the scaly coat. John slowly touched the bull with his shoe. There was no movement. It was then that I noticed the gunbearer close behind us with the double rifle.

"I thought you had forgotten that," I said. John grinned and shook hands.

"Not very bloody likely," he laughed. "Damn good buff. Should go forty-five inches. Nothing for the book, but a hell of a head for Botswana."

There was sunlight and there was stillness. The buffalo, inert, still looked lethal. I handed the gun to the tracker, who grinned and shook hands. The gunbearer shook hands and also grinned.

"Whew!" I said. There didn't seem much of anything else to say. Tsetse flies buzzed all about us. I couldn't have cared less.

Ed came walking up with his camera and slowly circled the bull.

"I thought he was never going down," he said.

"I had the same sensation," I said. "Those full-jacket solids don't shock much."

"It's a bloody good thing they don't," John said, kicking the bull in the shoulder. "Your first shot took the top of the heart out. It's the size of a football, you know. The second broke the right front leg high and went through the lungs. A lead slug would have splattered against that hide and never gotten through the bones of this ugly beast. As a matter of fact, the metal-covered solid wouldn't have gone through the stomach, if you had been a few feet farther back—not with all that grassy food in there."

Ed took some pictures before the skinners began their work on the buffalo. Then we began walking toward the hunting vehicle. Halfway, we stopped, and Ed looked back.

"All by himself," he said. "I wonder what that old bull was doing out here in the brush all by himself." He turned toward the Land-Rover, shaking his head.

"I guess he came to meet me," I said.

He stopped and looked at me for a moment, then slowly smiled.

"I never heard a better reason," he said, as we continued walking in the noon heat.

Tips on Safari Hunting in Southern Africa . . .

Safari! The very word suggests adventure, magic, a close-to-the-bone "moment of truth," an experience of a lifetime. It is all these things and more, even in a day of easy access to game areas, somewhat restricted hunting, and comparatively plush, in-the-field accommodations.

East Africa is the area we tend to have in mind when we think of going on safari, and it still offers good hunting. But southern Africa—countries such as Botswana and South Africa—is where most of the action is these days. Sudan, in the north, is coming on strong, too.

Most hunting in southern Africa is done during our winter months, which is summertime in the area, a dry season during which game animals tend to travel in herds. A typical safari in the area lasts about thirty days, although shorter outings—some for as little as fifteen days—can be arranged. A hunter seeking one of the rarer or more difficult trophies can stay out as long as a month-and-a-half, the extra time being necessary to search for exactly the "right" animal. Overall, your time on safari varies according to what you're after and where you're after it.

A good, well-organized safari is highly mobile, tending to move between satellite camps, more or less permanent set-ups situated to dovetail with established game patterns. Or, depending upon the game sought, you could spend most of your days being jounced about in a four-wheel-drive vehicle, your nights in a small tent. In any case, the safari is designed to help you get what you're after. And you won't be alone. Assisting you will be a professional hunter, plus assorted trackers, drivers, skinners, gunbearers, cooks, and field and camp hands.

It's possible to book your own safari, but generally it's best to utilize the services of a travel agency that specializes in such outings. Not only do they know the ropes, but through experience and feedback, they are in a position to clue you in on the many little details that can make the difference between a good trip and a shambles.

Regardless of how much you trust that friend of yours who has just come off safari, complete with glowing tales of a given trip in a given area, keep in mind that what you propose to do involves Nature—with a capital N—in all its fickleness. Areas and outfitters change, often from month to month, even from week to week. That's why it's important to have the very latest information available and to put yourself in the hands of a knowledgeable outfit.

Also, each safari area—usually each country—has restrictions as to the number and caliber of the firearms you can take along. If you specify in advance, it's possible to rent appropriate firearms, but it's best to pack your own simply because you

presumably (in fact, had better) know them like the back of your hand.

You should pack light, medium, and heavy caliber rifles as well as a good shotgun (for upland birds and waterfowl). A good light rifle would be something on the order of a .270 or a .300. Such firearms would be good for light plains game. If you can only bring in one rifle, probably the best choice would be something along the lines of a .375 or .300 magnum fitted with a variable scope. Thus armed, you can not only take the lighter game, but also large antelope, lion, and so on. For the heavy stuff, you'll want at least a .416 caliber or more, perhaps a .458.

By all means bring along a camera, a good one. Reliving your safari on film is almost as rewarding as the original. A 35mm single-lens reflex featuring a built-in exposure meter and fitted with a telephoto lens in addition to the normal lens should serve you handsomely.

Bring binoculars, too, preferably seven or eight power units (7 × 35, say, or 8 × 30). You'll be on the move most of the time, and scanning with glasses of higher power is just about impossible, particularly from the seat of a jouncing Land-Rover.

The cost of your safari will vary, depending upon where and how long you want to hunt—and how elaborately. In any event, figure that a thirty-day outing costs between $7,500 and $12,000, *not* including either overseas or local charter aircraft, and utilizing the services of only one professional hunter. To this amount will be added trophy fees and the cost of preparing and shipping trophies to a taxidermist. You can hack it for less (by sharing a hunter, say), or you can live it up for more; the amounts mentioned are only average costs.

You could start planning your safari by getting in touch with Adventures Unlimited, or you might write to Hunter's Africa (P.O. Box 11, Kasane, Botswana).

8.
Alaska's Trout and Salmon

A chill Alaska wind was blowing into the mouth of Pavlof Bay—the bite of it cutting even through the layer of goosedown jacket and outer windbreaker. Across the miles of choppy water loomed Admiralty Island, hazy in the early morning sunlight, as we cast the heavy salmon flies into the teeth of the wind.

All around us jumped the silver coho salmon—slashing up the current, leaping with abandon, and falling back to the surface with a slapping sound as though someone had thrown a heavy spruce log from the bank. Fresh-run from the sea and strong with the urge to spawn, the great fish surged up the current heading for the big holding pools upstream at the base of a waterfall not more than 100 yards above. Like all spawning salmon they were not hungry fish, and there is probably no more exciting and at the same time frustrating sport in the world than fly fishing for them on the first wave in from the ocean.

I had caught an 8-pound fish half an hour earlier that had taken a big red-and-white streamer fly in about 3 feet of water, running swiftly over a bed of boulders. The rise—much like Atlantic salmon's—had been casual, almost nonchalant. Remembering what our guide Buzz Fiorini had said about the coho having a tough mouth after the years in the ocean, I had set the hook hard several times. The resulting explosion of power had been awesome. The salmon took off across the river in one wild, straight rush, stripping off more than 100 yards of line in a matter of seconds. Well into the backing by then, it took to the air in a series of twisting, thrashing leaps that sent shocks up through the 7-foot, $3^3/_8$-ounce split cane rod and into my right arm.

Twenty yards above me on the same shore, Bing Crosby stripped in his line, leaned his rod against a large rock, and walked down to watch the battle. I could hear Buzz's camera clicking behind me each time the salmon jumped.

The fish moved into the center of the current now and took a position below a large boulder where it began a savage shaking of its head, trying to rid itself of the irritating hook.

"Looked like a beauty," Bing said, the ever-present pipe clenched in his teeth and his fishing hat pushed back on his head. "That little rod is going to get a workout!"

It did. So did I. The little rod has taken a lot of salmon—from Scotland's Spey River to New Brunswick's Miramichi—but it had never been fastened to a gamer fish than this one.

Like all great contests with salmon, this one settled down to a battle of fish strength against the punishing pressure of the curved bamboo rod. And as is the way with those who love the great fish, no one said anything as the fight went on and on—quiet periods broken by a burst of thrashing power and speed as the fish took to the air over and over, running downstream several hundred yards and then fighting its way back up against the current.

"My God, look at that!" Bing said during a lull in the fight. Several miles out in Chatham Strait a pair of blowfin whales surfaced—their black backs glistening in the sunlight and a white spume of steam spurting high in the air before they both submerged and their huge flukes rose gracefully into the air before sliding beneath the surface.

"How big do you think they are, Buzz?" he asked.

"About fifty or sixty feet long," Buzz replied. "They stay in the Strait all year long, passing up and down. A couple of years ago I had one come up along a big ledge where I was fishing and rub off barnacles from its sides. It looked as big as a submarine."

We both shook our heads as I went back to playing the coho. It took twenty more minutes to subdue that fish. In the meantime, a pair of seals had moved into the bay right behind another wave of incoming salmon, and remained a few hundred yards from us, with just their heads out of water.

When the big coho was finally thrashing in the shallows at my feet, Buzz walked down and, as I gently guided its head toward shore, grabbed the fish by the tail and heaved it onto the bank. The fly fell out of the jaw as it flopped on the gravel bed and, after taking a few closeup pictures of the gleaming silver coloration, we eased the salmon back into the current and watched it swim slowly off. It had weighed $9\frac{1}{2}$ pounds on the pocket scale.

Buzz and I sprawled on the bank after that and watched Bing cast over the schools of leaping and rolling silver salmon. Here and there we could see the carcasses of bright red sockeye salmon lying on the bottom of the river where they had lodged after floating downstream to die after their spawning run. Along the edge of the river, behind rocks and at the base of riffles, smaller splashes occurred as the sea-run cutthroat trout slashed at the schools of tiny stickleback minnows. We had taken them for days on smaller wet flies when the salmon action died down. Some had weighed 3 and 4 pounds, and they put up a magnificent fight. Also fresh from the cold waters of the Alexander Archipelago, they tasted wonderful baked in the evening back at the lodge.

"Damn!" Buzz grunted beside me. "One hit the fly."

Bing grinned, shook his head, and started casting again. "It struck right at my feet," he shouted. "Followed it all the way in to the bank. It hit just like a big trout."

I was watching Nelson Bryant, far upstream, casting to a spot across the river, when I heard Bing's yell and saw him set the hook. His $8^1/_2$-foot cane rod doubled over and a wild salmon hurled itself from the pool and somersaulted its way across the current in a series of spectacular jumps.

"*Olé!*" Bing shouted as the fish tore line from his reel and headed upstream. His face wore a happy grin as he pounded up the bank of the big, boulder-strewn river in bulky chest-high waders. His pipe trailed a stream of blue smoke behind him as he went, and he was as happy a man as ever fished. This is the Bing Crosby few people know—the Crosby who grew up as a kid in Washington State with a cut birch pole and a hook and line, and who would rather fish and hunt in his spare time than do almost anything else, except perhaps play golf.

By the time he landed his 9-pound coho, after a battle of about 30 minutes, everybody was involved. Nelson had come downstream to watch and photograph; I was trying for action jumping shots; and Buzz was sticking close to Bing, warning him of slippery rocks underfoot that he was far too busy to see.

Bing, his face flushed from exertion and the joy of combat with the coho, grinned like a kid and decided to keep this fish for dinner. Nelson went back to his fly casting, while Buzz decided to try for one with his long rod and shooting-head fly line. Bing and I found a sheltered spot out of the wind, where the early August sunlight bathed the grassy slope, and began heating tea on a small portable stove. Later, as we sipped the scalding tea in aluminum cups and watched the other two men cast, Bing, like all outdoorsmen, talked of the fish he had caught (and missed) and the hunts he had made over the years.

Looking out over the expanse of Pavlof Bay, north of Juneau, on this clear day and hearing Bing talk of his life in the outdoors, I thought back to my image of Bing Crosby in those days prior to and during World War II. I remembered the happy dialogue of the "Road Pictures" with Bob Hope and Dorothy Lamour; the Irish songs Bing sang as a Catholic priest, and the duets with Louis Armstrong and Grace Kelly. And I remembered a long-past night in a makeshift hangar during the monsoon season in western China in 1943. There, a bunch of dirty, bearded guys from Claire Chennault's 14th Air Force listened in silent homesickness as Bing sang, on the screen, "White Christmas," while the rain lashed the corrugated roof above.

Well, the "Old Groaner" was seventy while we fished Pavlof Bay, and he is still going strong. In the days that followed, we flew by float plane down the Strait to Baranof Island and fished for rainbow trout. We landed on tiny Lake Eva to the north, across from Admiralty Island, and caught sea-run Dolly Vardens up to 4 pounds. We caught so many—releasing all but three for a meal—that our arms were weary. We caught more fresh-run salmon and cutthroat trout from Mitchell Bay on Admiralty, and the sun stayed out and the winds died down the last few days—not a common thing for Alaska.

As Nelson said one morning while we were donning waders after breakfast preparatory to climbing into the float plane, and Bing was standing on the porch, viewing the still lake and singing, "Oh, What a Beautiful Morning," "That ain't bad!" It also wasn't bad to hear "Der Bingle," fast to a 4-pound Dolly Varden thrashing the surface of a tiny mountain lake, singing, "Hello Dolly, Hello Dolly . . ." to the leaping trout.

Tips on Fishing in Alaska . . .

It would be hard to imagine anyplace on earth that is more of a sportsman's paradise than Alaska. To some of America's nineteenth-century pundits, Mr. Seward's famed purchase may have seemed folly, but to successive generations of fortunate outdoorsmen, Alaska was a far better bargain than the $24 supposedly paid for Manhattan Island. There aren't many salmon swimming up Broadway, my friend.

Consider the forty-ninth state's variety of game fish: chinook salmon (locally called king salmon), coho salmon, sockeye salmon, rainbow trout, cutthroat trout, Dolly Varden, Arctic char, grayling, northern pike, whitefish, inconnu (locally called sheefish), white halibut, and on and on. And where else on earth is one likely to work a salmon run with a few grizzly bears as fishing companions?

In fact, so vast and varied are the state's natural supplies of fish and game, a sportsman has to reorient his thinking before even dreaming about taking a crack at them.

For one thing, you will have to agree to fly, at times in aircraft Wilbur and Orville might have hesitated to enter. Few of Alaska's great fishing spots can be reached by car, even four-wheel-drive vehicles. Thus the bush pilot is king, and sportsmen seeking true wilderness have come to appreciate just how skilled and dependable such men are. At first, neither the man nor his machine may inspire confidence, but once he sets you down near a stream, say, that gives up an arm-jarring ten-pound steelhead, you'll deem him a genius on a par with Daedalus.

For another thing, and this is true particularly in early summer, you will have to deal with what has been described as "Alaska's most dangerous species"—the mosquito. You think you've seen and warded off big, tough, nasty mosquitoes, right? As Al Jolson used to say, "You ain't seen nothin' yet." Alaska's mosquitoes have been madder than snakes ever since human beings first showed up, and obviously they're still trying to drive mankind into the sea from whence he came. You may never have

pictured yourself working a stream while wearing gloves, but Alaska's mosquitoes will, at the very least, expand your awareness of insect power.

You will also have to accept and deal with the fact that temperatures along a given body of water can fluctuate by as much as 50 degrees in a 12-hour period. You can start a day's fishing bundled up like a polar explorer, and by noon find yourself wondering how come there aren't any palm trees in sight.

Finally, you will have to get used to the idea that there is no *one* spot you've simply *got* to fish. On any given day at the right time of the year, one body of water can be as productive as any other. Where you go depends upon when you go and what you want and how much you are willing to pay to get there.

In general, the best months to visit Alaska on a fishing outing are from May through October. July and August are the warmest months, but warmth is relative; if, on an August morning, you have had to break ice for coffee water, 57 degrees can seem like a day in the tropics.

Bring your own gear, particularly a good supply of flies, streamers, lures, spoons, spinners . . . whatever. There are well-stocked sporting goods stores in the cities and bigger towns, but in the bush or in small villages, you will be out of luck.

Bring hip boots or waders, a pair of rugged, comfortable hiking boots, rain gear, sunglasses, headwear, long johns, heavy duty socks, sweaters, a warm winter jacket, a pair of lightweight gloves, a pair of warm gloves, insect repellent, a headnet, and anything else you may need. You may never use it, true, but if you *do* need something, you will be glad you brought it along.

You can't plan a fishing trip to Alaska too carefully. Good Neighbor Sam may rave about the So-and-So River during the first two weeks in July, but you could show up on the third week and be sorely disappointed. It is absolutely necessary to seek and heed the advice of those familiar with local conditions. Alaskan sportsmen generally know what is running where, and they're not selfish about pointing you in the right direction. Like every other state, Alaska maintains a Fish and Game Department (see Appendix B) complete with rules, regulations, and bulletins—and advice, usually good advice, which is available for the price of a letter or a phone call. There is also something called the Alaska Visitor's Association, which can be helpful, and the various chambers of commerce have never been known to be bashful.

In addition, Alaska Airlines, Western Airlines, and Wien Consolidated Airlines—among others—offer packaged fishing trips, often including stops at camps, lodges, and other accommodations that the airlines themselves maintain. There are many privately-operated camps throughout Alaska, most of which maintain contact with travel agents and tour packagers; or you can get a list of them from the Visitor's Association and contact them directly. An outstanding example of such an operation is Thayer Lake Lodge (Box 4116, Ketchican, Alaska 99901). The head man is named Bob Nelson, and like most camp operators in Alaska, he really wants you to have the best fishing time of your life.

One final note: Don't wander off on your own, either on foot or in a boat. Alaska is—and, one hopes, always will be—a wild and rugged place of incomparable natural beauty, but it can be fatal to a tenderfoot. Not hiring a recommended guide is false and foolish economy. There are louts in the trade, true, but a good guide (and don't be reluctant to ask hard-nosed questions) can be worth his weight in gold, not only in terms of comfort and safety, but also for pure and spectacular fishing enjoyment.

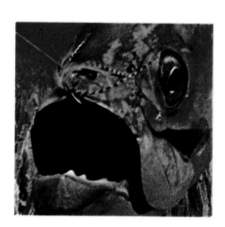

9.
King of the Keys

It was June and it was hot and the humidity was high—ideal bonefish and permit weather for the Florida Keys.

Permit are fine fish, and I had never caught any on a fly rod. I had caught two the year before at Chub Cay in the Berry Islands, but both had been on a spinning outfit, with sand crabs for bait. There is nothing unsporting about this method of fishing. It is an effective method, and a permit is more than likely to get away from you no matter what tackle you use. I just wanted to take one on a fly rod, and the Keys were the best place to try.

Oscar Godbout and I had been over in the Everglades for a couple of days trying to catch some big largemouth bass from an airboat out of Frog City on Alligator Alley, but the fishing had been slow. We had taken a couple of fair fish, but the big ones were sulking in the grass, and no popping bug or weedless plug could bring them out. Oscar had gotten a couple of good columns out of it for *The New York Times,* and Sid Latham had been puttering around us in another airboat taking some color shots. We had gotten back to Miami, and Sid was due back in New York for some meeting or other.

Since we had done a couple of stories on sailfish and kings off North Key Largo with Allen Self, we had pretty much all the big-game stuff we needed. Breakfast was almost finished and Sid was about to leave.

"Well," said Oscar, after putting away his usual three-course breakfast, "it's either we go to the pool and look at the stewardesses, or we fish."

We had been staying at the Miami Springs Villa, the home of a stewardess training school, and the scenery at the pool at all hours of the day had been pleasant.

"I worry about you two," Sid said, getting up and shaking hands. "It's been lots of fun. I think we may have some good stuff—both the largemouth and the sails." I shook hands with him as Oscar pushed his chair away from the table and stood up.

"So long, hotshot," he said.

"Good luck with the permit," Sid said, "although I don't envy you the heat."

We watched him thread his way between the tables before we paid the cashier and walked to Oscar's battered station wagon in the parking lot. The back was loaded with rod cases, tackle boxes, suitcases, camera gear, and assorted junk Oscar always threw in. We had checked out before breakfast and had the several hours' drive to Islamorada ahead of us. We had originally intended to drive down to Key West, but only had the day to fish and couldn't spare the time. Besides, guide Jack Brothers, a displaced New Yorker who had given up Fun City years before for the beauty and peace of the bonefish flats, had assured us there were plenty of permit about. Oscar had caught one the year before in lower Biscayne Bay, but this was his first trip to Islamorada.

The holes in the boat rack atop the station wagon set up a maddening moaning sound as we sped south of Homestead on U.S. 1.

"Why the hell don't you put tape over those holes?" I asked. "Or throw the rack in the back?"

"Oh, I don't know," Oscar said casually. "I kind of like the sound. And if I take the rack off, I'll just have to put it back when I put the aluminum canoe on."

"It sounds like your transmission's falling out," I said.

"It could be," he said lazily. "With the expense account the good gray *Times* gives me, I'm lucky to be driving instead of walking."

It was hotter than the proverbial hinges when we pulled up at George Hummel and Bill Pate's tackle shop to call the guide.

Jack's wife answered the phone and told Oscar that Jack had gone to Miami to pick up a new outboard motor. She said he would be back that evening.

"Damn!" said Oscar after hanging up. "That blasted Irishman forgot all about us coming down."

"When did you call him?" George asked. "That doesn't sound like Brothers."

"Call him?" Oscar asked. "Hell, I told him a couple of months ago I'd be here the first week in June. You can't depend on anything any more!"

"Christ," I said and looked at George.

"Any other guides around this time of the day?" I asked. It was almost ten o'clock.

"Nope. I was over at Bud and Mary's for breakfast when most of them went out. Everybody had a charter."

"What about boats?" Oscar asked.

"There's a couple at the dock for hire," George said.

"Fine," Oscar said. "Jack here knows the water. We can just tool out for a couple of hours and try for some fish. If it gets too hot or the fish aren't hitting, we can always come back and sit in a cool bar."

There was a 13-foot Crestliner with a $9\frac{1}{2}$-hp Evinrude and an 18-foot Mako with a big 85-hp Johnson for rent. We decided on the big boat because of the heat. Running speed cools one off in the hot weather. We got sandwiches made up, put some beer and ice in the chest, stowed the rod cases and tackle boxes, and finally set off down the narrow channel toward the flats. The high tide was expected at two o'clock, so there wasn't much water over a few of the bars as we headed for the flats to the west of the highway bridge, hoping to find some areas of turtle grass and shallow water where we might catch either bonefish or permit feeding on the incoming tide.

Oscar had his big rod rigged by the time I slowed the boat near a couple of small mangrove islands and tilted the big motor up. There was absolutely no breeze, and we floated on the glassy water as though in a large, muggy fishbowl. I could feel the sweat begin to pop between my shoulder blades as I slid the 9-foot fly rod from the aluminum case and started fitting it together. I took the big reel from a leather case and fitted it to the reel seat. I had rigged up a 15-foot leader to the 30 feet of shooting-head floating flyline before leaving the hotel. The tippet at the end tapered down to 3X—perhaps a little light, with a breaking test of about $5\frac{1}{2}$ pounds, for big permit, but they are a spooky fish and have good eyesight. There was about 150 yards of 12-pound linen backing on the reel. After stringing the No. 10 shooting head through the guides, I tied on a light-green keel fly Bing McClellan had tied up, one he swore was the best bonefish and permit fly around.

Oscar had on a yellow keel fly some guy had given him in Miami and was perched on the bow platform scanning the still flats. I picked up the wooden pole and eased the tip into the white sand. The silence was unbroken, except for the slight crunching sound of the pole each time it touched the sand, and the gurgling of water passing beneath the transom. Off to our right, a great blue heron took off with a hoarse croak and winged across the water to a less disturbed mangrove clump.

The heat was suffocating and the glare of the burnished sun on the water made me squint even through polarized glasses.

"Mud," Oscar finally said, pointing off to our right. I could see the milky puffs in the water where a school of fish had fed recently on bottom worms or crustaceans.

"Hard to tell whether it was bones or permit," I said.

"More than likely bonefish," Oscar said slowly, "the water as shallow as it is. Let's try a little more to the left toward that deeper channel. Maybe we can spot a school coming in on the tide."

I nodded and shoved the pole into the sand.

We saw nothing but an occasional barracuda and a collection of snappers for the next twenty minutes until suddenly Oscar pointed to our left, where the white sandy bottom shelved off into the blue channel.

"School of bones coming," he said, crouching a bit. "Swing the bow left a little. If they keep coming along the edge I may be able to reach them."

I swung the bow left, then shaded my eyes to look. I finally saw a school of perhaps thirty fish headed almost directly toward us. They were in about a foot of water and appeared to be cruising slowly rather than feeding. Oscar stripped line out at his feet and began false-casting as the school approached. I felt the old excitement as I watched the lead fish come closer.

Oscar dropped the fly well ahead of the school and let it sink slowly to the bottom.

"Good, good," I whispered. "They should pass right over it."

Just about the time the lead fish reached the spot, Oscar picked up the rod tip slightly and twitched the yellow fly. I could see it move slightly on the bottom. Strangely enough, three or four fish passed over it without making any move to pick it up. I thought they were not in a feeding mood, but suddenly one of the fish swung from the school, tilted nose down, and picked up the fly.

"Ugh," Oscar grunted as he set the hook, the rod held high over his head. The big rod bowed sharply and the reel sang as the fish took off across the flat to our right.

"Yeehooo!" Oscar laughed. "Look at him go!"

It was a good fish and it made four or five long runs. Oscar was a fine fly fisherman, having learned as a kid in his native Vermont. It didn't take him long to bring the fish alongside. I netted it and we held it up for a picture. It weighed 8 pounds on the pocket scale. We slid it back into the water and released it. The silvery fish swam off slowly at first, then suddenly took off on a straight run for the channel.

"Here," Oscar said, reeling in his line and stepping down from the forward casting platform. "Let me pole for a while. Let's see you top that bony."

He opened the ice chest and took out a beer. "Want one?" he asked.

"Nope," I said, stepping up to the bow. "It's a little early yet. Let's see if we can find another school and then I'll join you."

We poled across that flat for another half an hour without seeing any bonefish or permit. There was a basin off to our right where the bottom was covered with turtle grass. The tide had been feeding in through the channels for some time now and the water was getting considerably deeper. It was getting harder to stay in the shallows. I looked out to the right and noticed a disturbance on the surface of the water in the center of the basin about 100 yards away.

"Oscar," I said, shading my eyes with a hand, "what do you make of that?" I pointed. Oscar, can in hand, stood on the seat and looked.

"Holy cow!" he said softly. "Tarpon!"

I felt my heart speed up. "You're kidding," I said.

"The hell I am," he said, "I'll tell you what that is. Tarpon move in a circle like that in spawning season. They keep right on going around and around like that for hours. I caught the biggest tarpon of my life in one of those daisy chains at Big

Pine Key a couple of years ago. Sit down and hand me that rod. I'll reel in that line while you get the other spool out."

I nodded and handed him the rod. I dug the other spool out of my fishing vest. We had been fishing for sailfish a few days before with the other spools and I had 200 yards of 20-pound linen backing on the reel and 30 feet of No. 11 weight-forward floating flyline. The leader went down from a 3-foot section of 60-pound mono, where it was fastened to the flyline with a nail knot smoothed over with airplane glue so it would slide through the guides easily. After that came another 3-foot section of 30-pound mono tied to the bigger length with a blood knot. Another blood knot took it down a 12-pound section, then to a 18-inch length of 80-pound mono shock leader. Oscar was threading this through my guides as I fitted the big reel to the seat. My hands were trembling as I did it. I had caught several tarpon from New River at Fort Lauderdale and the St. Lucie Canal near Stuart, Florida, but none had been over 12 or 15 pounds.

Oscar snapped open his fly box and took out a red Keys Tarpon Streamer fly on a No. 4 hook and quickly fastened it to the end of the shock leader with a regular clinch knot. He reached into his tackle box and grabbed a pair of fishing pliers and tightened the knot as hard as he could.

"O.K., chum," he said, handing me the rod. "Now if we get lucky you are going to have the time of your life. I'll get you as close to those monsters as I can, but remember they can see a long way in this clear water and they may spook. Lay that fly slightly ahead of the one you pick, but don't let the leader come across its back. Fish him just like you would a trout. But the main thing," he said as he picked up the pole and began pushing the boat slowly toward the disturbance on the surface, "is to make damn sure all the line you strip out is coiled at your feet where you don't step on it. Keep the other coils in your left hand, and if one of those beasts takes the fly right after you set the hook, don't look at him. Keep your eye on the coils as they go out, because they are going to be going fast! When the coils are all gone, then you raise that tip as high as you can, look up if you still got him on, then hang on and play him with the brake. O.K.?"

"O.K.," I said over the pounding of my heart. I could see the huge shapes now as they circled slowly in about 6 feet of water. "My God, Oscar," I said. "They look like submarines! How big do you think they are?"

Oscar stopped poling and looked for a moment.

"Hard to really tell from here," he said softly, "but a couple of those big ones could go well over a hundred pounds."

My mouth was dry and I licked my lips as we inched up to the circling fish on the still surface.

"O.K.," Oscar said quietly. "Strip off all the line you need to make a cast of at least sixty feet and maybe more. Start your false-casting as soon as we get into range. Pick the one you want. Try to pick one that is sort of away from the others, not one that's swimming with his nose close to the tail of another. It can see the fly better."

I nodded and started stripping off line. When I had enough out, I started the casting. Only the swishing sound of the line broke the silence. The fish were moving as in a strange ritual dance. I saw one slightly off to my side of the circle swimming slowly, its dorsal whip out of water and the tip of its huge tail breaking the surface lazily. A couple of hauls and I shot the line at a spot about 6 feet in front of the fish. The line began hitting the surface about 30 feet out and the leader followed and slapped to the surface—like a telephone pole hitting the water, I thought, but perhaps it was just my imagination. The fly settled to the surface about 10 feet too short.

"Not quite," Oscar breathed. "Try it again. At least they didn't spook. Don't set the hook too hard if he takes it. I honed that hook as sharp as a needle. It will go in with luck. They have plates all over them. The only thing to worry about is busting that twelve-pound tippet."

I had the line back and started the casting all over again. I knew it had to be close to 80 feet to where the big fish swam. I picked another fish on my side of the circle. I tried to time it so that the fly would hit quite a bit ahead of the big head, but I misjudged it by a few feet and the streamer fly landed about 3 feet ahead of the fish and a foot or so to my side of it.

"Oooohhh," I heard Oscar breathe.

The big fish simply tilted its head up, opened its jaws the size of a peach basket, closed them on the fly and sank beneath the surface. I struck with a snap of my wrist and remembered to look down at the coils. I heard the sound of water being churned up as if by a waterspout, but I didn't look until the last of the coils had left my hand and the platform at my feet. When I raised the tip and looked up, the tarpon was suspended against the horizon 150 feet away on what must have been his third or fourth jump. The fish was twisting viciously in the air at least 10 feet above the surface. The sound of Oscar's wild yell mingled with the dry rattling sound of the big fish's gill plates and the crash of water.

My arm was nearly yanked from the socket when that fish hit the end of the billow in the line. I have seldom—with perhaps the exception of the bluefin—felt such unleashed power! Another and another jump across the surface of that lagoon until I couldn't believe the fish could keep it up! I had 100 yards of backing out and the fish showed no signs of slowing down when Oscar dropped the motor down, pushed the starter button on the console, and started after the fish.

The jumps became slower but the fish was still moving away from us at a terrific speed. I felt the boat pick up speed as Oscar added power.

"Reel, reel," he shouted over the motor noise. "He's not about to stop for a while!"

The fish had stopped jumping now but was swimming steadily toward the middle of the distant bay. I could see the many-spanned highway bridge, hazy in the distance to the east. The other side of that was the Atlantic.

"He's headed for the Bahamas!" I shouted above the noise, and Oscar laughed with glee.

"How you like big tarpon?" he shouted.

"My God!" was all I could say.

I gained some line in the next thirty minutes while we simply kept up with the swimming fish. It was indeed heading for the bridge—swimming against a strong bay current and a still-incoming tide. I applied the brake as much as I could and finally felt the fish tiring. It had been almost an hour and both my arms and back were numb from the strain when the fish suddenly decided that fighting the tide, current, and the big rod was tiring him too much. A mile or so short of the bridge he suddenly made a circle in front of the boat, and Oscar slipped the throttle into neutral. The boat coasted to a stop in the still water as the fish took to the air in another series of dazzling jumps.

"I think you got him whipped," he shouted. "I'm going to raise the motor in case he starts going under the boat."

I was too busy with the fish to watch him. The fish made several more twisting, frenzied leaps, falling back to the surface with a loud crash each time. Finally, he simply began to come in on his side, his huge gills flaring each time he took a breath.

Oscar reached for his camera as the fish came alongside. I heard him take several shots as the big tarpon lay on the surface not more than a few feet from the boat.

My rod was bent double and I looked at Oscar.

"What do we do with this thing?" I laughed a little unsteadily at the thought of gaffing it.

"Hell," Oscar said. "We can gaff it and haul it aboard if you want, but I don't know what you'd do with it unless you want it mounted. They aren't any good for eating."

I looked at the great silver length of it and shook my head. "No," I said, "I don't see any sense in having it mounted. It's a hell of a fish, though. How big you think it will go?"

"Oh, close to one hundred pounds," Oscar said matter-of-factly. "I doubt if it will go quite that, maybe ninety."

I looked at it again. "Well," I said, lowering the rod tip a little and letting the fish's head settle in the water, "cut him off. Let him grow to weigh one hundred and fifty pounds and I'll catch him again."

"No need to cut him off," Oscar said. He reached out, took the fly in his thumb and forefinger and removed it from the fish's mouth. The big silver king simply sank slowly out of sight in the milky water of the bay. I sat down.

"Congratulations, pal," Oscar said, shaking my hand. "You have just been kissed by a tarpon."

I looked at my hands. They were shaking from nerves and strain.

"Now," I said. "*That* is something else!"

"You bet your fanny it is," Oscar said, lowering the motor and punching the starter button. "And I have had all the excitement I want in this heat. Let's get back to Bud and Mary's and get into an air-conditioned room. One big tarpon is enough for any man in his life."

I don't know about that, I thought to myself as the boat began to pick up speed across the flat surface of the bay. *I don't know about that.*

Tips on Florida Fishing . . .

Years ago there was an old fellow who lived alone in a small house overlooking a backwater of Florida's Palm Beach. A visitor from the North, concerned about the old man being lonely, and solicitous as to how he passed his time, asked him if he ever went fishing.

"No," the old man said, "I don't have to."

Somewhat startled, the visitor asked what *that* meant . . . he didn't *have* to?

"Well," the old man said, "I caught a tarpon once. Weighed a little over a hundred pounds. I figured that was about all the fishing pleasure the Lord had down in the book for me, so I haven't wet a line since. Besides, if I ever hooked onto another one, I don't think my heart could stand it."

That's the way it is with tarpon. They are spoilers. Once you tie into one, most other fish become—in prizefight parlance—"mere opponents." For pure strength, tenacity, acrobatic display, and just plain no-holds-barred fighting, few fish can equal a tarpon, regardless of size. That they *do* reach sizes of up to 150 pounds or more should give anyone pause; they can literally kill a man. There have been several recorded instances of fishermen being done in by tarpon. At the very least, to hook one is to risk cardiac arrest.

In Florida, tarpon can be found in shallow waters along just about the entire coastline, east, south, and west. They are more abundant in southern Florida waters from about Vero Beach south to the Keys and around to Sarasota and slightly above, especially in the winter months.

Florida waters will also give up permit, mango snapper, king and Spanish mackerel, bonefish, jack crevalle, amberjack, bonita, pompano, snook, redfish, specks, billfish, and many other species. What you can get where is pretty much a question of seasons, but even a so-called off time can afford a dazzling catch of fish. Florida is one of the few states that find it necessary to prepare and issue quarterly or even monthly bulletins about its sport fishery.

An angler thinking about a Florida trip should keep a few things in mind:

One, it can get cold in the winter. Miami doesn't like to admit it, but temperatures in the high 30s are not unknown. And unless you've experienced being drenched by sea spray late on a January afternoon, when all you want is to get back to the dock and into a hot shower, you don't know what really cold is. In other words, bring a couple of sweaters, a jacket, and rainwear.

Two, bring canvas wading shoes. A sea urchin

spike stuck in your foot can introduce you to pain on a par with that of a medieval rack. Bring sunglasses and lots of anti-sunburn protection; a sea urchin spike *and* a severe sunburn (particularly late on a chilly afternoon in a small boat) is a preview of hell.

Three, while Florida may be the Sunshine State, it is also a haven for two-legged sharks. Only too willing to promise you the moon and deliver nothing—expensively—are some sharp operators who cruise the sportfishing docks preying on pale-faced tourists. Be sure you know who is guiding you where, and for how much—all things you should settle before you cast off.

The question of equipment isn't as critical here as it can be most other places. The entire state is fish-happy—both fresh and saltwater—so there are plenty of tackle shops, bait shops, and so on, many of which will rent gear on a daily or weekly basis. Charter boats, both sportfishermen and party boats, can generally provide anything you might need in the way of equipment.

Unless you know where you're going—and with whom—a good rule of thumb is to check with any office of the state's fish and game department. Florida likes happy tourists, and straightforward questions will usually elicit straightforward answers.

Facilities afforded fishermen are, seemingly, endless, so it is difficult to suggest specific accommodations. Deal with people whose self-interest requires that you enjoy yourself and get results. The airlines serving Florida, for example, want you to come back again and again, and some of their packaged fishing tours are first-rate. Just keep in mind that, invariably, you get what you pay for. For sound advice on Florida Keys fishing, write or contact Adventures Unlimited or World Wide Sportsman, Inc. (P.O. Box 787, Islamorada, Florida 33036; telephone 305–664–4615).

10.
Scotland and the High Birds

The first time I shot driven birds was in Scotland, and I learned a very valuable lesson.

I learned that it is not too smart an idea to try it with a .20 gauge shotgun, and I discovered a lot about leading birds I had not known before.

Arthur Oglesby, the European editor of *Field & Stream,* and I had been invited up to Seafield Estates on the northeast tip of Scotland to shoot pheasant and red-legged partridge. Our host was Eric Yates, a fine field shot and fisherman. His family estate was anything but modest, and by the time Arthur and I had been assigned our luxurious rooms by the doorman, Igor, and had bathed and changed clothes, I had already moved back several hundred years in time.

After dinner with the host, his wife, and half a dozen other shooting guests, plus a session in the huge library before a blazing log fire, a lot of my Scottish ancestry had begun to crop up.

My mother was born in Glasgow and came to America when she was eleven years old. Her maiden name was Jesse Steele Young and her father had been in the wrought iron business. I don't remember him at all as he died when I was very young after the family had moved to America and lived in Providence, Rhode Island, but I think I would have been very fond of the old man had I known him. I remember my grandmother making some references about him and "dirty friends" who would take off for the Highlands each year to fish for trout and salmon and would come home after days of not shaving or changing clothes. Anyone who did that every year couldn't have been all bad!

But to get back to my learning some lessons about driven birds. I had brought along a nice, light, Spanish AYA, a .20 gauge side-by-side which I had used for quail and pheasants for years in the States. It was a light gun, with 26-inch barrels, improved cylinder and modified, and had a selective single trigger. When I had asked Arthur what gun to bring he had simply said to bring a double—side-by-side or over-and-under. He hadn't said anything about gauge, only just not to bring an automatic as the English were a little touchy about them. I don't hunt much, except ducks and geese, and shoot trap and skeet with an automatic, so that was not too hard a request with which to comply.

We arose at a decent time in the morning and, after a light breakfast, headed out for the shooting grounds. The weather was damp and overcast with a chill wind blowing in from the North Sea just a few miles to the north of the town. It looked as though half the population of the small town of Cullen had turned out as beaters this day. There were 30 or 40 men and boys standing about with an assortment of dogs ranging from sheep dogs to labradors and spaniels. All wore the rough, country clothing of northern Scotland and appeared a happy lot—red-cheeked and sturdy. All wore walking boots and carried staffs.

The strategy was quite simple. The shooters were stationed in a long, spread-out line at the base of sloping fields—perhaps 60 or 70 yards apart—and the townspeople were to walk over the grain and beet fields in skirmish-line formation. The birds, and there were a lot of them on the hillsides and in the fields, would flush ahead of the line of beaters and would come sailing down the hills over the heads of the shooters. I was beginning to feel quite confident about the outcome of the hunt and was stamping my feet to keep them warm when the first birds flushed far up the hillside above me. They were pheasants, and after the first climb for altitude, they set their wings and came sailing down toward us. Arthur was to my right at the corner of a stone wall, and I turned to see him starting to raise his Purdey side-by-side. I swung back to watch a big cock bird head in my direction. The bird had its wings set and only occasionally would it flap them a few quick beats to keep up its momentum.

As it passed above and to the left of me, about 40 yards out, I swung ahead of it and pulled the trigger. I had started to lower the gun without firing the modified barrel—fully confident that the big cock bird would drop like a stone. Not a feather flew, and the pheasant landed just short of a patch of woods nearly a quarter of a mile behind me and ran into the thick cover. I looked at Arthur, who was casually inspecting the sky.

A few moments later another pheasant passed within range, a few yards farther out, but by no means an impossible shot for a .20 gauge. This time I carefully swung ahead of the banking hen and fired both barrels to make sure it came down dead—instead of flying on with its heart shot out as the first bird had obviously done. Not only did no feathers fly, but the bird did not seem to show any indication that several charges of shot had passed within inches of it. I glanced quickly at Arthur, who was dropping two new shells into his gun and looking at a flopping cock pheasant he had dropped about 100 yards behind us.

The next flight of birds was a group of three red-legged partridge that skimmed close to the surface of the ground as they came down the hill and then sailed neatly over the stone wall behind which we stood. There was no chance for a passing shot as there were shooters on both sides of me, so I took what appeared to be a fairly easy going away shot on one which had nearly taken my hat off as it went by. Both charges of shot may not have caught up with the bird at all as it sailed into the woods.

Arthur blew the smoke out of the barrel and glanced at the one partridge he had neatly dropped not far from his pheasant. I coughed and reloaded the gun after glancing at my shells. They were high base No. 6's and there was absolutely no reason why they should not be working perfectly.

I missed the next four birds in a row. By that time not only was my confidence in my shooting becoming shattered, I was getting damned embarrassed. An old gentleman to my left had not missed a bird, and Arthur had missed only one—and that one flew into the woods with wings set after losing a bunch of tail feathers. I was staring grimly at the approaching line of beaters when I heard Arthur's footsteps behind me.

"I say, Jack," Arthur said in what I detected was a slightly embarrassed manner. "Would you mind awfully if I made a suggestion?"

"Of course not, of course not," I said, trying my best to sound hearty about the whole business.

"You may be shooting a bit behind these birds," he said. "Have you shot driven birds before?"

"No," I said, "I haven't, Arthur, but I think I'm leading them enough. I'm using about the same lead as I would on a passing duck and that certainly should be enough, wouldn't you think?"

"Ummmmm," Arthur said. I had no idea what that meant.

"Tell you what," he said finally. "If it won't bother you, would you mind if I stood behind you for a bit? Perhaps I can pick up whatever it is you are doing wrong."

"I think I am standing too close to the hunt," I said.

"Eh?" Arthur said.

"Nothing, Arthur," I said. "Little American humor there."

"Oh," was all he said. "By the way, what sort of charge are you using?"

"High brass in the two-and-three-quarter-inch shells. I could have brought three-inch shells for this twenty gauge, but I didn't think I'd need them. It's chambered for three-inch."

There was a moment's silence.

"Did you say twenty gauge?" Arthur asked.

"Yes," I said, handing him the light gun. He leaned his against the wall and hefted the gun, then swung it slowly.

"What are the barrels?" he asked.

"Improved and modified. Twenty-six inches."

"Good God!" Arthur said.

"Good God what?" I said.

"Look," he said, trying to sound very earnest. "I assume you can select your triggers with this little button the Spaniards put on these . . . guns?"

I thought I detected a pause before he said the word "guns."

"Oh yes," I said.

"Good, good," Arthur said, almost absently. "Then I suggest you push that tiny button or switch or whatever it is and set it for the modified barrel. Just put one shell in that barrel. Don't bother with the improved one. You won't be needing it."

I looked at him for a second before removing one shell and pushing the selector switch to the left barrel.

"Very well, now," Arthur said. "On the next bird, pull ahead of it and just before you pull the trigger, pull ahead another five feet or so."

"Another five feet or so!" I said.

"That's right," he said firmly.

When in Rome, I thought to myself.

The next bird was another hen pheasant, flying in that same even glide which looked as though the bird were slowly floating by. I swung ahead of the hen, remembered Arthur's advice, and pulled ahead another few feet before firing. The bird dipped for an instant and left part of a tail feather floating in the air as it sailed toward the trees.

"Ummmmmm," Arthur said.

"What do you think?" I asked.

"I think several things," he said, frowning slightly. "I should have said six feet ahead of that bird, and you really should put that nice little thing away in the car and use my other double."

"Why?" I said a bit defensively. "I've shot a hell of a lot of birds with this gun and I like the way it swings."

"You may have shot a hell of a lot of birds with that gun, my friend," Arthur said politely. "But they were not driven birds in Scotland, and they were not coming down off these hillsides."

I looked at him for a moment. "Whatever you say, Arthur," I smiled. "You sure as hell should know what you're talking about. It's your country."

"Exactly," he said. "Now take this double. It is one of a matched pair. I always carry its mate in case something goes wrong with one. I shoot both at grouse when I have a loader and must shoot quickly."

"You're sure you don't mind me using it?" I said seriously.

"Of course not," he said, taking my AYA and starting to walk toward the car, which was several hundred yards away, before he stopped. "By the way, the barrels are thirty inches, full and full. Take a bit more than normal lead, even with that gun," he said and walked off.

I hefted the Purdey. It was a lovely thing with beautiful engraving, double triggers, and a very straight stock. It weighed considerably more than the light .20 gauge and the stock was a bit long for me, but otherwise felt all right.

The next shot I had was at a high-flying red-legged partridge which sailed, wings set, about 50 yards above me and to the left. I pulled ahead of it and touched off the trigger. The bird lost a handful of feathers and I pulled the trigger again. The gun did not fire. However, the partridge did fold in mid-air further down the slope and land with a thump.

"Damn!" I said aloud. I had forgotten there were two triggers. I only shoot single-trigger shotguns. I was going to have to concentrate on moving that finger back to the other trigger.

Arthur came strolling back with the other gun and grinned at me.

"Good shot," he said, pointing at the downed bird. "I watched you from the road. That was a good distance up, too."

"It was nothing," I said. "Range is no problem with a double rifle like this."

"You'll be bloody glad you have that 'double rifle' before the day is over," he said and clumped back to where he had been standing.

And glad I was. It took some time for me to get used to reaching back for that second trigger. But the gun did not kick much, heavy as it was, and it was beautifully balanced.

We left that particular field after the line of beaters walked to the bottom of the hill, then we all drove over to the base of another hill about a half-mile away. It was a big beet field and was full of birds. By the time the beaters walked down it, I had killed eight pheasants, a half dozen partridge, and had missed only four or five birds.

After a tailgate lunch in the field, we went back to shooting. One exceptionally interesting butt where the hunt master stationed me was in the bottom of a deep gully in the midst of tall trees. Most of the leaves had fallen from the trees, since it was mid-September, but there were enough still left on to make spotting the

11.
Bronzebacks of Quebec

"In the first place," said Ed Zern, upon whose word I have depended for years, "a smallmouth won't take a bug that small."

I nodded, fingering the tiny bluegill popping bug I had just removed from my bass case.

"And in the second place," Ed went on, "the wind on this lake is going to blow all day, the way it did yesterday, and no fish, not one single fish, under God's great golden sun, is going to see that little panfish popper in waves a foot high."

I wasn't going to argue with Ed. He has fished all over the world, and every fisherman is entitled to his own opinion. That, and the difference between guys who favor one horse over another, is what makes fishing—and horse racing.

We had run into some problems in taking smallmouth. There were all the northern pike around that anyone wanted. They hit trolled plugs and spoons about 25 feet offshore wherever we passed a likely grass bed, and the walleyes kept banging the deep-running plugs off the rocky points. We were fishing Lac Desert on the Gatineau, about 100 miles northwest of Ottawa, Canada. We had come up in the morning, via Air Canada, through Montreal, and then to Ottawa, where our fishing party—comprised of host Jim Rikhoff and guests Ed Zern, Gene Hill, Cornelius Ryan, Jack Saville, and me—were then transported to the lake via two float planes.

The fishing lodge owners had assured us that the fishing—now that the mosquito and black fly season was about two weeks past—was going to be just right. It had been and was just right—for walleyes and northerns. But in two days nobody had caught a smallmouth, although it was reputed to be one of the best smallmouth lakes in Quebec. True, the wind had been blowing fairly hard and the lake was large, so that there were few sheltered areas where one could cast a bass bug. Also, no one had brought fly rods but Ryan and me—mine was a $3^3/_8$-ounce split bamboo and Ryan's was a one-ounce bamboo rod—hardly suitable to the rambunctiousness of hefty bronzebacks.

I always pack a light fly rod just in case. We had thought the lodge owners would have a few, so the rest of the party had not bothered to carry them. There were plenty of spinning rods around and the standard equipment for the northerns, walleye, and lake trout was trolling gear. The guides were Algonquin Indians who knew the country well and fully expected the guests to be happy with the northerns, walleye, and lakers. If we had not known there were smallmouth in the lake, there would have been no challenge. There is not much that can beat the walleye as an eating fish, and for days we had feasted on the succulent fillets. The northerns had hit like the proverbial ton of bricks—had sulked behind the boat like sunken logs until they saw the hull, then had taken off and battled until netted. But the guides didn't think much of them and were not fond of separating the meat from the bones.

The second day we tried for the lake trout, but we had to go after them at depths of from 60 to 90 feet with big sinkers and "Christmas Tree" rigs. It worked, but by the time we got them to the surface, they were almost drowned, and there was little fight to them.

It was on the third day that Ed made the slighting remark about my tiny bluegill poppers. I had forgotten to bring along any large deer hair bugs or any cork poppers of the size I normally use for bass. I had taken a breakdown rod and level-winding reel for plug casting and trolling, but the bass hadn't shown one sign of interest in surface plugs or divers. We had cruised the rocky shoreline for hours, casting into likely holes, and the bass had ignored the offerings.

I knew the bass were there because Ed had hung one on a gold spoon the day before and had gotten two jumps out of it before the two-pound-or-so bass had shaken the hooks. But every time I tried to find a shore where I thought I could cast a bug, I found the wind either behind me or blowing in my face and—even with the tiny plastic panfish bugs—the rod was too light to get any distance. I was using a double-tapered floating line and a 9-foot tapered leader and it still was a task to get out enough line to reach a shore 30 feet away. I finally gave up—mostly because both the guide and Ed were getting bored with my rocking the boat while standing up and trying to reach the shore.

We went back to trolling and took some nice walleye for dinner before I finally got the itch again.

"Zern," I said, realizing I was treading on some fairly thin ice, "I have an idea about these smallmouth."

There was an ominous silence.

"Look, Ed," I said, taking a deep breath. "What if I guarantee you a smallmouth in, say, ten minutes?"

I got a grunt for that attempt.

I went all the way. "How about betting me a buck I take a smallmouth on the first cast?"

A glimmer of light appeared in the dulled eyes of a man who has fished the greatest salmon streams of the world and the private rills of nobility across Europe.

"A buck?"

"A buck."

"You're on," was my reward.

"O.K., Mathew," I said to our Algonquin host. "You remember that cove about a mile back that emptied into the lake? The one with the channel and the moving water, where the rocky shore came right down to the water?"

My host nodded slowly.

"Take me back there," I said, "and as you enter the cove, slow down that nine-and-a-half-horsepower motor and just let it idle. I don't want to move too fast."

Mathew looked at Zern. He knew who had the brains and seniority in the group. Zern shrugged and began reeling in his trolling line, with which he had been slaying walleye for hours—with obvious sadistic pleasure. I had a feeling the dollar played a part in the decision.

It took about fifteen minutes to get back to the mouth of the cove. The wind was blowing like blazes, and the waves were washing up on the rocks with splashes audible for 100 yards. Casting was a waste of time because the back cast would have had to be into the teeth of a 15-knot breeze and I have had too many hooks embedded in the back of my neck for that.

"On the first cast," Zern said, with all the uncertainty of a Greek shipping magnate negotiating for a secondhand skiff.

"On the first cast," I said, with all the confidence of a hung over skid-row derelict applying for a job as an alpine guide.

"O.K., Mathew," I said. "When you get into the cove, run that motor at idle and make a slow turn. I just want to get this little bug over that channel."

His eyes lit up a little. I began to think I had an ally. I got out about 20 feet of line and cast in toward the rocky shore. Zern gazed indifferently out toward the middle of the lake, obviously planning where he would wantonly spend the ill-gotten dollar. I left the bug in the water, but I twitched it a couple of times.

"Take her in a little, Mathew," I said. "I want to get a big billow in the line where that water calms down over the channel."

The only other honest man in the boat nodded solemnly.

"You said one cast," said Zern sternly.

"I only made one cast," I observed.

"Trolling is not a cast," he said.

"Trolling is a cast," I said, equally as sternly, "until one picks up the bug or fly and makes another cast."

"Semantics," said Zern.

"Smallmouth and one buck," I said, which caused a strange silence on the part of Zern—who must have been reviewing the grammatical aspects of semantics and fishing lore.

The line began to billow out behind the boat as Mathew started to make his turn, and the relative calm of the cove gave me some relief from the battering waves. As the line began to curve on the surface, I began to move the tiny popper bug in short jerks. Nothing happened. Zern nodded approvingly.

Mathew had made two-thirds of his turn and I had begun to mourn the loss of face—not so much the dollar—when there was a surface boil and my popper disappeared.

"Yeowww!" I yelled.

Zern did not answer.

Out of the water came a beautiful smallmouth bass, somewhere in the 3 to 4 pound class, and began to jump.

"Yeowww!" Mathew yelled.

Zern inspected a jagged fingernail and looked bored.

At the seventh or eighth jump, Zern decided maybe the 3⅜-ounce bamboo rod might hold the bronzeback and resorted to psychological warfare.

"Lower the tip," he advised, "the rod can't take the strain."

I ignored the advice—in the midst of near-hysteria—with almost complete indifference.

"When he jumps again," said my benefactor, "let him have slack. That leader is fragile."

I nodded, my arm getting numb.

"Thanks, Ed," I said, "at times like this it's nice to know I have someone rooting for me."

"Would you consider fifty cents?" asked Zern. "There is a real good chance you are going to lose this fish and in that case, it won't be a total loss." I began to gain confidence.

The smallmouth bored into the depths for about the seventh time, and I was really beginning to wonder if the leader could take the strain. Also, I had tied an improved clinch knot and I was beginning to wonder about the durability of that good knot.

Ten minutes later, I brought the smallmouth alongside and Mathew netted it, ignominiously, with the big northern pike net—not that I couldn't have done it by running my finger through the gills and hauling it aboard. It was the dollar that stayed me from that rash act.

To his everlasting credit, Zern handed over the tattered, weatherbeaten dollar he received for his first humor column in 1898 from *Cap'n Billy's Whiz-Bang,* without a whimper. A big man is a big man.

To make a long story short, I caught three more smallmouth. I caught them all the same way, too—trolling the small popper bug through the cove and across the channel. And when the bug passed over the deep channel, up came a bronzeback and whacked it. I asked Ed if he wanted to try using the rod, but he maintained a stoic silence—developing a sudden ornithological interest in the Canada jays which were flitting from spruce to spruce.

After the fourth 4-pound smallmouth came aboard, Mathew informed me that there was a four-to-a-boat limit to bass. It was then that Zern agreed to try my fragile rod, obviously figuring that if he missed a strike he was doing it because he was law-abiding. Unfortunately, he caught a beauty of a smallmouth by the same trolling method—right in the same channel—and had to suffer the indignity of having it netted, brought aboard, and released.

After that—though we made four more passes at the channel—we got no more strikes.

"It is very easy to explain," Zern said, reeling in the floating fly line after we decided to return to camp for supper.

"Oh?" I said.

"Certainly," said Zern. "I will explain bass psychology to you in a matter of seconds, and I will charge you nothing for the lesson—which is a concession I seldom make."

"Proceed."

"That last smallmouth I caught was the only one released today, right?"

"Right."

"O.K., that bass went down into that deep channel and he talked to his chums, and you know what he told them?"

"No."

"Well," Zern said, "here is what he said. He looked his cousin George right in that fishy eye, and he said, 'George, you remember when Aunt Louise took that black and yellow wasp two summers ago, and it stung the living bejabbers out of her?'

" 'Yup,' George said.

" 'Well, I have news for you,' said that bass I caught. 'Compared to that wasp, there is a little black bug up there on the surface that is unreal.'

" 'What I mean, Man,' said my smallmouth, 'is that this little black bug does things you can't believe. First of all it grabs you by the lip, jerks you all over the blasted cove, finally hauls you to the top of the water, yanks you out of the water, slams you on the bottom of some kind of big log, grabs you by the cheeks and pulls something out of your mouth, and then throws you way out and back in the cove. It's just plain unfriendly, undignified, for a smallmouth to be treated that way. Furthermore, it smarts. Stay away from that bug!' "

"That's what he said?" I asked.

"That's exactly what he said," said Zern.

"Mathew," I said, "what you say we go back to the lodge for dinner?"

"Good idea," Mathew said, putting the engine into forward. "I learn a lot about bass today, that's for damn sure."

"Well," Zern said modestly, "we all do what little we can to help."

Tips on Fishing in Quebec . . .

At the heart of Quebec's Mistassini Park, over 5,000 square miles of plain old wilderness, are two lakes—Mistassini itself and Lake Albanel—fed by a network of rivers both large and small that afford some of the best and most varied freshwater fishing in the world. In the lakes and the rivers and streams that feed them are whopping bass, generous walleyes, and hefty, slashing pike, plus a large population of native brook and lake trout. In this country, you'd have to be an incredibly inept *klutz* to get skunked.

Weather in the area is varied and quite changeable. You're above the 50th parallel, which means that while it can be warmish during the day, it can be bone-rattling cold once the sun goes down, particularly in late August and early September (in fact, don't be surprised if it snows in early September). So pack plenty of warm clothing and a good rainsuit.

If brook trout are what you have in mind, bring along a couple of fly rods and all your fly fishing gear (most of the rivers are restricted to fly fishing during the peak season). Include a wide selection of fly and streamer patterns, and floating, sinking, and sinking-tip lines.

Both lakes are full of fish, including lake trout that cruise close to the surface in June and September, but go deeper in August, which will call for a trolling set-up. Spinning tackle will take lake trout in the mouth of the Albanel River, northern pike just about anywhere. For pike, figure on at least 10-pound line,

heavier if you're new at the game. As for an appropriate pike lure, the ubiquitous Dardevle probably has taken as many as anything.

Although the brook trout fishing is good from June on, the peak season is the last week in August and the first two weeks of September, when the spawning runs start. If you're thinking in terms of trophy-sized brookies, you might go somewhat off the beaten path.

Vieux Poste Lodge, located on an island in Lake Mistassini, offers short flights to satellite camps situated right on several of the spawning rivers. The satellite camps are tent affairs, far from fancy, set up to accommodate four to six fishermen. Food at such camps is invariably good (usually prepared by the resident guides), and, of course, the fishing can be fabulous, be it by wading or from an outboard-powered canoe.

If tenting isn't exactly your style, the Lodge itself offers comfortable cabins, albeit toilet and shower facilities are separate. The best way to reach the Lodge is by air from either Lake Cache, near the southern end of Mistassini, or Temiscamie Base, to which you can drive.

The park and its lodges are controlled by the provincial government of Quebec, so prices are fixed and reasonable. However, space for guests is limited, so get in line early. Write to the Quebec Ministry of Tourism, Fish and Game (12 St. Anne's Street, Quebec, Canada).

12.
East Africa: Land of the Tigerfish

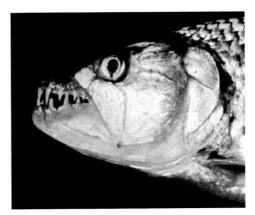

We first began hearing about the great fishing in Rhodesia's Lake Kariba as we came out of Botswana after two weeks of hunting for cape buffalo and greater kudu. The customs man at Kasane said he had been taking some fine tigerfish from the swiftly-flowing Cuando River, which flowed into the Zambezi a few miles to the northeast. He said that he took his fish on large silver and brass spoons, using spinning tackle, and that we needed to use wire leaders. He was certainly right about the wire leaders!

I was battling my first tigerfish on Lake Kariba two days later, and I don't recall any game fish which strikes more savagely or has a better chance of cutting the line.

"Better keep him out of those limbs," said Jim, my guide. "That's light tackle you're using and these fish are brutes."

I was almost too busy to hear him, but I nodded and tried to steer the zigzagging fighter into clear water. My light spinning rod was bent as far as it would arc, and I had loosened the drag on the reel so the plunging fish would not break the 8-pound mono. The fish had been on for at least five minutes and showed no signs of tiring. It had smashed a live minnow bait lowered into the top of a dead tree. The tops of dead trees were everywhere—killed from the waters of one of the world's largest man-made lakes. The tree tops harbored schools of bait fish, and the tigerfish—which travel in marauding schools themselves—tend to circle the submerged tree tops to prey on the fry.

The fish suddenly streaked for the surface and jumped. I had no time to take up all the slack and reeled as hard as I could to gain back line.

"Look out!" said Jim, as the fish broke water. "Keep the tip up and don't give him any slack!" Every guide and friend with whom I have fished for years has given me the same bit of advice every time a fish has jumped, whether it was trout, salmon, or marlin. However, it is exactly the right advice, and I suppose I have given it myself a few thousand times. I did just what I was advised to do and—thanks to the gods who watch over all fishermen—the tigerfish did not shake the hook on that jump or the two more it made in quick succession.

"Here he goes again," I muttered as the fish made another deep dive toward the safety of the submerged tree limbs—whipping the tip of the rod almost under the boat. I swung the rod tip behind the stern and led the fish into deep water again, where it continued to circle at will.

The tigerfish is endemic to Africa and is found from the Lower Nile River to such lakes as Albert, Rudolf, Marguerita, and such Gold Coast rivers as the Niger, Volta, and Offin. It is also distributed through Lake Tanganyika, the Upper Zambezi, Olifants, Crocodile, and Komati rivers in eastern Transvaal to rivers and lakes in Rhodesia, Botswana, and the Republic of South Africa. It is a superb game fish but is not considered much of a delicacy as food because of its many bones. However—much the same as the bonefish of the Bahamas—it can be and is eaten by native people who have learned ways of preparing it. Its weight has been recorded as up to 30 pounds, and it has a habit of tearing up even heavy tackle.

For centuries tigerfish had inhabited the mighty Zambezi River as it plunged through a seemingly fathomless gorge for 225 miles south of the incomparable Victoria Falls. Eroded through the centuries, the sheer rock walls of Kariba Gorge defied exploration and bridges. It was an awesome place known throughout central Africa and by the local, primitive Batonka tribesmen as the unassailable domain of Nyaminyami, the wrathful god of the river who lived in a citadel where huge rocks thrust up through the swirling currents at the deepest and darkest whirlpool. Today, the home of Nyaminyami lies more than 300 feet below the surface of a lake contained by a massive concrete-arch dam wall 420 feet high forming an inland sea of 2,200 square miles, with a maximum depth of 390 feet and a length of 175 miles. The huge lake today forms the border between politically troubled Rhodesia and Zambia.

And the god Nyaminyami? Many Africans, besides the Batonka people, believe he still sleeps a troubled sleep in his deep, submerged gorge—biding his time for revenge against those who dared to challenge his power.

"I think he's tiring," said Jim, as the tigerfish began swimming to the boat in ever-decreasing circles. I nodded and reeled slowly, being sure not to put too much pressure on him. Jim reached for his long-handled net and stood up in the boat—leaning slightly to peer into the clear depths. The fish came up gradually until I could see the glint of silver and gold in the water below me. The early morning sunlight pierced the depths and made black finger traces down through the water where the shadows fell from the dead tree branches.

The guide eased the net into the water as the strong fish circled close to the hull, and suddenly—with a boil of water—the tigerfish again streaked for the depths as it saw the net enter the water.

"Damn," said Jim and sat down to wait a bit more. I tried to keep the diving fish from the sunken trees and gazed toward the shoreline about a quarter of a mile south of where we were fishing near Bumi East—about halfway between the town of Kariba at the east end of the lake and Bumi Hills, a resort hotel five miles or so up the lake from the dam site at Kariba. A solitary bull elephant fed contentedly on a small island just to our left—more than a quarter of a mile from shore.

"How do they get out here?" I asked, nodding at the elephant.

"Swim," Jim said.

"Really?" I said. "All the way out here?"

"Oh yes," Jim said. "They swim very well and for great distances. I remember last spring passing one several miles from shore. It was heading for another island where it thought the food was better. They swim very strongly, with the tips of their trunks sticking up for air."

"I'll be damned," I said. "I never would have thought an animal that big would want to swim for any distance."

"You should have been here when the lake was filling up in the early fifties," Jim said. "It was really incredible!"

When the engineers began their assault upon the Kariba Gorge in 1955, he said, the only inhabitants for hundreds of miles around were the elephant, rhino and hippo, the tsetse fly, malaria mosquito, uncounted small game and birds, and the primitive Batonka people. As the waters rose at the sealing of the dam, the silence of the land was broken by the agitated buzzing of insects, the anxious chattering of

rodents and monkeys, and the frightened cries of big-game animals trapped on the many small islands formed by the encroaching waters of the man-made sea.

Every year, for countless centuries, wildlife had suffered the same fate due to the annual flooding of the mighy Zambezi, but this time it was being caused by man. As the news quickly spread to many parts of the world, governments and conservation organizations flooded the country with telegrams of concern and many sent money and personnel to help evacuate the wildlife. The S.P.C.A. in Johannesburg contributed a large boat to help in lifting game animals from the myriad islands dotting the 800 miles of lake shoreline. The smaller game was caught in nets and transported to dry land by boat. Elephants and other large game were driven into the water and assisted in their long swim to shore by constant ramming with long poles. But it will never be known how many animals perished in those few years while the water rose to make Lake Kariba one of the largest lakes in the world—surpassed only be Lake Bratsk in the U.S.S.R.

"He's coming up again," I said. "See if we can't scoop him from the surface. He seems to be getting tired, and I'll try and get him alongside the boat and on his side on the surface."

The guide nodded and I brought the fish close by—where it coasted, gills rhythmically opening and closing and its head held slightly out of the water by the pressure of the rod. The guide made an even, almost casual sweep with the net and the tigerfish was ours!

As it came aboard I swung my feet off the floorboards and placed them on the gunwale. The guide laughed as I did so, and the fish pounded against the bottom of the boat.

"Not a bad idea, that," he laughed. "They have a nasty set of teeth, but after a while one gets to know how to handle them without danger."

With that he reached down, grasped the big fish behind the head, righted it on the boat bottom, and whacked it solidly with a short wooden club he carried near the bow of the boat. The tigerfish shuddered and died instantly. Then the guide untangled it from the webbing of the net and, with a finger stuck in the gills, held it up. The sunlight glistened on the alternating gold, black, and silver stripes of the beautiful fish.

"Lovely thing, isn't it?" he said. "Bloody good fighter, too, as you just found out."

"It is that," I said. "Got a scale?" He reached into a pocket and hung the fish on the small, silver-plated pocket scales. He jiggled it for a moment.

"Let's see, must convert it to pounds for you blokes. That's between seven and eight pounds. Closer to eight. Very nice fish—especially for your first one."

He handed it to me and I hefted the fish. "That's quite a fighter," I said. "No point in keeping any more now that we have this one for a photo and mounting—since they are no good for eating."

"Right," said Jim. "The rest we can release. I release all mine and only keep bream for food."

"What's the largest tigerfish you ever caught?" I asked.

"Eighteen pounds," he said. "That was in 1965—during the summer months. We fish for them differently in the hot weather—trolling deep with spoons. The big ones are caught at that time of year, but the weather is bloody awful. Temperatures are over one hundred degrees, and the humidity is very high. Lots of rain, too. I caught that big one on one of those red and white spoons you Americans use. A chap gave me several the year before, and I used the large size—he said he used it in salt water. I had to take the treble hooks off it, though. These tigerfish have tremendous strength in the jaws. They can literally crush a treble hook. The way we have to catch them is to put on a single hook so that when the fish strikes, the single hook slides between the teeth and it cannot break it by grinding it."

"What kind of tackle were you using?"

"Heavy," he said. "A bait casting rod, level-winding reel, and twenty-pound mono with a wire leader. It still took half an hour to land the monster."

"Have they taken bigger ones?"

"Oh yes," he said. "A chap I know took a twenty-two pounder some years back, and they say they go up to thirty pounds, but nothing like that has come out of this lake yet. Of course . . ." he got that look in his eyes all fishermen get . . . "the lake has only been built since 1958 and one never can tell . . ."

I smiled.

"Let's see if we can do it today," I said. "Hand me another minnow."

"Not very likely in May," he said. "After all, this is our late fall here, you know. These cold nights and mornings keep the lake water temperature quite low. The fish are not as active . . . still . . ." He shook his head and we both grinned.

We did not set any records that day—although we caught several dozen tigerfish. The largest was almost 9 pounds, but the average was 4 to 5 pounds. The sun climbed high into the sky to the north of us—a strange feeling for the month of May. We tied to a large, dead tree and had lunch at noon—roast beef sandwiches and cold bottles of Castle Pilsner beer from an ice chest.

Later in the day, after catching enough tigerfish to satisfy any angler, we toured the irregular shoreline near Sanyati West and Fothergill Island—where we watched wildlife through binoculars for hours. Herds of elephants came down to the water to bathe and drink, completely unconcerned about the boat within a few hundred yards of them. Cormorants flew overhead in irregular Vs and the incredibly-colored malachite kingfishers perched on dead limbs close to the shore. At one point on the way back to the Kariba marina, we floated with the engine turned off and watched a herd of more than 100 cape buffalo come down to water—the calves and cows spooky at the sight of us and the ring of huge bulls staring at us belligerently as they snorted in anger and distrust. Dainty lechwe antelope, impala, and waterbuck pranced near the shoreline, not certain whether to flee or watch us chug by.

And just before the sun began to sink—bright orange above the northwest horizon—we came upon a huge fish eagle perched in a dead tree in shallow water. As it flew off, its white head, neck, and chest gleaming in the last light of the sun, it uttered a ringing scream that echoed across the still lake . . . home of some of the best game fishing in all of Africa.

Tips on Fishing in Rhodesia . . .

Perhaps the most aptly named fish in the world is Africa's tigerfish. Any angler who has ever had one on the end of a line is to be tolerated, excused, and gently soothed if he starts to rant wildly during his description of the experience. The tigerfish is a fighter *par excellence,* a dedicated leaper whose sharp teeth can make hash of all but the stoutest lures. A wire leader is a must if you ever hope to land or boat one.

Rhodesia's Kariba Lake, an approximately 200-mile long artificial impoundment formed by damming the Zambezi River, is famed, and justly so, for its tigerfish. Individual catches of from 6 to 9 pounds are fairly common, and 15-pounders are more than a now-and-then thing. Most of the fishing is done from boats, but one can fish from the banks. However, fishing from Kariba's banks can present an angler with uniquely African hazards—hippos and crocodiles.

Other fish found in Kariba's waters include several species of *tilapia,* a variation of what we call bream. Two of the species—the largemouth and the olive—will go for artificial lures, and individual catches have been known to run over 10 pounds.

It is possible to fish throughout the year in Rhodesia, but you'll be a lot more comfortable if you plan your trip for sometime between April and September. That time of year is the dry season, and the days are a bit cooler.

Lake Kariba can be reached by air from Salisbury via Air Rhodesia, the national airline, or you can drive the 230 miles or so, again from Salisbury. If you have the time and a taste for possible adventure en route, making the trip by car can be a rewarding experience; the roads from Salisbury take you through some very interesting country.

Once you get to Kariba, there are several places to stay, in a variety of price ranges. The Kariba Hotel is good, as is the Cutty Sark. Both establishments will help you make fishing arrangements. There are two motels—the Lake View and what is really a boatel called Venture Cruises. On the south shore of the lake is the Bumi Hills Hotel.

If you think Kariba's tigerfish might be your meat, you'll find Rhodesian Safaris, Ltd. (P.O. Box 191, Salisbury, Rhodesia) prepared to answer your questions. A three-day outing for a single client will cost about $300, about $400 for three clients. Included in the package price are room, meals, guide service, a boat and tackle (but clients are advised to bring their own gear), and all transportation. If you want a real armchair adventure, try telephoning Rhodesian Safaris, Ltd., at 27815 in Salisbury or contact Adventures Unlimited.

13.
New Mexico: Elk of the High Country

There had been the climbing for more than an hour, and—as always in the snow-encrusted meadows near timberline—a feeling of not making much headway; the heart pounding in the chest and in the temples, and every few steps bringing labored breathing in the last light from a setting sun—silhouetting Ash Mountain into a black etching on the western horizon.

There had been a time, a dozen years earlier, during which time New Mexico had been home, when climbing at 10,000 feet would have hardly caused the heartbeat to speed up. But by the fall of 1975, I had already been city-bound at sea level in the soot-encrusted canyons of New York for ten long years. Even with periodic spurts of freedom to hunt big game, birds, and to fish every now and then, the leg muscles and lungs of a desk-anchored editor do not stay tuned up for high-altitude climbing.

Sliding the .270 Colt Sauer from my shoulder, I eased to a sitting position and, with the rifle barrel resting in the hollow of my left shoulder, raised the binoculars and began a survey of the opposite slope of the wide canyon. Elk tracks were everywhere, as they had been for four days. The high country on the border of Colorado and New Mexico was home to literally thousands of elk, but those who have hunted this great game animal know that an elk can disappear into the slightest cover and remain there most of the day.

And there was more than just slight cover on the spines of the big ridges and canyon slopes of this high country. Below me, mesa tops of massive ponderosa pine stretched to the foothills in all directions. The ridges were choked with wind-twisted juniper and spruce, and at the top of each header canyon, the patches of dense aspen could conceal a herd of several hundred elk. The open slopes were covered with several inches of hard-crusted snow from a fall a week before, and elk tracks crisscrossed the open areas in all directions.

The bright red of the pickup parked on a narrow cattle trail a thousand feet below me was easy to see. The guide's blaze-orange hat showed through the windshield as he sat watching the last rays of the sunlight bathe the peaks above. He had asked if he was needed on the last climb of the day, and I had said no. I had wanted to spend the last few hours alone in the high country. The next morning was time for a return to the office, and there was precious little of this solitude and grandeur there. Also, he was probably glad to rest. We had hunted hard the last four days, and several times had been within moments of seeing elk. We had come upon steaming droppings and tracks so fresh the snow was still falling into the imprint, but the elk remained hidden.

There had been several times—in the few moments just at dawn—when there could have been elk slipping like spirits into the edge of the blue spruce blowdown timber. There may have been. There is little to differentiate between illusion and an elk silently gliding into cover.

Dozens of mule deer does had appeared on the ridges and on the early-morning sunny slopes where they fed on the sparse mountain mahogany. There had been no good bucks. The mule deer hunting in northern New Mexico was not good in the fall of 1975. This was true all the way from the Four Corners area and the Jicarilla Apache country across the state to the high country of the Pecos Wilderness and eastward to this area—near Raton and Cimarron. Some of the oldtimers said it was cyclic, which was certainly possible, and others said the reason was a combination of too much grazing of cattle, horses, and sheep, and too much hunting pressure. Years ago there wouldn't have been much truth in the hunting pressure theory—considering the vast domain in which mule deer roam. But each year there are more off-road vehicles cruising the remote high country. It is a poor way to hunt—settling for comfort when climbing on foot would not only be more sporting but more satisfying.

Most good sportsmen today will only hunt on foot or horseback for big game—the way we all did before the development of gadgets that pamper the body and take away the pure enjoyment of hunting.

The sun began to drop behind the black mountain, and the bottom of the slope near the small stream took on a rosy glow of dusk. I rose and shouldered the rifle. I wanted to take a look at the slopes of a canyon to my right—a vast expanse of snowy slopes that stretched up to a rock wall half a mile above to the north. There were only a dozen yards to go to reach the top of the ridge. The heart was hammering again by the time I made the small saddle that formed a notch in the ridge. Tom Thornber, a hunting companion, was somewhere on a ridge across the canyon to the right. We had agreed to work up as close as we could to the wall—hoping that one of us would get a shot if we put elk out of either canyon that headed up against the wall.

Leaning against a lichen-covered boulder, I began a methodical search of the slopes far below, covering the open patches of snow near the thickest stands of timber. The big animals would wait until just before dark to come out and graze on the meadow grass. There would be no moon tonight, and they would eat until the first light just before dawn and then would fade back into the heavy timber to spend the day. An elk is an incredibly difficult animal to hunt afoot. Few hunters have ever successfully stalked them afoot in heavy timber. They have keen eyesight and acute

hearing and are capable of moving through the thickest maze of standing and fallen timber swiftly and without a sound. Years ago I had been seated on a spruce log in thick timber tying a lace on a boot while hunting for blue grouse in the Sangre de Cristo Range above Santa Fe. Another hunter with me had startled a bull elk and two cows several hundred yards to my right and all three animals had run by in a tangle of trees so thick a man could not walk through it without traveling at a half-crouch. And yet all three animals went by at full speed—not more than a dozen yards away—and never snapped a twig. The picture of that huge bull—his horns laid back against his massive shoulders and his nose thrust high in the air—remains as clear today as it did on that day decades ago.

The sun had gone completely behind the mountain. It was 4:30 in the cold stillness of an October dusk, and it would be almost too dark to see in another fifteen or twenty minutes. There was nothing moving in the large fan of slope at the bottom of the valley nor on the meadow opposite. My scrutiny shifted to the top of the valley to my left. A red squirrel began chattering a short way up the ridge—sounding loud in the stillness. That and the occasional croak of a raven circling high up near the top of the wall were the only sounds to be heard.

And suddenly there were the elk. Where a moment before there was nothing, there were now two cows and a yearling coming slowly from the dense stand of aspen near the head of the canyon. They were at least 500 yards up the canyon and were the first of the herd to venture out into the open. It was necessary to get closer for a good shot, and yet the slightest sound from my direction would send them back into the aspens where they would wait until darkness.

There was the need to move and the need to do it quickly and without sound. The best method was to drop slowly off the saddle to the left where the spine of the ridge would hide me until within good shooting range. It was also a matter of coming back on top of the ridge at precisely the correct place because the chances of being spotted against the skyline were too good.

The snow crust breaking sounded like bombs going off. It was impossible for the elk to hear the sound with the ridge separating us, but nevertheless the noise sounded deafening. As it always does at the stalk and the chance for a shot, the dryness started in my mouth and the pounding of the heart returned—not so much from the lack of oxygen but from the age-old excitement of the stalk.

Each yard seemed like a mile and each stick and small rock passed, without snapping it or tumbling it down the slope, seemed like a miracle. There was no wind, and the squirrel had stopped its chirring sound as though it, too, was waiting for the outcome of this most ancient of rites between man and big-game animal. At about 300 yards—and after at least three stops to let the hammering heart slow down—I eased up to the top of the ridge and lay prone in the snow. The herd was all in the open below. Some of the animals were grazing, others pawing the snow to get at grass, and the rest were walking slowly across the pale white of the slope. They were several hundred feet below and approximately 300 yards distant. Several bulls fed near the center of the herd and another small one grazed at the extreme left. There were several dozen animals altogether. The heaviest timber was to the left at the foot of the slope. The herd would run for heavy timber at the shot—rather than risk going for the scanty cover of the aspen stand from which they had come. There was a maze of spruce trunks between me and the herd. Although they were small trees, the mass of lower, brittle branches presented something of a problem in getting a clear shot. It would be necessary to move several yards to the left and slightly forward if there was to be more than one shot. Inching to the left, each step sounded like splintering wood to me as the thin snow crust broke.

Something—either my outline against the burnished sky of sunset, or the crunching snow—alerted the herd. In an instant, each head jerked up and every elk in the herd was staring at the ridge top. As it always does at such times, everything went into slow motion. I had remembered to set the 3 to 9 variable scope on position 4—for just such a sudden emergency.

There was the jar of a shoulder against the roughness of a spruce trunk as I sought for some kind of a rest. The herd was in full motion across the snow to the left—each animal moving with that unbelievably swift and fluid motion of elk running at full speed.

The safety seemed to take an eternity to slide off. There was a profusion of spruce trunks as I tried to sort out a suitable running animal. The crosshairs finally picked up one of the larger animals toward the tail end of the herd—running nose up, its front legs rising and falling like those of a trotting horse, and everything in slow motion.

There was the remembering that the .270 had been sighted in to hit 6 inches high on the 100-yard range at Camp Fire Club. That would put it about 3 inches high at 200 yards and approximately on at 300 yards with the 150-grain shell. Swinging slowly and swinging evenly and remembering that a running elk is moving faster than it appears to be. The crosshairs—wavering as always across the distance and under the pressure—held just on the front edge of the chest as the pull was slowly, ever so slowly begun as close-up spruce trunks moved across the face of the scope in blurred shapes.

The crash of the shot and the slam of the recoil against the cheek coming as a surprise—as it always should if the trigger is not jerked. And lifting the cheek from the stock to see the results, hearing the sharp "whack" of the striking bullet carried from the opposite slope on the cold air. The elk stumbling and going down—to roll over sideways once and then attempt to rise. Knowing how far an elk can go if the shot is not in a vital area, the rifle coming down, steadying, and the recoil slamming back once more as another bullet hits and the elk, thrashing once more, lying still.

And from the peaks—now a faint rose color against the darkening northern sky above—the echo of both shots, slamming back and forth against the many faces of the towering cliff and reverberating across the snowy slopes, now empty of all movement. Then there were the echoes—slowly rumbling away among the peaks and canyons—a sense of exhilaration that gradually ebbed until the hands stopped shaking and there was simply the sense of accomplishment.

Tips on Hunting Elk in New Mexico . . .

Possibly, only possibly, there is a greater thrill for a sportsman than to be in the high country of New Mexico's mountain ranges and to hear the echoing bugle of a bull elk. But it's doubtful.

No outdoorsman on earth, alone and working his way through vast and fragrant stands of aspen, spruce, and ponderosa pine—the air searingly clear—can fail to appreciate Nature's bounty and noble design. It is an incredible and lasting experience.

For a hunter, the peak of the experience is the knowledge that an elk is a more than worthy adversary. Not only is he alert and wary and crafty, but he seems to appreciate and react honorably to the hunter's role in the drama. He manifests, somehow, an awareness of what is happening to him, and accepts it with a seeming determination to bring out the very best in the hunter.

The hunter who spots, tracks, and takes an elk in such a locale may well be tempted to retire from the field, secure in the knowledge that the sport can afford him few, if any, more rewarding prizes.

New Mexico's big-game season is limited to the month of November, and limited even further within that 30-day span. In 1975, for example, big game could be taken only during separate periods of two, six, and nine days. Days during which you may hunt—perhaps even the season itself—will vary, so before you make any plans, get in touch with the New Mexico Department of Game and Fish (Appendix B).

Most of New Mexico's big game is found in the northern portions of the state. Two prime locales are around Chama and Raton, near the Colorado border. Vermejo Park, 750 square miles of scenic beauty tucked away in the Sangre de Cristo mountains, has one of the largest herds of elk in the United States. Farther west, near Chama, in the San Juan range of New Mexico's Rocky Mountains, is what is probably the largest private elk herd in the world.

Vermejo Park is a working cattle ranch of nearly half a million acres covering terrain which ranges in altitude from 6,000 to 13,000 feet. You can wander around it all day—sometimes even for several days—and never see another soul. There are accommodations at the Park's headquarters, as well as three guest lodges on the ranch—Costilla Lodge, Cressmer Lodge, and Shuree Lodge. Costilla Lodge, a log cabin overlooking a scenic valley, complete with streams and a 200-acre lake, can accommodate up to fifteen guests. Cressmer Lodge, a favorite of hunters, can accommodate twenty. Shuree Lodge, which can handle up to thirty-two guests, is used only during the hunting season. Each lodge is fully staffed and offers all the amenities, including indoor plumbing. For detailed information about the Park, including current rates, write to the manager of Vermejo Park (Drawer E, Raton, New Mexico 87740; telephone 505–445–3097).

Another private facility offering outstanding elk hunting is the Chama Land & Cattle Company, also a working ranch and an incredibly scenic spot. In fact, the ranch's overall beauty has twice been featured on nationwide television. The hunting lodge at the ranch is new, and accommodates up to twenty sportsmen. It offers everything that comes to mind when you picture such a place—awesome views, a huge, broad-beamed trophy room, a mammoth fireplace made of native rock, western-style cooking—the works. The Chama Land & Cattle Company is about a two-and-one-half-hour drive from Albuquerque, or, if you have your own airplane or can charter one, there is a 6,000-foot sod landing strip right on the ranch. For current rates and more detailed information, write to the general manager of the Chama Land & Cattle Company (P.O. Box 85, Chama, New Mexico 87520; telephone 505–756–2133).

Accommodations are limited, so if you might be interested, get your bid in early.

14.
Bahamas:
The Unpredictable
Bonefish

Like the delicate and much sought-after brook trout, the bonefish has attracted a following amounting to an elite corps—particularly among the ranks of fly rod anglers.

But unlike the brookie—which sticks fairly close to the rules of the game—the unpredictable bonefish can act like anything from a battling gentleman to a carp with an inferiority complex.

The last statement is guaranteed to raise the hackles of many a bonefish stalker—particularly those who have been indoctrinated by resort owners in many parts of the world where the silvery scrappers abound. The fact that the cost of some bonefishing expeditions can be akin to paying one's income tax could explain some of the big buildup. Nevertheless, at the risk of losing friends from West End to Islamorada—and I have waded and poled for bonefish on just about every flat between them—I have to repeat that a bonefish can be a real slob when it wants to.

Nobody gets a bigger thrill than I do from that first great run of a big bonefish, particularly if I have been lucky enough to take it on a fly. Also, I have yet to fail to get a heart-thumping feeling when a streaking "bony" rips off about 100 yards of 6-pound monofilament on an ultralight spinning rig.

But if you think all the things a Bahama, Florida Keys, or West Indies guide tells you about bonefish are true, you are not only naive, but you have some surprises in store. And if you believe all you read in the promotional brochures about bonefish from these same areas, you need your head examined.

Sure they spook easily. Try fishing for them in an aluminum boat on the flats, and every time you drop the rod on the bottom of the boat, bonefish schools for 100 yards around will head for deep water. Wear a bright-colored hat and wave it within 30 feet of a "tailing" school of bones, and they will boil the water getting to the dropoff.

Cast a shrimp or sand crab bait 5 feet too close to the lead fish of a school, and you'd think you tossed a hand grenade into the water.

Slap a 15-foot leader, tapered to 3X, on the surface 10 feet from the cruising, silver torpedoes and they won't stop until they have passed the first deepwater sportfishing boat.

Try any number of things a guide warns you about—talking too loudly, coughing, popping the tab on a can of soft drink or beer, closing a tackle box lid too hard—and you will see bonefish leave the area.

But there are a few things one finds out about this frequenter of the flats, after years of fishing for it, that are not always mentioned in literature attempting to lure one to the crystalline waters of the Bahamas or West Indies, or the milky waters of the Florida Keys.

Ask any native kid in Bimini how long it would take him to get a dozen bonefish. You may be surprised how fast he could produce them, and I don't mean frozen. The kid would make a beeline for the nearest channel where—from his battered little wooden skiff—he would proceed to handline in the required dozen bones. He'd do this in water anywhere from 6 to 20 feet deep and he'd take them on a big hook loaded with chewed-up conch. Not only would he get you the dozen, if you greased his happy little palm enough, but he would get them in the exact size you want. The wrong sizes he would throw back.

All you have to do—if you take umbrage at this statement—is to follow any savvy kid, or grownup, for that matter, at any island in the Bahamas when he wants to catch bonefish.

I have sat evenings on rock jetties, wooden docks, and sandy beaches with Bahamian pals of mine and watched them handline in bonefish up to 10 pounds, using conch for bait. And I've watched them do it during the day, from schools of bonefish that were cruising below us among the dock pilings, while kids swam in the water and half a dozen boats were starting and stopping engines.

The simple fact is that bonefish are only wary and a real challenge to an angler when they are on the flats. The reason for this is simple: on the flats a bonefish is vulnerable to enemies—predatory birds such as ospreys, pods of barracuda, and certain species of sharks fast enough to catch them. They move onto the flats because that is where they find their favorite food—shrimp, crabs, and mollusks.

An osprey shadow will send bonefish churning for deep water the same way the shadow of a small plane will. An osprey takes a lot of bonefish from the foot-deep clear water of the flats and has been doing so for millions of years. And well he should—this being his way of doing things. There are a lot of bonefish in this world and not as many ospreys as I would like to see—thanks to DDT and other inventions of man.

Barracuda, working in packs, can and do slash through bonefish schools like silver blades—confusing them, splitting them up, and devouring them as singles. Sharks, capable of moving like lightning for short distances, take schools of bonefish unaware, particularly when they are tailing, or feeding in coral marl with their snouts in the sand and their tails out of water.

So it is no wonder that bonefish don't wait around to find out what makes the splash, flash, or sudden sound. By the time they do find out, with some natural enemies, they could be half-bonefish.

A bonefish can really move. It can probably outdistance most fish in any race, traveling an estimated 30 mph, but it can do the same thing in deep water, too. In deep water, it has the same enemies—sharks, barracuda, and a few other predator fish—but it has more room to maneuver. The osprey, pelican, sea eagle, and other aerial predators don't bother the bones a bit in deep water. I am sure many a bonefish falls prey to sailfish and white and blue marlin in deep water. Otherwise why do most native skippers consider bonefish a choice trolling bait for billfish?

Nobody is knocking the courage, the strength, or the sporting qualities of bonefish taken on the flats. It is a magnificent game fish and its first few runs are breathtaking. So are the rest of its runs if it is hooked on light tackle.

I guess I've heard too many would-be bonefish experts and resort promoters talk about how difficult and how elevating it is to catch a bonefish. Sometimes it gets a little too esoteric, especially when fly purists get into the act.

There are a couple of rumors handed out to the gullible angler that can be thrown out the porthole before going after bonefish. One is that a bonefish will not come close. Another is that it won't take anything but a well-presented bait resembling its natural food. Another is that only an experienced fisherman or guide can spot bonefish—that you only see the shadow, not the fish. I have spotted bonefish—with polarized glass, I'll admit—70 feet away. The fish show up against varying types of bottoms, their stripes standing out vividly.

Consider the experience I had with A. J. McClane one overcast day on the flats of a Bahama island which has long catered to the affluent and purist bonefish chaser.

Hefting a large, bulky wooden plug of the type used for tarpon, snook, and Lord-knows-what-else, Al gazed absently at the foot-deep water on the flat from where he was standing in the stern of my 17-foot boat.

"What are you going to take with that monstrosity?" I asked, staring at the battered yellow lure.

"Don't know," said McClane. "Lots of things might take it on this flat—tarpon, barracuda—never can tell. Bonefish have been known to hit things this size."

"Bonefish!" I snorted.

Whereupon McClane, who knows as much about fishing and fish as any gent I know, flipped the plug out about 50 feet, where it slapped to the surface, throwing water several feet into the air. He jerked it once and water erupted in all directions as a fish smashed it on the first twitch and headed generally east at full speed.

McClane, who was using a short fiberglass breakdown rod and a level-winding reel with about 200 yards of 8-pound mono on it, yawned casually and handed the rod to his wife.

"Bring him in, Honey," he said, resting against the gunwale as his attractive wife proceeded to whip the adversary. "That bonefish might go six pounds."

As it turned out, it weighed 8 pounds. Since a wife cannot testify for or

against her husband (and *nobody* will believe an outdoor writer) I can count on another witness, the president of a major lure manufacturing company. Since the plug was made by one of his competitors, I am pretty sure no one will doubt his word that the whole thing happened.

"I've always claimed," McClane said later, "that a bonefish will eat other fish when it's hungry. That plug just represented a bait fish and that's what it hit. Of course," he added, "they only seem to do that when they are fairly big and cruising, either alone or in pairs. School fish won't do that."

As for bonefish not coming close to man, Tony Watts, an English friend of mine, and I used to wade for bonefish on the flats early in the morning off North Bimini. We used a special yellow fly—the type with the hook riding upward to prevent it from becoming tangled in the rubberlike grass of the shallow flats.

Many a time I have had bonefish come so close to me that I couldn't cast,

knowing the movement of my arm would spook them. I have, by remaining
motionless, had a bonefish school pass on both sides of my legs. Casting to them after
they pass, incidentally, is a waste of time, I found out.

One time, fishing the flats below North Cat Cay, I had two big bonefish chase
a white fly right up to my feet and battle to see which one would get it, churning up
the sand as they searched for it. One grabbed the fly and I caught it—a 9-pounder.
Another time, wading the seemingly endless bonefish flats of Chub Cay in the Berry
Islands of the Bahamas, I was trying to untangle a knot in the line from a spinning
reel when a school of several hundred bonefish swam up to, around, and past me while
I muttered unprintable words at my reel.

Another time, fishing the "blue holes," deep holes near the edge of
mangroves on the flats beside Grand Bahama Island, I took a bonefish on a spinning
rod while using a small red-and-white striped spoon. I had been trying for mangrove
snapper for dinner that night.

I also had the unpleasant experience of still-fishing, the way the natives do off the north tip of big Andros Island in the Bahamas. Given half a chance there, a guide will tie your boat up to a mangrove root, rig your hook with a big shrimp, and toss it out in the milky water. He will try to sleep until a cruising bonefish comes along and picks up the bait, unless, like me, an angler gets impatient and leaves the boat to wade for them.

All of which points out—with no malice toward my old friend, the bonefish—that it will take whatever it wants, when and where it wants to.

Even the most dedicated fly fisherman will admit that the kid down the block can make you look like an amateur by dropping a night crawler into your favorite trout stream. The trout is not insulting you when it takes a gulp of that worm, any more than the bonefish is when it gobbles a hunk of conch from under a dock or snatches a big, gang-hook-rigged plug on the surface.

It doesn't detract from the ability of the angler or the thrill of the sport. All I am trying to do here is to get some bonefishermen to take themselves a little less seriously. It's a great sport on fly rods and light spinning gear. But there is no need to make a cult of it, especially when much of the attempt to make it an elite sport comes for those who most benefit from it commercially.

The truth is that bonefish are really just fish—although fine game fish. They are not much as far as eating is concerned, unless you know how to yank them until their vertebrae are realigned, as do some of my Bahamian friends. The realignment of the bones makes it easier to separate the bones from the meat while eating. But even so, I don't consider the bonefish much of a delicacy.

The real truth about bonefish, then, is that they're a lot of fun to catch when they're up on the flats, and they can require some fancy stalking. But don't get too caught up in the mystique some anglers have woven around them; they're a prize, sure, but not a Holy Grail. They break too many rules to be that sacred.

[For further information, see Tips at the end of the next chapter.]

15.
Walker's Cay: Barracuda on the Flats

Most big-game fishermen consider the barracuda a damned nuisance. I do at times—especially when the quarry is tuna or billfish, and barracuda cut off trolled or live baits on the kite lines.

Regardless of the size, there is never much trouble subduing a barracuda on big rods. These predator fish strike savagely, and many an angler has thought he had either a big wahoo, king, or yellowfin tuna on for the first few moments. But a barracuda, at least in deep water and on heavy tackle, does not put up much of a battle after a few initial bursts of speed. It is for this reason that it has never gained much of a reputation as a game fish. After I found out about its game-fish qualities, I was delighted to read that Zane Grey and his brother used to fish for them with light tackle at Long Key before World War I, and considered them one of the best sport fish around. Van Campen Heilner also caught them on light tackle and thought them terrific fighters.

I knew nothing of this, however, until I had a chance to fish for them on the bonefish flats of Cat Cay with light spinning gear. My three sons were living in Fort Lauderdale, and I had the small boat over at the island during the Christmas holidays. Johnnie and Donald came over for a week each, and we caught lots of fish. Both boys enjoyed barracuda fishing best. I am sorry I couldn't take Jimmie over, as he has always been the most enthusiastic fisherman of the three, but he was only about eight then.

We used light spinning rods and 8-pound monofilament line. We fastened wooden silver and cobalt-blue plugs to the lines with a light 8-inch cable leader to keep the barracuda's teeth from cutting the lines. The 6-inch-long plugs were equipped with two sets of treble hooks, and when trolled across the flats would dive to a depth of about a foot and stay there. The water depth would vary from a foot to several feet, depending upon where the various channels were from the lighthouse on the rock jetty to the southern end of South Cat Cay. Fortunately there is little in the way of coral rock on the east side of the two islands, or I would have had to replace props fairly often. As it was, the blades were well chewed by conch shells as the prop churned up a wake of white marl every so often.

I would watch for the big predator fish through polarized glasses as one of the boys stood between the two light rods stuck in the console seat rod holders. Barracuda usually travel either in pods of four to six or in pairs, but sometimes a lone fish would sight the wriggling plugs from at least 50 feet away. The fish would streak about halfway to the boat and then stop to get a better look. That's when I would shout for the boy to get ready, and usually just about then the incredibly fast fish would be almost upon the lure. At that depth, the strike was an explosion of spray and coral sand as the huge jaws clamped down on the plug and its sharp hooks. Anyone who has caught these great fish only on big rods in deep water would be astonished at the fight they put up. The bigger fish are up to 5 feet long and weigh 30 to 40 pounds on the average. Many will leap into the air on feeling the bite of the hooks and soar 20 feet or more on the first few jumps. We had some smaller ones jump as many as fifteen times in a row—jumps that would make a fly-rod-hooked Atlantic salmon look slow in comparison.

The boys and I were not trying for records, just fun. It took fishing pliers and a tight grip behind the head with a heavy glove to release these big, toothy battlers. We released most of them—sometimes to catch the same fish a few days later. They never grew smart enough to resist those wriggling plugs. A good fish would take twenty-five minutes to whip, and even after getting them close to the boat, they would make sudden last-minute runs that tore line off the small reels. We kept a few each day because Curly, the bartender at Cat Cay, loved to eat them. He tossed them into the freezer room and later sawed the frozen lengths into steaks. He had no concern about the occasional instance of ciguatera, the poisoning possible from eating large, old fish (presumably because the barracuda had eaten smaller fish that actually carry the toxin themselves, such as the puffers and others). He admitted he had heard of people getting sick from eating them and even losing all their hair, but he said he liked eating them too much to worry about it.

I hooked a heavy barracuda in the channel between Cat and Gun Cay one day as I was going out for marlin. I was using a red-and-white-striped saltwater spoon about 8 inches long on one of the light boat rods and a 9/0 reel filled with 12-pound mono. The spoon had one double hook on the aft end. That barracuda was well over 6 feet long, jumped only twice—falling back with a tremendous splash each time—and got away when I stupidly let it get behind the coral reef jutting out from the dump on the north tip of Cat, and the line parted. I have always wondered how much that rascal would have weighed. Nelson Bryant, who was with me at the time, hazarded a couple of guesses, but I suspect it was to make me feel worse at losing the fish.

One of the biggest and most spectacular barracuda I ever saw was one Pat Smith caught when he and I were bonefishing on the tiny flat near Walker Cay in the Bahamas. The wind was too high that day to let us go after marlin and sailfish with Les Flato aboard the *Sea Lion,* but we had both taken billfish the day before—me a nice blue marlin and Pat a good sailfish.

We had hoped to make it a grand slam the next morning by taking a white marlin, but the wind turned and blew out of the northeast, ruining all the blue-water plans. Rather than spend the day in the bar and at the swimming pool, Pat and I found a guide and pounded across the stretch of open water to the small bonefish flat a few miles away. The tide was wrong, and we caught no bonefish, although we saw several small schools. As we were about to leave in the afternoon and return to the marina, Pat found a pod of about six big barracuda lying in about 10 feet of water in a channel. Several casts to them with spinning rods and small spoons drew only a half-hearted follow from several of the medium-sized ones. There was one huge fish in the school. Standing on the bow of the bonefish skiff, I could make it out lying close to the bottom in light blue-green water. Pat was fascinated by the size of that fish. He wouldn't leave until he tried everything in his tackle box. I finally got tired of watching him cast to the unresponsive monster and walked back down the bank toward the skiff to get a cold beer from the ice chest.

"I think I'll try bait," I heard Pat say as I walked on the white sand. I stopped and looked at him. "What kind?" I asked.

"Oh . . ." He looked in a plastic sandwich bag he had tied to his belt. It contained some shrimp and pieces of conch the guide had chopped up for him to use for bonefish. "I think I'll try conch on him." I shook my head as he fastened a big piece of the rubbery conch on the bonefish hook. He had 10-pound mono on the medium-weight spinning reel. I walked toward the boat, idly thinking about getting a camera and taking some scenic color shots while Pat ran out of ideas to catch the big barracuda.

I never saw that fish take the bait. Later Pat said he cast the glob of conch ahead of the barracuda, let it sink slowly until it reached about the right depth, then moved it in a series of short jerks. He said the big fish simply turned, rose slightly, and swallowed it. He was so surprised he didn't set the hook until the fish settled back to the bottom. When he did set it, I heard a whoop of excitement and saw the guide, ahead of me, point back to where Pat stood. I turned just in time to see that fish at the top of a jump that must have been 25 feet straight up! Because of the small pool it didn't go far horizontally, but it hurled itself into the air and climbed for altitude. When it came down it sounded as though a 12-foot skiff had been thrown into the water.

I made a run for the camera, but the fish was too big to make more than about two jumps. By the time I got back to Pat the long, loglike fish was thrashing in the center of the pool. When that didn't get rid of the hook it made two streaking turns of the 30-foot-long pool, yanking the rod almost out of Pat's hand. Half an hour later Pat had the fish in the shallows, and it still fought him as he walked it down toward the boat where the guide had a long-handled net. That guide, however, was having none of a barracuda in the shallow water! Pat finally had to slide it up on its side, where I socked it with a big gaff and finally got some pictures. I don't recall if we weighed that fish when we got back to the dock, but it was more than 5 feet long and

heavy-bodied. We both agreed if I had gotten an action shot of that first jump it would have been some picture.

My biggest barracuda was never weighed either, but it was close to 6 feet long and was caught at Treasure Cay on Abaco. We were making a bonefish movie with A. J. as the angler, and had tried for two days to get some good fly rod sequences, but the weather had been against us. It remained overcast, making it hard to spot fish, and thundershowers kept passing over us every hour or so. The barometric pressure was low, and the fish were not feeding too well. A. J. was fishing from a bonefish skiff with an old friend, guide Joe Sawyer, acting as his pole man. Two camera boats glided along near him as he stood in the bow looking for bonefish schools. I had given up on the bonefish and was on a larger 24-foot boat anchored in the mouth of a small channel on the east end of a small island. The current had our boat facing upstream on an outgoing tide, and the water, gurgling at about six knots, poured past us and fanned out on an expanse of flat to the east. I was tired of doing nothing, so I picked

up a glass rod belonging to Bud Brownell, who was sunning himself on a forward
deck. I dug in the skipper's battered tackle box until I found an old wooden floating
plug with rusty treble hooks. From one sailfish wire, I made a leader about a foot long
and fastened a big swivel on the end, and after sharpening the hooks with a piece of
torn sandpaper, I stood up on the transom and flipped the plug out on the flat. I let it
run out several hundred feet with the current before flipping the bail closed and
twitching the plug. As the floating plug reached the end of the arch, I twitched it
again. There was a sudden bulge just beyond the plug and a flash of silver, but it was
too far away to see what had made the commotion.

I cast at that same area for half an hour until I began to think there was nothing there. I decided to make a few more casts and to let the plug float farther out on the flat. By that time the plug was in about a foot of water and there was not a thing in sight on the expanse of white bottom.

I will never know where that big barracuda came from, but it erupted from beneath the plug and took off across that flat in a series of jumps that could be heard up on the foredeck where Bud was. I heard the pounding of feet as he came over the top of the cabin and dropped to the deck behind me.

"What the hell was that?" he asked, shading his eyes to see where my line was stretching. "It sounded like a marlin out there!"

It jumped like a marlin, too. It took almost an hour to land that fish—what with the current aiding it and only about 150 yards of 10-pound mono on the reel. It was a huge barracuda, and it took both A. J. and me to get it. I transferred to the skiff and, with the help of Joe, poled out to fight it.

There are all sorts of stories of barracuda attacking swimmers and wading anglers. I have never seen a documented case, although Bahamian friends swear it has happened. I have been down close to them in scuba gear and have had them follow me slowly while snorkeling for lobsters. They are somewhat unnerving—remaining still in the water and watching when one looks at them. If you swim toward them they will back up slowly—much as a pickerel or a big northern pike will move in reverse—but I have never seen them attack. I know their unbelievable speed and am never really at ease when I am in the water.

One of the most eerie barracuda stories was told to me by Captain Henry Phillips, a longtime skipper who worked for Hatteras at Highpoint, North Carolina, and spent many years with the boats in the Bahamas. He was en route one day from Florida to one of the cays—West End, I think—and it was a calm summer morning with the sea glassy and a hot sun shining. He was running a big Hatteras sportfisherman alone. He began to feel hungry and decided to stop for lunch. He shut off his engines and slowed the boat to a stop in about 15 feet of clear water over a white sandy bottom. Henry told me he wanted to stretch and get off the bridge for a change of scenery. He got a sandwich from the galley and walked back to the cockpit, where he sat on the gunwale next to the transom and unwrapped the sandwich. He was about to take a bite when he glanced into the water. On the bottom, like so many logs, were hundreds of huge barracuda. They just lay there, baleful eyes looking up in the clear water. He estimated some at 7 feet and longer.

Henry said he knew the sportfisherman was 45 feet long with a fiberglass hull. He said he sat there for another moment, looking at the sky and the sleek boat and feeling the hot sun beating down on his bare arms. There was no sound on the big expanse of calm Gulf Stream surface. He told me he slowly rose to his feet, climbed to the bridge, started the big marine engines, and headed for the islands . . . feeling relieved only when he was doing about 20 knots on a calm sea.

Tips on Going for Bonefish or Barracuda in the Bahamas . . .

There are fish . . . and then there are fish.

The nugget contained in that somewhat obscure observation may be elusive, but once a man ties into either a bonefish or a barracuda, it all becomes gloriously clear. Pound for pound, like Sugar Ray Robinson, a healthy example of either species can rattle an angler's teeth and dazzle him with footwork.

They are, of course, fighters of the very bluest steel, providing action guaranteed to send a fisherman to his bed weary of arm and at peace with his soul. The contemplative man will appreciate that their fury stems not so much from meanness (although a barracuda on a feeding foray is far from a Samaritan to his lesser fellows) as it does from indignation; hooked, that fish is fighting for his life, obviously, but what he is really manifesting is outrage at being in the fix in which he finds himself. To the fish, it's demeaning, and he doesn't mind letting you know it.

Of all the waters in which these superb fighters can be encountered, few if any surpass those of Deep Water Cay and Walker's Cay in the Bahamas. Both islands offer miles of sun-warmed flats in which bonefish and barracuda cruise in great numbers. In addition, the waters of both islands offer everything from a blue marlin to a mutton snapper. There are also white marlin, blackfin and yellowfin tuna, wahoo, amberjack, bonito, mackerel, permit, jack crevalle . . . even sailfish, all of which justify ranking the Bahamas an angler's paradise.

If you go, bring along just about all your gear . . . everything from a couple of fly rods to heavy-duty trolling tackle. You can try to convince yourself you are interested only in bones, say, but you'll find it just about impossible to ignore a chance to take a marlin or a yellowfin. If you are on the flats, you are likely to encounter almost anything, so you'll want three or four rods rigged and ready to go. You can rent just about everything you'll need, but there is an undeniable something extra involved in taking fish on your own

gear. It is possible to pack too much, of course, but if you deny yourself what may be a once-in-a-lifetime crack at something because you're not equipped to handle it, you'll never forgive yourself. On the other hand, if you *do* get to take a bone or a barracuda on, say, a fly rod, you'll become a boring old windbag.

If you check in at Deep Water Cay Club, leave your fancy duds at home. Knockaround fishing stuff is worn all day, and nights don't call for much more than a reasonably clean shirt and a lightweight sport jacket—no tie needed. You'll want rain gear, a pair of trunks for swimming, a pair of canvas wading shoes, and a sweater or jacket to ward off an occasional chill. Bring sunglasses and a good supply of anti-sunburn lotion. In any event, keep your non-fishing-related stuff to a minimum; you'll be flying to the Club via small aircraft, so precious pounds and ounces should be given over to fishing gear, not an attempt to land you on a Ten-Best-Dressed list.

You'll find Deep Water Cay Club comfortable. The main lodge houses a bar, a dining room, and a spacious lounging area in which to swap stories. Guests are accommodated in duplex cottages complete with modern private baths. Available at extra cost are two-bedroom cottages equipped with kitchenettes and bar facilities. Fuel and a limited supply of fresh water are available for visiting yachtsmen. A 2,000-foot strip can handle light aircraft, but arrangements to land on it must be made beforehand. The Club also has a concrete ramp to handle small amphibious aircraft, but again, arrangements must be made beforehand.

The Club's basic bonefishing package— room, meals, boat, guide, tackle, and bait (if needed)—comes to about $70 per day per person for a party of two. A week for a party of two will come to about $425 per person. Charter flights from West Palm Beach or Miami will cost about $40 per head.

Here again Adventures Unlimited can provide details, or you can write to the Club (P.O.

Box 1145, Palm Beach, Florida 33480; telephone 305–655–2988).

Things are a little fancier at Walker's Cay—more of a fishing resort than a fishing camp. It's luxurious, and in the evening you may want to dress accordingly. You can, however, get by very well with slacks, a sport shirt, loafers, and a sport jacket. Again, bring rainwear and a light jacket and sweater; nearby Florida occasionally exports a cold front in the winter.

Accommodations at Walker's Cay Club include large, air-conditioned rooms with private terraces, or private villas. There are two swimming pools, a big dining room, a large lounge and bar, a TV room, and a billiard room. There's also a first-rate marina and a 2,600-foot landing strip, both of which offer fuel and appropriate services.

Winter room rates, which include breakfast and dinner, are about $40 a day per person. The villas go for about $150 a day, including breakfast and dinner. A 15 percent service charge will be added to your bill.

Boat charters, including guide, tackle, and bait, are extra. Depending upon the size of the boat, daily prices can range from about $50 (for, say, a Boston Whaler) to $175 to $200 for a sportfishing cruiser. Daily dockage rates vary, again according to the size of your boat; a 30-footer would cost about $15 a day, and you can figure about $0.30 for each additional foot of length. If you arrive in your own boat, a guide for the day will set you back about $30. Any extra services are—you guessed it—extra.

For details, you can contact Walker's Cay Club (P.O. Box 22493, Fort Lauderdale, Florida 33315; telephone 305–522–1460) or World Wide Sportsman (P.O. Box 787, Islamorada, Florida 33036; telephone 305–664–4615).

16.
Surprise Bass of Japan

"Fishin'," was all that Fred had said the day before and that was enough for me. I had gotten him to divulge that it was a freshwater lake, that it was about ninety miles south of Tokyo, and that the elevation was close to 2,500 feet above sea level. I had hung up the phone and had started digging out the spinning rod and tackle which I had carried over half the Far East. Having found American-imported rainbow and brook trout in the mountains to the north and several species of Japanese native trout on previous trips, I had learned to come prepared for anything. Thinking that the Japanese might have some form of lake trout, I had packed a tackle box and plenty of lures. After supper, the houseboy had taken the car down to the garage and had had it checked; extra spare tire, tools, extra water, and gas. Japanese roads are not the best in the world, though most are paved, and the distances between filling stations can occasionally prove frustrating.

Fred showed up at the office about noon, and we loaded the car. Several hours later, as we swung to the southwest below the town of Odawara, I hadn't gotten much more out of him about the lake or the fishing. A Turk, who had been born in Kobe, Japan, Fred has spent most of his life in the Far East. He speaks Japanese like the native he is and is a wonderful companion for hunting and fishing trips, not only for his linguistic accomplishments, but because he is as enthusiastic about the game as I. I did get him to admit that he had fished the lake before and that he had caught fish.

"What kind?" I persisted, trying to miss a foot-deep hole in the rough road.

"Hell, I don't know. The Japanese have a name for them . . . Funa. They're good eating, and they fight well. What else is there to know?"

I thought this one over for several hundred yards and was reflecting on what there really is in a name, when Fred pointed ahead.

"This is Yumoto," he grunted, indicating the cluster of fragile houses bordering the narrow, crooked street. "Pull up over there on the left, and we'll get some bait."

"What kind?" I asked, braking the car beside an open shop that had the decided air of a fish market.

"Shrimp," he said casually, getting out. "Best bait for Hakone Lake."

He stood at the front booth of the store several feet away and, after several minutes of heated discussion with the woman behind the counter, he returned.

"No shrimp," he said resignedly. "Maybe we can get some at the lake. Let's go."

We swung into the dirt road again and began to climb into the foothills. The heat and dust grew less severe as we gained altitude. A few miles farther we crossed a small stream that paralleled the road from then on; a clear brook that rumbled steeply down between the high valley walls. The air grew cooler, and forests of pine were thicker on the slopes. The small villages we passed through were now spotlessly clean. Mountain water was channeled through the towns in a narrow cement canal, and the houses, as well as the people, looked freshly scrubbed.

Half an hour later, we topped the pass and looked down on Hakone Lake. Perhaps four or five miles long and a mile wide in most places, it rested in what appeared to be a giant crater, surrounded by jagged hills silhouetted against the late afternoon sky. The steep, pine-clad slopes dropped abruptly to the clear water below. We sat, the jeep motor idling, and breathed the clear air.

"It's a good lake," Fred said quietly. "Water as clear as a mirror. You can see the bottom twenty feet down."

"It's a beautiful thing from here," I said.

The last few miles were spent in winding around the hairpin turns to the water below. At the town of Hakone, Fred tried two bait stores and found that there were no freshwater shrimp to be had.

"What else do they use?" I asked as he climbed back into the car.

"Best thing to use, if we can't get shrimp, is minnows. The guide can catch the minnows in the shallow water for us before we go out."

The hotel was several miles down the shore and built up to the edge of the water. A small boat dock jutted out into the lake for several yards, but there were no boats there.

"What about a boat?" I asked as we unloaded the gear in front of the door.

"Looks like they're all out. They only have three or four and it may be too late to get one tonight. I phoned to have one in the morning so we may have to fish from the bank for the few hours we have left before dark. That is," he turned as the boy carried the tackle into the hallway, "if you want to fish tonight."

I looked at the surface of the lake, still as glass and reflecting the steep hillsides.

"No. . . ." I said, trying to sound convinced that it was too late, "might as well get set up and eat. Tomorrow morning early will be all right."

Fred grinned. "You'd go out right now, and so would I if we had a boat. . . .
Still, there's not much sense in fishing from the bank. We have to get out off those
rocky points to do any good. Might as well wait 'till morning." He shrugged, and we
followed the boy upstairs to the rooms overlooking the water.

After a meal of Japanese food on the small porch over the lake, I sorted the
tackle while Fred made arrangements for the boat and guide in the morning. Since
the arrangements were to get up at four-thirty, we decided to get to bed early. After a
short walk along the shore, we turned in on the light mattresses placed on the
"tatamis," or Japanese floor mats. The cool breeze from the lake and the silence, after
the sounds of Tokyo, put me to sleep easily.

The alarm clock went off like a bomb, and I stuck an arm out for it
instinctively. It was barely light and I lay back to rest for a few more minutes.

"None of that," Fred grunted from across the room. "You'll wake up at about nine-thirty if you don't make it now."

I grinned, with an effort, and sat up. There was no sound in the hotel. Fred was shoving an arm through the sleeves of his khaki shirt.

"What are the chances for some breakfast?" I muttered.

"I'll wake one of the girls downstairs while you wash up. It's too early for breakfast, but we can probably get some tea and cakes."

The wooden stairs creaked loudly in the still morning as Fred made his way down to the kitchen.

Half an hour later the guide, drowsy and silent, reached the dock and began untying one of the heavy, flat-bottomed boats. About 20 feet long and steered with a long sculling oar in the stern, it floated heavily on the still water. As we moved out from the dock, sending long Vs from the bow, Fred checked the minnows in the bait bucket.

"We've got enough of these," he reported.

The light was getting stronger and the pines on the shore stood out clearly. The long boat moved silently toward a point of land about half a mile away.

"What's the plan?" I yawned.

Fred jerked a thumb at the guide sculling in the stern.

"He says that it's been good off that point ahead. There are some sunken trees and big rocks. He says we may do all right with the minnows, but that shrimp would have been better. Can't get any, for some reason. It must be a bad season for them or something."

The guide slid the boat within 20 feet of the shore and slowly lowered a heavy stone anchor on the end of a length of light cable. The boat slowed gradually until the small waves moved to the bank and the surface was again glassy.

Fred began stringing the line through his guides.

"Got a cork?" he asked.

I looked up from rummaging in the creel. "No," I said. "That's one thing I don't have. Why, is it necessary?"

"It's better. These fish take the bait slow at first. It's easier to see the bite."

"Whatever you say," I said, resignedly. "I haven't used a bobber since I fished for sunfish as a kid."

"Well," he smiled. "You can do as you like, but they all use them here."

"When in Rome." I grinned. "Throw me one."

We baited up with minnows and put out the rods. I lit a cigarette and watched where the sun was beginning to edge its way up from behind the hilltops to the east. No fish broke the surface around us and the morning was still and beautiful. The only sounds were the first sleepy calls of birds in the thick pines. The smoke from my cigarette swirled in a faint layer close to the boat. I looked contentedly at Fred.

"Good time of day," I said.

"Best part," he smiled.

For over an hour we sat in the stillness and watched as the scene brightened around us. The guide got one bite that suddenly bobbed his cork, but the fish, whatever it was, didn't hit again. Shortly afterward, Fred nodded over his shoulder.

"Look behind you," he said softly. "Old Fuji is pokin' his head out for a look."

I turned and looked to the northwest. There, high above the mists of the foothills, white in the sky, the snowy peak of Fujiyama towered over the land. It was enough to take my breath away, and I stared for a few minutes before I thought to reach for the camera. Fred chuckled as I fumbled with the case.

"You'll never get it. It only stays out for a few seconds in the morning at this time of the year. In June the mists gather around it all day. See . . . it's already going."

I watched as the great peak faded behind the whiteness of the morning sky.

"Well," I sighed, "the picture probably wouldn't have done it justice anyway."

After another half an hour the sun had risen and the waiting was beginning to get tiresome.

"What about another system, Fred?" I turned on the wooden seat. "This may be fun for the guide here, but it can get a little dull after a while. Ask him if he has any other suggestions."

Fred turned and began to talk. The guide nodded periodically—and just as periodically he shook his head. After a few minutes, Fred turned to me.

"He says some mornings are good and some are bad."

"Look, friend, I didn't have to come on this trip to know that about fishing. I learned that when I was ten years old. Ask him if he knows any other method of catching these fish."

He turned to the guide and began again. After several minutes, the guide suddenly moved to the center of the boat and picked up a small wooden box with a glass bottom. He lowered it gently over the side and peered into the clear water. For several minutes he gazed down, then motioned to Fred. Fred took the guide's place and bent over the side for a time. Finally, he straightened up.

"He says they are just not biting, but you can see a couple of them swimming around down there. Not big, but fish." He motioned to me. "Take a look for yourself."

I took the box and eased it into the water. Below, the blue depths showed clearly, and I could make out the shadows, the outline of rocks and a tree trunk. Suddenly, about 10 feet below, a small fish swam lazily out from one of the rock ledges and rested, fanning the still water. I looked at it carefully and then straightened up.

"Ask him what he calls these fish in Japanese, Fred," I said.

He and the guide held a long discussion. At one point I picked up a word that sounded like "funa."

"Is that it?" I asked.

"Yeah."

I felt a tinge of excitement.

"Ask him where they came from."

"Came from?"

"That's right . . . were they always here or were they planted some time ago . . . ?"

Fred shook his head, but began to talk. The guide answered, scratched his head, and waved his arms toward the lake.

Fred looked a little more interested.

"He says he hasn't been here more than ten years, but that the old guides say these fish were stocked in the lakes maybe twenty . . . thirty years ago . . . what's this all about?"

"I'll tell you, laddie. These rascals, unless I have forgotten what a lifelong pal looks like, are largemouth bass. Apparently they were imported to Japan a long time ago and have made a go of this lake. . . . " I chuckled in spite of myself. "That puts a different light on things."

"What are you up to?" Fred asked.

"Unless these rascals have undergone a change of attitude since they were brought to the Orient, I'm going to show you something."

I took off the cork and hook. Then I dug into the box and came up with a small rubber worm and tandem spinner. Fred looked dubious as I tied it on.

"That thing?" he said as I stood up in the boat. The guide squatted and grinned.

I dropped the worm several feet from the shore, close to a dead trunk, and began to retrieve it in short jerks through the clear water. As the lure hit the edge of the deeper water I saw the shadow streak up from the large rock just below and to the right. It was like meeting an old friend. I struck as the bass hit savagely from the rear of the lure, and the fish came clear of the water, spray glistening in the morning sun. I grunted as the rod arched, and Fred came to his feet with a shout.

"A fish!"

"You can say that again!" I grinned happily. "Get that net ready."

He fell over the seat several times before he unwound the net and crouched at the boat's edge. The fish was not large, but was digging deep into the clear water. The light rod bent almost to the surface. The guide still squatted in the bottom of the boat, but an openmouthed gape had replaced the grin. Fred dipped the tiring fish into the boat and then held up a 12-inch bass. His sharp face wore a wide smile. . . .

"Hah!" he gloated. "That's a good one."

"Not too big, where I come from, friend," I laughed, "but I've never been happier to see one of these roughnecks!"

The guide had picked up the worm and spinner and was holding it in his hand. He shook his head slowly and muttered in Japanese.

"What's he say?" I asked.

Fred's laugh carried across the quiet lake. "He says, 'Fish no eat!'" He laughed again. "No eat, hell!" he snorted. "You got another one of those things?"

From then on we had a picnic. The guide, his amazement changed to wholehearted cooperation, sculled us quietly along the rock- and brush-strewn shore while we cast. Fred took his first bass on an artificial lure several minutes later, and it is safe to say that that made him a confirmed bass fisherman.

The fish made two passes under the boat before I netted it, and by then Fred was convinced that both he and the bass had gone mad. By noon, when we decided to quit, we had taken nine fish. None of them ran over 13 inches, but they fought savagely in the clear, cold water.

Fred jumped onto the dock as the bow touched the shore. He turned to reach for the tackle box. I was leaning comfortably against the seat and looking at the lake.

"Come on, let's go get some food," he said. "I'm starving to death. . . . what are you looking so smug about?"

I turned from looking at the water and grinned.

"I was just thinking of my next trip up here. I'm going to find a casting reel and some plugs if I have to send to the States for them. I have an idea this place has got some real lunkers in it and next time I'm really going to show you something."

Fred shook his head wonderingly.

"Nothin' would surprise me after today," he grinned. He picked up the tackle box and began climbing the path to the hotel.

I watched him climb for a second and then stretched. The sun felt good. The boat moved slightly as the waters nudged it gently against the bank.

[For further information, see Tips at the end of Chapter 25.]

17.
Montauk: Days of the Striper

When the first chill winds of November shriek past the old lighthouse on Montauk and the seas churn white against the jagged rocks at the base of the eroded cliffs, the big bass of the Atlantic migratory stock reach the peak of the movement around the ancient point.

And it is then—with the occurrence of the full moon—that striped bass fishermen on the East Coast experience what I personally think is the greatest time of the year to fish for these magnificent game fish.

There will be those who say the rocky shores of Rhode Island provide better sport in the spring as the schools pour northward from the breeding grounds of the Hudson River, northern New Jersey, Barnegat, Great Egg Harbor, the mouth of the Mullica River, and even from as far south as the huge spawning area of the Chesapeake. There are others who claim there is no striper fishing that compares to hurling a tin squid or surface plug into the surf off Hatteras or to drifting over the rip and the rocky ledges off Sandy Hook, dragging a freshly dead mossbunker close to the bottom. They all have a point. I have fished them all. I have stood on the wet sloping sandy beach of Martha's Vineyard and felt the striper smash a topwater plug in the gray and curling seas and laughed with the sheer joy of combat as the big bass stripped off my line—my laughter whipped away in the howling winds of fall.

I have set the hook—rigged lightly through the lips of a live eel and drifted slowly close to the jetty rocks of Cold Water Inlet at Cape May—and had huge stripers break 20-pound-test monofilament like dental floss on the jumbled rocks near the sound buoy. I have cast a plug into the midst of an acre of feeding stripers not 50 yards off the beaches of Wildwood and Ocean City and cursed as a small bass got to the lure before a really big bass.

But for truly magnificent striper fishing, give me a cold November evening—with the sun just setting and a running tide churning up whitecaps over Shagwan Reef off Montauk and the herring gulls, Bonaparte gulls, and terns shrieking and diving into the white water to pick up the bits of baitfish left by the voraciously feeding schools of big southward-moving striped bass. In the few hours of remaining light and on into the silver brilliance, as the full moon comes up red from the eastern sea, the stripers seem to go mad with the urge to feed.

I have trolled over the reef using a surgical tubing lure and have had a half dozen arm-wrenching strikes before one finally hooked itself and the battle was on. If the tide and the moon are right, a man can literally fill a boat with bass—ranging from 10 to 12 pounds and up to 50 pounds and God-only-knows what weight.

I fished the reef at this time with Al Ristori and Nelson Bryant—both experts on striped bass—Nelse with his lifetime of fishing his native Vineyard and Al with a career that followed the stripers from New England to Georgia. We fished the reef one night in Al's 24-footer and caught so many fish we were literally knee-deep in stripers. After the first half an hour of battling the fish—arm-weary and satiated—I took over the controls and just watched the other two men fight bass. Nelse used a big surface plug and Al was using a bucktail jig. It didn't matter what we used. I am convinced that I could have caught bass on a stone if it had been rigged with a hook. The excitement was contagious, and there was hardly a moment when there was not a fish on.

The system was to move the center console boat about 50 yards above the rip—running against the tide at about half power; then, keeping the bow into the choppy sea, to let the boat drift through the rip with just enough power to enable one to steer. It was easy to see where the fish were feeding: there was a line of diving and screaming gulls all along the white water that marked the beginning of the rip, which extended for about 100 yards until it again became relatively calm water. As soon as we glided within casting distance of the line of feeding birds, both anglers would drop the lures into the tumbled water of the rip. Almost invariably the strikes were immediate. Several times I saw feeding bass knock Nelson's surface plug into the air as it touched the surface—only to have it land a few feet away and disappear in a boil of water or a burst of spray. About two turns of the spinning reel handle was all Al usually got as a bass smashed his bucktail jig. It was not at all unusual to have two fish on within a few yards of where both lures landed. Some stripers were lost in the first few moments of battle and both men tried to let the small bass shake themselves off after getting a look at them on a first jump.

Now and then either Nelse or Al would spell me at the controls, and I would catch several bass before handing a rod back for them to fish some more. The night was full of the hissing of a cold northeast wind, the pounding of seas against the fiberglass hull, the cries of gulls overhead, and the laughs and shouts of saltwater fishermen having the time of their lives. And strangely we were one of the few boats out that night. To the west could be seen a few running lights of boats hugging the shore beneath the old landmark lighthouse, and along the shore twinkled the myriads of beach campfires where hundreds of heavily dressed surf fishermen warmed their hands between spells of casting into the breaking seas.

Earlier in the day we had walked down to the point and sat watching the surf casters—literally shoulder-to-shoulder—hurling tin squids, plastic eels, jigs, and dozens of other traditional surfcasting weaponry into the churning surf, breaking against the rocks at the base of the cliff. There had been dozens of boats, large and

small, weaving back and forth just beyond the breaker line—some fishermen casting into the beginning of the surf and others trolling back and forth across the famous striper water, lines getting fouled and skippers and crewmen shouting and shaking fists at each other as they have been doing for as long as American striper fishermen have fished Montauk.

But that type of fishing is no longer for me. I did it for decades, from my childhood days on Narragansett Bay through the years of fishing the Long Island and New Jersey coasts. Now I want that perfect time when the stripers are feeding full and with a frenzy and where one can concentrate on the fish and the sheer joy of the sport—and not have to watch out for someone else's swinging squid close to an ear or have to reel in a surgical tube or umbrella rig because some novice boatman has cut across close to the stern of the boat.

Like a lot of striper men I know, I will ride the beaches all day until I find that isolated school feeding close to the shore. I have been known to hang off a number of bridges where the big stripers come up the estuaries to spawn—but I no longer go where they hang over the bridges shoulder-to-shoulder. I like to go to the ones with few people—and where, perhaps, not many fishermen know there are fish.

And I find solitude and happiness at the end of a rock jetty early on a misty morning when the tide is running just right and my reel spool slowly moves as a striper takes the rigged eel and swims confidently away, not knowing I am waiting for him to swallow that eel just a little bit more before setting the hook and beginning the fight.

There is a healing aloneness about fishing after dark—waist-deep in a moderate surf—with salt drying on the lips and black water churning around the legs of waders that few but the striper fisherman are privileged to share. It is where the cities and the problems and the annoyances seem far away and insignificant—not only seem to be, but really are. And for the true surf fisherman there is no need for an audience as a 20-pound striper is eased into the sudsy foam of the shallows. That the fight was good, the fish strong, and the angler satisfied is reward enough.

But the best—at least for me—is when the sea runs white and mean and fast over the rips at the end of the day and the striper schools will hit anything that moves—from schools of bunker and porgies to croakers and sea robins churned up from the bottom by the raging tide. It is there—when a man never knows whether the next cast will bring the smashing strike of a 5-pounder or a 65-pounder—that I find the real essence of striped bass fishing.

And so the great silver moon climbs slowly into the night sky, and the wind bites even through the waterproof gear and the goose-down jackets and trousers beneath. Hands that an hour before could crank the reel handles now begin to stiffen up with the cold, and footing in the laden boat is difficult with the layers of fish slithering about as the boat pitches in the pounding sea. There is the usual difference of opinion about when to quit, and finally it boils down to a majority vote. Nelse and I are for making the run for the marina and Ristori, who, like his late, great friend Al

Reinfelder, would never quit fishing as long as the bass are hitting, votes to continue after our striped bass foes.

So the rods are stored and the boat slams into the running seas as power is added and a course is taken for the lights at the tips of the twin rock jetties. It is a kidney-jarring, spray-filled, and freezing twenty-minute ride to the shelter of the jetties, and a following sea does nothing to help keep the boat on an even keel as we slide between the rock walls and finally enter the basin.

But there are the lights and the curious faces; the laughter and the heaving of stripers onto the rough dock planking; the hosing down of the boat; the cleaning and storing of gear; and making the boat secure against the night winds. And after that it is a warming and bracing drink, hours of filleting a winter's worth of striped bass for the freezer, the laughter of friends, and the stories of other great days on the water.

And finally, after a hot shower and a change of clothes, there are the fresh fillets of striper cooked by Nelse with his own favorite recipe: boiled in a deep frying pan, simmering in the contents of several cans of stewed tomatoes, laced with salt and pepper and just a few freshly chopped-up onions. Leave it to a Vineyard man to cook striper the right way, while the freezing wind moans around the frame motel room and the schools of striped bass feed throughout the night off Montauk, as they have done for millions of years.

Tips on Striper Fishing at Montauk Point . . .

If anyone ever gets around to writing *the* definitive treatise on surfcasting for stripers, he could do worse than pick Long Island's Montauk Point as the appropriate locale. For more years than a lot of dedicated New York area surfcasters would care to remember, the waters immediately off Montauk have given up whopping big fish.

What's more, and probably of equal importance, the aesthetics are right—the beaches themselves, the roll and roar of the surf, the squawking seagulls circling overhead, the feel and smell of the wind, the action itself. Perhaps best of all, the scene is graced by the presence of the famed Montauk Lighthouse, a pictorial punctuation mark that serves as an overall complement to the entire adventure.

An aesthetically soothing atmosphere and backdrop is necessary when surf fishing for stripers because the fish themselves can drive a man crazy. They must be among the most unpredictable creatures in the sea. Extremely finicky as to diet, they'll bang hell out of one type of bait for days, then—with the next cresting tide—switch to something else. Trying to figure out what they'll hit at a given time can be frustrating. As a result, there is very little striper lore that holds true from one day to the next.

Experienced surf anglers can be certain only that stripers running in a school tend to feed either at dawn or at dusk, preferably a couple of hours before and after the tide crests. Individual fish, however, will violate even this rule, some battlers having been taken at high noon when the tide was dead low.

If you're getting the idea that going after stripers is a matter of dedication and patience, you're right. It's also a matter of knowing the territory.

Regardless of whether you plan to work the surf, or offshore from a boat, it's a good idea to scout an area at low tide first. When the water is low, you can mark sandbars, inshore holes, waterways through which cruising fish are likely to pass when the tide is high. Well worth working are bars and points at which coming and going tides rip, however briefly; at such times, the roiling waters stun natural prey, and predators—in this case, stripers—can have a field day gorging themselves.

There are surface signs to look for. Stripers often work close to a beach, and you can see them chasing bait fish, which will tend to leap right out of the water in a frantic effort to escape.

Overhead, gulls and terns can tip you off as to striper feeding activity. If the fish are on a tear, you can almost count on seeing circling sea birds over the hungry diners.

Striper fishing requires persistence and, frankly, personal experience. True, you may have beginners' luck, but chances are it will take a few outings to strike pay dirt. And then you'll have your own theories, freely expounded and believed by no one except yourself, on how to catch stripers.

If you go after Montauk's stripers, you'll want a good 8- to 10-foot surf fishing rod (either of bait casting or spinning type), at least 250 yards of about 20-pound-test line, a pair of full-length, heavy-duty waders (and ice creepers if you get around on the rocks), some kind of flashlight (to be used only when absolutely necessary), foul weather gear, a compartmented bag in which you can carry lures, leaders, and just plain handy "stuff," and a sap of some kind to subdue a thrashing fish.

Montauk *is* fishing—pure fishing, and all fishing—meaning you won't want for facilities, boat charters or rentals, accommodations, or company. Fishing talk is hard to avoid; you'll find even a restaurant waitress has a few theories as to how, when, and why stripers can be caught. A few forays on your own, and you won't believe any such talk, but it's all part of the fun. And who knows . . . you might learn something.

18.
Scotland: Salmon and the Wee Stick

It hadn't rained for three months in Scotland. Arthur Oglesby, the European editor of *Field & Stream,* met A. J. McClane and me at the airport in Edinburgh as we came in from London after a nine-hour flight from New York.

We had come to Scotland in the last part of September for the salmon fishing and a few days of shooting driven pheasants and red-legged partridge. We had carried our cased, light rods aboard the plane—much to the consternation of the stewardesses, who probably thought they were cue sticks for an international billiard match or sword canes with which to hijack the jet to Dublin.

Arthur was not in the best of spirits when we disembarked at Edinburgh. He is a fine trout and salmon fisherman, and the author of a number of books on the subject. He is also a constant contributor to the *Fishing Times* and *Shooting Times* of London. It was not the early hour that disturbed him, but the low water. No true fisherman is happy when the chances of catching fish are poor.

"Awfully sorry," Arthur said, in what must have been the understatement of the century. "The damned rivers are all low, and if a salmon took a fly, it would be because it had gone daft."

I looked at McClane and he at me. Both of us being of Scotch ancestry, there was not much else to say.

"Do you suppose," said McClane, "there would be a good inn that had fine kippers on the way north?"

"Now there," answered Oglesby, "is the first intelligent question we have come to. I think I can guarantee that."

With due ceremony we stashed the rod cases and gear in the car and headed north.

The Tweed was indeed a disaster. We stayed in a fine hotel—where the kippers were as good as reputed—and both McClane and I spent a fruitless hour and a half trying to interest some tired salmon which had been lying in the same pool for months. None showed the slightest inclination to rise to a fly, although they periodically jumped as salmon on a spawning run will do. The Tweed is a magnificent river; but it is one which will break the heart of a fly fisherman when it is too low, and the salmon are not in a taking mood.

We ended up driving back to Edham House and enjoyed a fine hour or so talking to other disgruntled fishermen who had been there for weeks and had not had a strike. The English and the Scots seemed to have a lot more perseverance than North American trout and salmon fishermen. It may be because when the fish are not striking these men have no other place to go on their tight little island, while North American anglers can take off for provinces or rivers reputed to be better. At any rate, we all agreed there was no question about the reason for the lack of activity. The streams were extremely low and the fish had been staying in the holding pools for a long time. Even when they jumped one could see that they were getting dark red—almost black—and were late spawners.

The following morning we drove farther north and stopped at noon on the Tay to see what it was like. The river was one of the most beautiful I have ever seen, but it, too, was very low, and the fishermen we met at the local inn at lunch had the same report that the men had on the Tweed—low water and no action.

The only option left was to drive as far north as we could and hope to catch the run on the Spey, on the northeast coast. The salmon there might still be coming in from the North Sea and might be less affected by the low water and lack of rainfall.

We arrived at Seafield Estates, a fine shooting and fishing preserve at Cullen, a beautiful, small town on the sea coast. Our host, Eric Yates, had the foresight to leave the bar open with instruction that we be revived with some of the excellent Scotch whisky from the many distilleries dotting the landscape of northern Scotland. It probably saved our lives after the seven-hour drive across the moors.

The following morning found us on the Spey, one of the most magnificent rivers I have ever seen. The late-September weather had turned the aspen and birch leaves to gold and red and the water, low as it was, was filled with salmon fresh from the North Sea and on their way up the great stream. They had been coming into the Spey since spring—a continuing surge of life.

At about 10 A.M. we arrived at the stretch of the Spey which our host had said was the best of the approximately twenty-seven miles of the river owned by the estate. Our ghillie was a man named Georgie Williams, a dour-looking Scot whose looks belied his nature. Dressed in the traditional knickers and stalking cap, he looked at my tiny 3⅜-ounce, 7-foot, split-bamboo fly rod and shook his head.

"You're not goin' to do much on this river," he said, "with that wee stick."

McClane had a 7-foot glass rod which weighed only an ounce or so more than mine. Because we had been converting big-rod men for years from the Bahamas to Quebec, I said nothing. I did note, however, that Arthur had unleashed his 12-foot English "telephone pole" and had waded into the rapids. I found out in the first few moments, however, that Arthur could do a roll cast with the big rod that was called the "Spey cast" and literally shot the line across the big river.

I am sure the big rod is a great advantage—especially in the spring when the water is high. But I cannot help it; I am a light-tackle devotee.

It was not more than half an hour before Arthur had a strike and was hooked up. We all waded ashore to watch the battle. The fish was a good one, and Georgie stood behind Arthur and said very little, recognizing an expert at work when he saw one.

After about ten minutes the fish began to tire, and Arthur brought it into the shallows. It was a beautiful fish, about 8 pounds, still silvery from the salt water and full of strength. Georgie tailed it and held it up for photographs before we released it to swim back into the current. Arthur went back upstream to try for another, and Georgie, with a pitying glance at McClane and me, retired to a wooden bench to smoke his pipe and watch us cast. I had tied on a nondescript black wet fly which had been tied by a first-class trout and salmon angler back home, Eric Peper. He never did tell me what it was called, nor did I ever ask. It looked a bit like a Green Butt, and he told me it had worked for him on the Miramichi.

I had a 30-foot shooting-head fly-line on the small reel with 75 feet of 12-pound monofilament tied to it with a nail knot. The backing was 100 yards of 18-pount-test braided Dacron. With it I was able to cast a pretty fair distance; a fact that did not escape the notice of Georgie, although he did not make any great effort to acknowledge it.

If he ignored my casting, he made a special effort to show disinterest at A. J.'s casts—which were reaching close to the far bank. There are not many fly fishermen in the world who can equal the McClane when it comes to heaving a fly. Arthur knew this, as did I, but we had not so informed Georgie. He did notice it, however, and missed a few puffs on the pipe when Al made a particularly beautiful cast—which was often.

The take on my cast to a bit of rough water was as gentle a take as I have felt in many a year of salmon fishing. The fish never broke water. If I had not fished for Atlantic salmon before, I might have thought I was hung up on a snag. But, knowing the ways of the fish, I set the hook gently and waited to see what would happen. As I expected, there was a slight movement to the middle of the stream as the fish felt the hook. I had no butt extension on the tiny rod and raised it high overhead and cupped the reel with my left hand for the expected run.

"Hey!" A. J. shouted from above me and began backing out of the river, reeling in his line to give me room. "Fish on!"

Arthur splashed ashore from below me as Georgie got up from the bench and strolled casually down to the shore behind me.

"Now, don't fight him too hard, lad," he cautioned. "That wee stick will never hold him if he takes it into his head to run downstream."

A. J. had moved down beside me and was unlimbering a camera to get some action shots. He winked as I glanced at him, and I felt better. The little rod had not let me down on the Miramichi, the George, and the Icelandic rivers. I was fairly sure it wasn't going to fail me on the Spey—Georgie or no Georgie.

The salmon came out of the middle of the current suddenly when it finally realized it was in trouble. The reel whirred, and the handle scoured my palm as I

cupped it. The little rod bent double as the fish headed downstream, and I moved to my left—trying to keep a footing on the slippery and rocky bottom of the Spey.

"He's going into the big pool below, lad," Georgie shouted, doing a semi-dance behind me. "Keep the tip as high as you can." (If the tip had been any higher I would have looked like Wilt Chamberlain.)

The fish made a spectacular jump—switching ends in midair—and came down with a resounding splash.

"Oh, look at him, look at him!" Georgie shouted. "What a beauty!"

I was too busy at the moment to appreciate the local dialect. The fish was fairly heavy. I couldn't tell how big it was, but it was a nice fish, and the river current wasn't helping me as much as it was the fish.

The salmon made several more jumps, but I really wasn't worried too much about losing it for lack of line, what with the backing on the small reel. My only real worry was that it might find a sharp rock or underwater snag.

I kept moving downstream and was followed by a retinue of ghillie, Arthur, and A. J. taking pictures. I began to notice my right arm tiring from the strain, but that was nothing new with a good fish on. One thing about the small rods—they are fun, but they don't give one a chance to rest.

"There's a bar down about thirty yards," Georgie cautioned. "If you can keep him in the big pool for a while until he tires, we can perhaps lead him onto the sand—as long as you can hold him with that bit of a rod," he hastened to add.

At this point, Arthur laughed. "I have a feeling, Georgie," he said, "that wee stick, as you call it, is going to be enough."

Georgie grunted something in Scottish, which I was too busy to try and translate.

The fish fought long, and it fought well, as do all Atlantic salmon. When it finally tired and got close to the sandbar, I waded out to try to get it close to me. Suddenly, I realized that Georgie was wading beside me—leather shoes, woolen stockings, knickers, and all. I was wearing chest waders.

"Now, now, lad," Georgie said softly. "Lead him a bit toward me. Easy now, *easy!* Don't rush him . . . . easy, easy . . ."

He had no tailer, just his hands. I began to watch him, rather than the fish. He was bending over from the waist and staring into the water, carefully watching the fish.

"Aye, aye," he advised. "Just a bit closer now. Ease that wee stick a bit to the left. Aye, that's it. Just a bit more now, lad. Fine, fine . . ."

And suddenly, he reached down and had the salmon by the tail—a fine, beautiful, vibrant, silvery fish of about 12 pounds—wriggling as he held it aloft. I heard Arthur's jubilant shout from behind me and also heard the repeated clicks as A. J. took pictures of us both standing thigh-deep in the cold, calm, clear water.

And after that, it was putting the beautiful fish back into the shallows—moving it back and forth until the gills worked well—until it swam strongly, and finally letting it go back into the mainstream to join its upward-bound brethren.

I reeled in the line and sloshed out onto the grassy bank.

"Georgie," I said, "what in the hell did you have to wade into that freezing river for? It's going to take you hours to dry out."

Georgie stamped his feet for a bit on the sod and grinned. "If this water could have hurt a member of the Williams family it would have killed my great-grandfather and his alike, all the way down to me. We've been ghillies on this river for a great many generations." Arthur laughed and beckoned us to the wooden bench up on the bank.

"I have a little toast," he said, "seeing as this is your first salmon in Scotland."

He had put four tiny silver shot-sized glasses on the bench and was filling them with Scotch whisky, seventy proof and distilled not more than seventy miles from where we were standing. He handed Georgie four plastic cups. The ghillie, without any need of instruction, walked down to the edge of the river and filled all four with water from the Spey.

We all raised the glasses, and I caught the twinkle in Georgie's eye.

"To your first Scottish salmon, laddie," he said. "May it never be your last."

I swallowed the whisky and followed it with a sip of Spey water.

The warmth spread in my stomach, and I grinned at the tall Englishman and the wiry Scot, standing in his soaking shoes, socks, and knickers.

"If it's my last, Georgie," I said. "It will be enough."

We all emptied the tiny silver glasses as the noontime sun glinted on the surface of the Spey and the incredibly clean September air blew in from the North Sea.

Tips on Fishing in Scotland . . .

Scotland and salmon fishing are pretty much synonymous, with four rivers—Tay, Spey, Dee, and Tweed—coming to mind most often. There are, however, many other productive salmon waters there, including the Oykel, Nith, Glass, Awe, Beauly, and Thurso. Brown trout are common to just about every Scottish lake, stream, and river, and sea trout run from early in October to about mid-March.

The season on salmon varies. Some rivers open as early as mid-January, and just about all of them are open by mid-April. The same variation holds true for closing dates. All rivers are closed by the end of November, though, and, throughout the year, there is no fishing allowed on Sundays.

Most Scottish salmon waters are whacked up into beats, or lengths of the river upon which fishing is permitted. The extent of each beat varies, and usually only a specific number of fishermen (or rods) are allowed to work a given stretch of water.

The Ballathie Beat on the Tay is limited to six rods over its 1½-mile length. Actually, the Ballathie is divided into two parts which are fished alternately. Most fishing is done from a boat, the Tay being a big river, but fish can be taken from either bank. When the water is low, it's possible to wade.

The season on the Tay opens in mid-January, and closes in mid-October. Their most productive periods are August, September, and the first two weeks in October.

All salmon stalking on the Ballathie is under the supervision of a man named John Bennett. Bennett suggests long fly rods with enough backing on the reel to handle wide-ranging fish that average over 11 pounds in weight, but can weigh in at 20 pounds and more. You can also use spinning tackle, but Bennett suggests rigging it to handle 12- or 15-pound test lines.

Accommodations for fishing the Ballathie Beat can be arranged at Ballathie House Hotel, a lovely country house featuring large bedrooms and private baths. Meals, complete with a fine selection of wines, are outstanding. The hotel is in Stanley, near Perth.

Prices for a week's fishing on salmon waters in Scotland vary, depending upon the time of the year they are being fished. During the peak time on the Ballathie, a week's fishing will run a little over $1,000 per rod, which includes room, all meals, guides, boats, the loan of fishing tackle and waders (if necessary), and transportation between the hotel and the airport.

Lower in cost—about $700—is a week on the Taymount Beat, just below the Ballathie. Again, it's about 1½ miles of prime salmon water divided into two beats offering outstanding fly fishing runs.

The Taymount Beat, also under the supervision of John Bennett, is limited to five rods. Fish taken in these waters recently have averaged 14 pounds. Again, accommodations are at the Ballathie House Hotel, with cars providing transportation to and from the beat, and again, the overall fee includes all services.

The Tulchan Beat on the River Spey is one of the most famous stretches of salmon water in Scotland. It is divided into four beats, each about 1¼ miles long, and, while spinning tackle is permitted, most fishermen work its great width with fly rods. The beats are fished alternately.

Most fishing on the Tulchan is done by wading, both banks offering easy access. Chest waders are a must. The season runs from mid-April through the end of September and offers good to excellent fishing throughout. Salmon average about 10 pounds, sea trout (for which the Spey is equally known) about 3 pounds. Rods on the Tulchan Beat are limited to five, and fisherman and guests are accommodated at Tulchan Lodge, an elegant Scottish country home situated on a 21,000-acre estate about 8 miles from Grantown-on-Spey. The Lodge offers double rooms with private baths and gourmet cuisine.

There are other beats along the Spey, and arrangements to fish them can be made locally in such towns as Fochabers, Archiestown, Craigellachie, Aberlour, and Grantown. Prices vary according to beat fished and time of the season.

If you're thinking about a fishing trip to Scotland, don't be misled by what it says on a calendar; August in Scotland is nothing like August in, say, Hannibal, Missouri. Just about any time of the year in Scotland is chilling enough to make necessary a dram or two of the potable for which Scotland is justly world-famous. True, you may not need them, but pack long johns and a pair of gloves.

For further information, contact Adventures Unlimited or Arthur Oglesby (European Editor, *Field & Stream*, 9 Oatlands Drive, Harrogate, England; telephone 0423–83565 or 0904–27234).

19.
Prince Edward Island: The Incredible Bluefin

It was the last day of the tournament, and the Canadian team was leading with six fish. We, the eight members of the American team, had managed to land only three of the big "horse mackerel," and the weather on this, the last day, wasn't making life or the prospect of winning the annual tourney at Prince Edward Island any easier.

At 11:00 A.M., five miles out of the tiny port of North Lake, the rain was drenching us in the pitching 35-foot diesel-powered plank boat, and the 4- to 5-foot seas were making life generally miserable even for seasoned big-game fishermen.

I was teamed up with Fred Archibald, a Florida big-game fisherman of no mean repute, who had lost a big bluefin the day before after four grueling hours in the chair. The American team had been hooked up seven times and had lost four fish in the past three days of the contest. We had been scheduled to compete four days, but the winds had been so high Wednesday that even the hardy commercial boats would not venture from the narrow harbor mouth into the massive, cold and gray August seas that pounded the entrance to the jetty. So it had turned into a three-day tournament, and this was to be the last day. The official quitting time, determined by our International Game Fish Association (IGFA) judges, was to be 4:30 P.M.; nothing hooked up later would count.

We were taking half-hour stints in the fighting chair and trying to heat the chill in our bones in the cabin between bouts with the downpour and seas. I had not gotten a strike in the tournament. For reasons known only to the patron saints of big-game fishermen, none of my partners the last two days had either. Boats all around us had been raising fish, losing fish, and boating bluefins, but the boat on which I fished appeared to be jinxed. It was probably my imagination, but I sensed that the other team members were beginning to look at me strangely.

Fred lurched out of the chair and groped his way back to the cabin—his lips blue and his hair plastered down by the cold rain.

"Your turn," he muttered, reaching for the offered hot black coffee and waving toward the crude chair. "I don't blame them for not hitting. They want to stay down there where it's warmer and drier."

My deep love for big-game fishing notwithstanding, I moved back toward the battered chair with no great enthusiasm. I had on the official tournament jacket over a heavy waterproof flotation jacket and several layers of wool sweaters and long underwear. The weatherbeaten plank fighting chair was a far cry from the plush and padded luxury fighting chairs sportfishermen used in the States. There was just the flat wooden chair seat, an ancient cracked leather-and-canvas kidney harness, and a welded steel footrest, probably resurrected from some discarded barber chair. The two reels were not exactly the latest—a battered, vintage Ocean City 14/0 and an old 12/0 Penn. But both were well cared for, and each held 800 yards of 130-pound braided nylon.

The mate helped snap the swivels to the big reel and to adjust the footrest to the proper length. After he had moved back to the shelter of the cabin roof, I hunched my shoulders, looked at my watch to verify the time, and stared at the two "daisy chains" of rigged mackerel skipping astern in the sullen and gray sea. The No. 13 hook was buried in the last bait on the chain. One chain of a half-dozen foot-long mackerel rode the swells on the starboard side approximately 30 feet back, skipping off to one side from a clip fastened to a line from a 20-foot bamboo outrigger jutting out and up into a sodden sky. The other bait chain skittered as a flat line lure not more than 15 feet from the rough, salt-pitted transom of the aged boat. It bounced in the center of the churned wake—a practice no American big-game fisherman would try, believing that the wake spooks fish.

There were several other tournament boats in sight on the horizon, and once we passed close to a big dory with two sou'wester-clad fishermen handlining strings of small mackerel over the gunwales. The red beaches and rolling green slopes of Prince Edward Island were barely visible off to our port side through the rain.

One moment there was nothing, and the next a wall of water pushed up into the tumbling white wake.

"Here he comes!" I heard the skipper shout, and automatically I reached for the rod in the right-hand holder as a tremendous explosion of water came over the transom and the bait chain disappeared into a vast cobalt-blue maw. I saw the dorsal fin and sickle-shaped tail as the big fish went under, and the reel shrieked as the line tore off the spool.

There is almost no way to describe the feeling of that much power packed into a big fish. The steel-tipped rod butt slammed into the seat gimbal and I leaned back, left hand clenched on the felt rod grip and my gloved right hand resting on the star drag. Hooking up to a bluefin feels like being fastened to a speeding train. There is nothing the angler can do on those first few runs but exert as much pressure on the fish as the tackle will stand. The sound of the reel was an ear-splitting scream by now, and the cockpit was full of action. The mate swung the old chair until he had me

facing the direction of the streaking fish. Fred had jerked the line from the outrigger clip and was reeling the other bait string in as rapidly as possible to get it out of the way.

Three hundred yards of line had left the reel in a matter of seconds, and I eased the star drag slightly.

"No, no!" The mate shouted in my right ear. "Don't give him any more. You'll break him off!"

I nodded but continued to add slightly more drag. Most big-game crews hate to see a fish lost, because the more they boat the better they look. But I always remember the voice of Bill Carpenter, president of the IGFA and a man who has caught more than a hundred bluefins in his life.

"Stop 'em or pop 'em," he said to me once at Cat Cay during the annual tuna tournament. He was standing with Annie Kunkel, the fine woman big-game angler who has caught more than a hundred bluefin tuna. She had nodded in agreement.

The first few runs of the big fish are the crucial ones. If the fish senses it has a chance, the fight will probably be a long one. If one can exert enough pressure in the first few dashes for freedom, psychologically, the fish will already have lost the battle—even though it may still take considerable time to get it in.

The harness was cutting into my back and the fingers of my left hand clenched tight as I lifted the rod and leaned back with all my strength, legs straight against the metal footrest. The fish was taking a lot of punishment from the drag, the heavy, bowed fiberglass rod, and the movement of the boat.

It seemed hours before the mate grunted and leaned close to my ear.

"He's stopping, he's slowing down," he said hoarsely. The reel spool was barely turning now.

I lowered the rod tip almost to the horizontal, took three or four quick turns of the reel handle, and leaned back into the pull.

"He took more than six hundred yards of line on that run," the mate said. His voice was a faint background sound.

Now, as always, came the sheer, pure joy of physical combat with the fish. Forgotten was the cold, slashing rain, the throbbing of the diesel engines, and the gray seas dumping water into the cockpit. There was just the pumping of the big rod; the exhilaration of feeling the huge fish's head shake in anger and frustration; the cranking of the big reel handle; and the pleasant ache of straining leg, back, and arm muscles. But most of all, for me, there was the uncomplicated thrill of battling an adversary which had most of the advantages on its side—it being in its own element and much stronger than I.

I found myself again in that special world where there are no grays—just black and white, win or lose. It is this simplified world, far removed from the confused one in which we all live each day, that keeps me big-game fishing.

The reel spool began to wail, for the third or fourth time. I added a fraction more drag and leaned back to let the heavy rod absorb the power of the fish. In a few moments, the run slowed and the fish began to shake its head from side to side. It was in about 60 feet of water.

The shocks of the thrashing head traveled up the line, into the rod and into my left shoulder. With each shake, the reel spool spun and the rod bent. And suddenly it was all over.

"He's off," I said quietly. The feel of the cold rain on my face returned.

"What?" the mate shouted.

I held the rod up and pointed to the tip. The big rod was still bowed, but only from the weight of almost 700 yards of heavy line.

"Reel, reel!" the mate said. "Maybe he's coming toward the boat."

I shook my head. I felt the pitching of the boat and could smell the diesel fuel. I turned half in the chair and glanced at the captain over my right shoulder. "Full ahead, skipper," I shouted. "He's off, but let's make sure."

The captain nodded, and the roar of the engines filled the cockpit. The angle of the line streaming astern changed slowly, but there was no more power on the other end—just dead weight. The skipper gradually slowed down, shifted into neutral, then reversed and began to back down as I started the long retrieve of line. Cranking in 700 yards of 130-pound line can be as difficult as bringing in a fair-sized amberjack or grouper. While the muscles of my right arm had not telegraphed the strain of the fighting fish, they protested against the work of bringing in the inert line.

"Fish broken off on the *Princess Anne,*" was the voice of our IGFA judge speaking into the radio.

"Name of angler, please," came back the response from the tournament boat.

"Samson, American team."

"Right," came the answer. "Reason for loss?"

"We won't know for a bit. Line still coming in."

"Confirm time of hookup as 12:20 P.M., please."

"That's right," said our judge. "Breakoff time 12:46 P.M."

I glanced at my watch. It was 12:57. My God, where had that time gone?

The strain had lessened and the double line finally came over the transom. The mate ran the heavy line through his gnarled hand until he came to the break. It was where the double line had been fastened to the wire leader. "Damn," he said and shook his head. I unsnapped the swivels from the big reel and slid it back into the rod holder on the chair. I got up and walked to the shelter of the cabin roof as the mate began to rig up the line again. There was the taste of bile in my mouth, and fatigue washed over me.

"Broken at the double line," said the judge, a Canadian, into the radio. "Noted. Rotten luck. Our best to angler."

I nodded. Fred rested a hand on the shoulder of my soaked jacket.

"I know how you feel," he said simply. I thought of his four-hour ordeal the day before. He knew.

"Thanks," I said. "I could use a drink."

The skipper fished a flask from beneath the wheel and handed it to me. The brandy felt like scalding water as it went down—warming me almost instantly. The disappointment began to fade, as it always does.

"Well," I said to Fred, "there're still three and a half hours to go. Let's see you haul one of these monsters in."

He grinned, slapped me on the shoulder, and made his way back to the chair. The mate and I helped him into the harness. I put out the other outrigger bait while the mate rigged up another bait chain for the flat line from the mackerel, which had been soaking in a pail of brine to keep them tough.

The rain let up an hour later and the wind began to die down as the afternoon wore on. We removed several layers of sweaters and ended up wearing just the light official jackets over long woolen underwear. We had both been in the chair several times, but there had been no action. Baitfish schools had churned up the surface of the sea in many areas as we trolled back and forth along the coast of the beautiful island. Several other boats were hooked up, but the fish were lost—one in a matter of minutes and another after almost two hours. One of our team members lost his after the reel handle came off and he fought it with a large nail inserted in the metal arm as an improvised handle. There was to be a victory and awards banquet starting at 7:00 P.M., and I had begun to think about a hot shower and a couple of drinks before dinner.

It was 3:50—forty minutes before official quitting time—when the big bluefin smashed the bait chain behind the transom. The wall of water doused Fred in the chair and caught us by surprise. We had all been thinking of starting back, resigned to the loss of the one fish.

I jerked the line from the starboard outrigger and began pumping in the bait chain as Fred grabbed for the same rod I had before and hung on as the old reel began

its wailing complaint again. The mate swung the chair as the huge fish headed north toward the cliffs about three miles away.

"Hookup on the *Princess Anne*," our judge shouted into the radio. "Three-fifty P.M., angler, Archibald, American team."

"Roger," came the answer. "Noted. Hell of a time to do that."

Fred leaned back and held the rod aloft, the big stick bowed against the afternoon sky.

"Tell that to this big bastard!" he laughed.

Fred was about 6 feet, 2 inches tall, weighed close to 200 pounds, was in his early thirties and in excellent physical shape. I shook my head and went forward for a bottle of cold Alpine beer and a camera. Even if the fight went a little long, I thought as I reached into the ice chest, we would probably still be back in time for the dinner.

At 4:30—when the official tournament boat contacted all the competing boats to tell them the baits must be taken from the water and that the tournament was officially over except for those anglers fighting fish—the big bluefin was still out over 500 yards from us and still taking line when it felt like it. One other angler on the Canadian team was hooked up and had been for almost three hours.

Twenty minutes later the tournament boat came by and stood off several hundred yards as photographers from the local newspapers and television cameramen took still shots and some film footage. A short time later they wished us luck over the bullhorn and headed toward the harbor, visible down the coast.

At some time after 6:00 P.M.—with Fred stripped of his jacket and down to a woolen undershirt top—the Canadian angler boated his tuna to make it a total of seven for their team. With only four boated for the American team, we couldn't win even if Fred succeeded in bringing this stubborn fish to gaff, but—in the spirit of big-game fishing—this had become unimportant now. It was the fish that mattered.

The sun dropped slowly toward the western horizon, and the surface of the sea had become glassy, with a burnished-bronze cast. I took some fine color pictures of

Fred and the mate silhouetted against the sun, as the giant fish bored through the deep water—its great scimitar tail propelling it against the tide and its tremendous strength apparently undiminished. Just before dark a number of small boats came out from the harbor and drifted several hundred yards away from us. They were filled with townspeople watching the battle. They watched for almost an hour, then left—headed for the cluster of lights marking the harbor and jetty.

I got a flashlight from the forward locker and stood behind the mate, who continued to swing the chair in the direction of the fish. I played the light on the line so Fred could see the angle of line at all times. Several times we had the fish up close to the boat, but each time it came up under the transom on the port side, and the captain was forced to increase the power to keep the line from being cut by the propellers. At the same time he had to swing the bow to port to keep the fish from under the boat. And each time the double line and the wire leader would move back behind the boat, and the big fish, having seen the boat, would begin another surging run.

Fred—now in the fifth hour of his fight—was drenched with sweat. His face was set in that expression big-game fishermen know so well—not fatigue as much as a combination of anguish and resolve. He had been operating on reserve energy for some time—after several cups of hot tea, a soggy sandwich, and several beers had been handed to him.

The flashlight batteries began to lose power after 9:00 P.M., and the skipper radioed the dock for help. A boat was dispatched with a powerful flash which could be run off the boat batteries. It took the boat nearly half an hour to find us, and a youngster handed our judge the flash and cord over our bow, to prevent coming near the line and fighting fish. My arms had long ago gone numb from holding the flashlight on the rod tip and line, and my legs ached from constantly standing behind the mate or walking around him as he swung the chair. I could imagine how Fred felt.

Sometime after 10:00 P.M.—the big fish had just made another incredible run and then had thrashed on the surface about 200 yards back in the darkness—Fred rested his forehead on his stiffened left elbow.

"Give up," he said, evenly, as if to himself. "Give up, damn you, give up." Then he raised his head, took a deep breath, and began pumping the rod.

Around 11:00 P.M. the beer, sandwiches, coffee, tea, and crackers were gone. A box of sugar cubes remained to give the big man in the chair an occasional surge of energy as the big fish continued to swim evenly through the black water. A slight wind began to come up and I asked the judge to put the heavy padded jacket on me—not daring to take the light from the line lest Fred lose sight of the all-important direction and angle.

We had drifted about a mile east of the harbor and were in fairly close to shore as the hands of my watch crept slowly around the hour of midnight and we entered into a new day. The fish had been under the boat several times and almost lost to the spinning propellers. It was a never-ending nightmare of pumping it close to the boat; sighting its huge, silver-blue image with the flashlight in the clear depths below and to the port side of the transom; watching it start to come up; and then having to swing the boat and add power to keep it clear. I had long since ceased to feel any physical sense of fatigue, hunger, anxiety, thirst, or anger at the stubborn fish. There was only the gleam of the white, braided line in the light beam, the labored breathing of the man with the heavy rod, and the muttering of the diesel exhaust ports in the water at the stern.

A while later, the depth finder indicated 18 feet of water and Fred groaned.

"What's the bottom like?" he asked wearily.

"Sandy," the mate muttered. "Don't worry. Not many rocks."

I knew Fred was thinking the same thing I was. I could see the huge bluefin, nose-down at the bottom, trying to rub the leader on rocks. In spite of the shallow water—the boat was not more than a quarter-mile from the harbor entrance—the tuna continued to take out line on another run.

The big man braced his legs against the footrest, leaned back in the chair, and hauled on the rod with what must have been a tremendous effort.

"Die, damn you," he said, as the reel spool continued to revolve slowly. "Give up, you son of a bitch," he said through clenched teeth. "Give up, because . . ." He placed both hands on the rod. "Because I'm not going to. You hear me. I'm not."

I watched the angle of the line slowly change as the fish drew farther and farther from the boat.

And suddenly the reel slowed to a stop. I felt no emotion, nor, I think, did the mate or Fred. It was simply a fact.

The big man lowered the rod tip, took his right hand from the rod, took the reel handle, and began to turn it. Slowly at first, and just a little faster as time went on, he kept turning it. His breath was coming in gasps and he grunted with each long pump on the rod.

"He's coming in," the mate said. I nodded, knowing the mate was right and yet not really understanding how we knew.

I glanced at my watch. It was 1:40 A.M. The fish was out in the darkness about 300 yards away.

By 1:50 Fred had the fish less than 100 yards away. The steady pumping kept up, and I could tell by a splash now and then that the bluefin was on or near the surface.

The mate looked at me. Then he turned to the captain.

"I'll clear the gaffs," he said slowly. "When I see the double line I'll call out. Leave her in idle and take the long-handled gaff. I'll take the wire leader and try and sink the flying gaff at the same time. Keep the light on him at all times if you can," he said to me.

I nodded. The judge moved back into the cabin area to give us room.

"Double line," I said as the swivel gleamed in the blackness. Fred continued to pump, his breath a rasping sound in his throat.

Then there was the double line up close; the glint of shiny wire as the swivel came up.

The mate left the chair, reached down and picked up the flying gaff, reached out on the starboard side with a gloved hand, and grasped the leader.

"Neutral, Skip," he shouted.

And there was the huge fish, coming up in shallow water—an immense torpedo of silver and dark blue, lying on its side. Its huge eye, as big as that of a horse, rolled in the light of the flash.

The mate reached out with one quick movement and sank the flying gaff into the back of the bluefin. With that the fish thrashed and hurled water over the entire boat. I tried to keep my footing but went down on the wet deck. I saw the skipper reach out with the second gaff and got to my feet in time to see him sink it into the silver underbelly. The fish began to thrash violently against the side of the thick hull.

Fred hurled himself from the chair and grabbed the rope of the flying gaff and braced his feet against the gunwale.

"Hold the light," I shouted to the judge, who took it from me as I grabbed the long-handled gaff from the captain. The fish almost tore my arms from the sockets.

"Get a meat hook into him, Skipper!" the mate shouted. "I'll try the tail rope."

The mate finally got the fish tail-roped, but not before the tuna almost broke his arm in the process. The captain had sunk another steel meathook into the back of the fish, passed a rope through its handle and fastened it to a cleat. He then passed a half-inch nylon line up through the gill slits and out through the mouth of the still-thrashing giant tuna. It was not until he fastened that line to a forward cleat and the mate had tied the tail rope to the base of the fighting chair that I knew we had won.

I raised my head from the gunwale, where I was still clenching the wooden gaff handle and trying to keep bruised ribs from the rough gunwale wood.

Slowly Fred raised his head from between his arms, which were still straightened out, holding the thick rope of the flying gaff. He looked at me in the light of the flash and a grin slowly started to grow. "O.K., lads," the mate laughed, "you can let go now. We got the mean, ugly son of a bitch!"

Fred let go of the rope and sprawled back in several inches of water on the cockpit deck. He started to laugh.

I sat down and leaned back against the cockpit. I thought I was too tired to laugh, but then I started to—and after that I couldn't stop.

And then it was handshakes and slaps on the back and falling down in the cockpit again and again as the crew and angler team, and the IGFA judge, joined in a wild victory dance on a wet plank boat gently rolling in the black water and darkness of a tiny harbor.

Even after the skipper had broken out the secret bottle of brandy he kept for special occasions and everyone had taken several large swallows and the boat was halfway to the harbor, whose twinkling lights grew larger by the minute, the great fish continued to thrash, pounding over and over against the planks of the hull.

It had taken more than eleven hours to subdue the bluefin. It wasn't a record fish, nor that huge a tuna. The Canadians' biggest had weighed 788 pounds, and this stubborn young "green" bluefin finally weighed in at 655 pounds. But this fish was probably between ten and fourteen years old, in the prime of its life, and far stronger than some in the 1,000-pound class.

The banquet had been over long ago, and the competing teams—after drinking up most of the beer and liquor of the tuna club at the harbor—came weaving down to the weighing dock to greet us as we eased into the slip. It was 3:00 A.M. before we had the fish hoisted on the towering iron scales, and even then the strong fish thrashed as it was being hauled tail-first up the concrete launching ramp.

Gone was the fatigue, the hunger, the cold, and the dampness; and in their place was the quiet, triumphant glow that comes with winning the battle with huge ocean fish. Between Fred and me there was only a simple handshake and a drink in salute. But that was enough.

Tips on Tuna Fishing off Prince Edward Island . . .

A fisherman who can recall the smiling parental exhortations to "Catch a whale!" when he first ventured forth armed with a cane pole, a kite string, and a bent pin will find the odds at last in his favor if he ever gets a crack at bluefin tuna off Canada's Prince Edward Island. Bluefins aren't whales, of course, but they can be enormous, and hooking and boating one can put a man in a rest home—his body a battered wreck, his mind a shambles, his mouth in a fixed grin. The experience is incredible.

A little over a decade ago, the sport of going after these mammoth fish was pretty much unknown in Prince Edward Island. Today, however, anglers from all over the world regard trying to catch the Island's giants a must. The annual tuna tournament attracts many of the world's best game fish devotees—and with good reason; record-sized fish have been taken off North Lake, and other areas of the Island have tremendous potential.

The bluefin season usually opens when the local lobster season ends. That can be anytime from late spring through early summer, but July is usually the month things get under way. The biggest of these huge fish are usually landed in September and October. Near-record specimens, however, have been boated in late August.

Going after bluefins, like game fishing for sharks, is a rather specialized affair, so it's best to place yourself in the hands of experienced locals. You can, of course, bring your own tackle, but the boats of the sportfishing tuna fleet are well-equipped and their skippers knowledgeable.

You will need to bring warm clothes and heavy-duty foul weather gear, including a pair of serviceable knee-high rubber boots. Throw in a pair of rubberized work gloves, too, preferably the kind with a knobby or gritty surface.

Charter tuna boats are available at North Lake and also at Alberton, Covehead, and Malpeque. Eight hours of fishing for a party of six anglers (larger groups would clutter things up, when and if a tuna is hooked) will cost about $100. The boats usually leave their berths about 10 A.M. and return about 6 P.M. No lunches are supplied, so bring your own—and bring plenty. You can book a boat a season in advance, and, if weather washes you out, there's no charge.

Even though tuna are what you have in mind, don't overlook the many Island waters in which you can take rainbows, Atlantic salmon, and brook trout. Different seasons apply to different species, so check it all out before you sandwich in a little freshwater fishing.

Accommodations near the tuna grounds range from farmhouses to hotels and motels. Rates for a room can be less than $10 per day or as much as $20.

Prince Edward Island tries hard when it comes to tourists, and your best bet for both general and specific information is the Prince Edward Island Tourist Information Division (P.O. Box 940, Charlottetown, P.E.I.; telephone 902–892–2457).

20.
Texas:
Hunting the
Hard Country

It's been said that everything grows bigger in Texas, and there's not much to argue about in that statement if you've ever hunted the Big Thicket Country west of San Antonio.

For the good Lord not only made everything big, He made it rough, tough, hard, prickly, sharp, hot, cold, wet, dry, and full of things that bite, sting, stab, gouge, and hang on till the last minute. But most of all, He made it beautiful.

He made it beautiful in a way only someone who truly loves the outdoors and space could appreciate. And after He made it, some say, He didn't tell anybody about it for a long time except those who love to hunt. Because he knew nobody would ever really appreciate it as much as those Indians, Mexicans, and early Texans who stalked the whitetail deer and the javelina, the waterfowl, the doves, the quail, and the wild turkey in the jillions of acres of mesquite on both sides of the twisting, brown river. The Rio Grande enters Texas about 300 miles to the northwest at El Paso and finally spews its silt into the Gulf of Mexico at Brownsville, another 300 miles or so to the southeast, and is the international boundary between the United States and Mexico.

But the land doesn't know this and therefore doesn't change at all on either side of the huge meandering river. The almost impenetrable mesquite which stretches from horizon to horizon is gashed every few miles by roads cut through the red clay soil. The roads connect towns with names dating to the time a handful of Texans made a heroic but hopeless defense against General Santa Anna's armies in 1836—towns with names like Yancy, Dilley, Big Wells, Carrizo Springs, Crystal City, La Pryor, Del Rio, Leakey, and Laredo.

The dusty trails also connected those same towns six weeks later when aroused and angry Texans, remembering the sacrifice at the place named after the cottonwood tree, the Alamo, defeated the Mexicans at San Jacinto. Those towns are connected today by paved roads, as are scores of others with historic names that conjure up the early days of the great West, such as Langtry, where the legendary Judge Roy Bean dispensed his law west of the Pecos in a saloon built in honor of the Jersey Lily.

But it is the hunter and the fisherman who have learned to love this land— even more so today as "civilization" and "progress" move the developers ever farther West. The earth mover and the bulldozer raise clouds of red dust over the brush country, but it will be many a decade before the developer makes much of a dent in the big thicket. And in the meantime, the mourning dove and the whitewing skim over the ranch tanks and the clumps of joshua trees, and the javelina feed on the yucca and prickly pear. The hunters with the welded tubing towers built up on jeeps and pickups will cruise the ranch roads on their way to the deer camps each fall, and the riflemen in the high deer towers dotting the rolling country will continue to scan the vast land for that elusive 10-point buck that slips through the mesquite at dawn and dusk. It will be many a year before the deer hunter stops using discarded antlers to "rattle up" bucks ready to do battle in the rut, and many a year more before the whistling flights of pintails, mallards, gadwalls, greenwing, bluewing, and cinnamon teal cease to make hearts pound as they slant out of the morning and evening sky toward the decoys set in the ranch ponds.

There will be many a shopping center built and paved near the bigger towns and cities, but there are enough coveys of fast-running scaled or blue quail and bursting coveys of bobwhites to keep the average hunter happy for a good many years to come.

Coming out of the heavily-paved East and the cement canyons of Manhattan into West Texas in December is like opening a conning tower after being forced to cruise under the sea in a World War I submarine for ten years. The airport guard at La Guardia, who looked at your gun case as though you were certain to hijack the jet, was replaced at the San Antonio airport by a uniformed security guard who grinned as you retrieved the case.

"Goin' to do a little huntin'?" he asked casually as you handed him the baggage checks. "Weather should be good the next few days. Lots of luck." Resisting the reaction to faint from shock, you heft the case and realize the country has not all gone mad and that hunting is still considered normal in the real world.

On the highway from San Antonio, west toward towns named Hondo and Sabinal, there are the rec vehicles and pickups and 4 WDs rolling along the wide highways, with gun racks in the rear windows, and loaded down with tents, food, and sleeping bags. In the fields fat doves streak over the grain crops, broom corn, and the truck gardens. Harris hawks, sparrow hawks, and rough-legged hawks perch on innumerable telephone poles as the car speeds past.

A couple of hours later the car pulls up at a deer camp—a Christmas deer camp at that—in the brush country, and New York might as well be in India. Someone has decorated a 3-foot-high Christmas tree with tinsel, next to a camping trailer. A long board table is set in the bright sunlight and anyone can dip into a pan of hot chili or cut off a slice of cold venison roast or smoked turkey. Few out here hunt from a ranch house. This 26,000 acres of ranchland is leased by the year for hunting rights, and the camp will only be here for a week—maybe two. A couple of house trailers contain hot showers; there are two camp cooks who can work miracles with quail, javelina, venison, duck, or wild turkey, and, if that fare runs short, steaks.

And suddenly the worn Levis and the scarred and comfortable hunting boots replace the city clothes. Old friends appear and the laughter and the chiding takes the place of the reserve brought on by urban living. The cold cans of beer are dipped from ice-filled coolers and deep lungfuls of clear air finally displace the remnants of carbon monoxide and hydrocarbons coating bronchial tubes unused to such luxury.

Temperatures in the 70s and 80s during days of hard sunlight under cloudless skies drop to well below freezing each night. The mesquite bush was not designed to be kind to man, except in one way: an old, thick mesquite root burns with a hot flame for a very long time. A man can stand against a mesquite fire—turning every so often to keep each side even—for as long as friends want to stay up and talk at night. And long after all have turned in, the logs will burn with a steady flame until dawn shows up as a line of pale blue under the blackness of the eastern sky. Except perhaps for the smell of piñon wood, nothing has a finer smell than burning mesquite.

Morning is a time for coffee—the black brew kept clear with half a dozen eggshells tossed into the huge porcelain pot—and ham and eggs and pancakes, sausages, hot biscuits, and preserves. For the knowledgeable, there are strips of canned green chili to cut up and mix with scrambled eggs.

Some of the deer hunters go out before dawn to climb into the elevated blinds while the vast land is still and bathed with darkness and brittle cold. A heavy parka, a hot thermos of coffee, rifle, and binoculars are all that is needed. The shooting time is brief before a guide or ranch hand comes rattling down one of the red dusty roads to pick up the hunter an hour or so after sunrise. The bucks move at dawn and dusk, and then only to feed or to seek out a herd of does. It is the rutting season and most of the bigger bucks are thick-necked and their antlers glisten from sharpening them on brush or in combat. Shots are long ones in this country—no 50-yard snap shots using rifled slugs fired from shotguns, as in much of the heavily-populated East. One hundred and fifty yards in mesquite country is considered a cinch shot. Most of the smarter and bigger bucks are only brought down by shots of 300 yards or more, and these are made while they are either circling in the brush at a fast pace or running flat-out after scenting danger. A look at the calibers of local hunters' guns gives one the clue: the .30/06 is standard, but there are a lot of .270s, 7mm magnums, .257 magnums, and .243s—long-range, flat-trajectory rifles and all well scoped. Both the successful and unsuccessful deer hunters are back in time to salvage some breakfast and—even though the quail coveys beckon—a morning nap feels fine after being awakened at 4 A.M.

Hunting quail in thicket country is a far cry from the leisurely "mule-and-buckboard" tradition of the Old South. Nash Buckingham and Havilah Babcock would cringe beneath the Spanish moss of the old plantations if they could see how the bobwhite is hunted in mesquite, cactus, and yucca country. Pickup trucks and jeeps are rigged with seats for two hunters right over the front bumpers, allowing the shooters to see fairly well in the thick brush, but, most important of all, enabling them to bail out in a hurry when a covey is sighted. In addition, a seat is fastened to the top of a derrick of welded pipes over the roof of the pickup cab—or the same distance up over a jeep. Usually two hunters ride topside, standing so as to have a better view. The driver simply handles the vehicle. He has no view to speak of, but latter-day Texas hunters have devised a buzzer system, activated by a push-button switch in the tower. When the hunter on top spots a quail covey, he pushes the switch, and the buzzer sounds in the cab. At the sound, the driver—who has been inching along the rutted trails in low gear—jams on the brakes. Before clambering down from the tower the top gunners point the direction of the covey. The driver and whoever else is riding in the cab, the shooters in the front seats, and both hunters from the tower then dash madly into the mass of mesquite needles, cactus thorns, yucca spines, and razor-sharp rocks in pursuit of the running quail. The fastest runners get the first shots at the flushing birds. If the covey flushes as a unit, it may fly for hundreds of yards before landing and running again, so that will be all the shots the party gets at that particular covey. However, if the birds scatter on the covey rise, then the party can spend some time kicking brush and grass clumps to flush the singles.

The Texas bobwhite is by far the easiest quail to hunt this way. The big scaled or blue quail tend to run much faster, will not flush as easily, and when they do flush, may fly a quarter of a mile before landing again. Leather chaps and sturdy leather boots are needed for this kind of hunting. If not chaps, at least some form of heavy canvas or leather-fronted trousers should be worn as protection against the spikes, thorns, and razor edges. Almost all the shotguns are full-choked, as few hunters get much of anything but a straight going-away shot.

Why not hunt these quail with pointing dogs, asks our gentleman friend from the East or Deep South. Because Texans, suh, are gentlemen too and love their dogs. In addition to getting them all scratched and torn up in such country, the thicket is a haven for rattlesnakes most of the year.

And so the bright pre-Christmas days are filled with the quest for quail, and sleep at night is easy as aching muscles relax after the mad charges through the brush. Talk around the blazing fire is of the fine Tom turkey George Coe got with one shot from a 7mm magnum; the spectacular double on streaking scaled quail Stan Studer made while balancing on one leg halfway over a barbed-wire fence; the symmetrical beauty of a ten-point buck Bob Kuhn dropped in a long-range shot from his tower blind; and the big javelina boar young Jimmie got—the first of his life.

No food tastes like food eaten under a star-studded sky as a cold wind blows the campfire ashes and men talk about other hunts in other times and in other places. No one down through the centuries has cared more about wildlife than has the hunter, and the talk is of what the bulldozing of habitat has done to the whitewing dove populations below the border, the successes of Ducks Unlimited, the progress of Game Coin and how to raise more funds for education, wildlife management, and conservation. Jim Midcap worries that anti-hunting groups have raised $14 million and are trying to prove hunting—instead of habitat destruction—is hurting wildlife. Harry Tennison, who collects friends, is concerned that school children don't know that the sportsmen of this country are the ones who have protected and paid for the preservation of our wildlife. "Yet each man kills the thing he loves," Oscar Wilde knew.

And there is talk of today's hunt and of what the hunts will be like tomorrow, of those of us who are here now and of those who have gone on ahead—to where the hunting is always better. The American Indian knew.

No days pass as quickly as the hunting and fishing days, the days with friends. There are several special moments—suspended in the eternity of memory—that will last.

While Bob Holloren and the kid lawyer were stalking a flock of pintails resting on a small ranch pond, Harry and I sat quietly in the seat of a pickup,

watching the last rays of the sun slowly change the colors of a low ridge. The only movement was that of a female marsh hawk as she quartered back and forth over the mesquite in a last-hour search for food. Our world stretched from horizon to horizon, and there was no sound. Harry shifted in the seat and nodded at the vastness.

"It ain't all bad," he said and smiled. Nobody but a Texan could describe the brush country that well.

Just before the red orb of the sun rose across a lake one morning there was the whistle of wings as a flock of pintails banked over the blind, spooked at the decoys, and climbed for altitude. The over/under kicked twice, and two ducks spun from the flock. The look on John Thompson's face as they pinwheeled from about 60 yards up made all future misses unimportant.

The eight-point buck was a long time in coming out of the brush. Hours had gone by and the binoculars had grown heavy sweeping all the way to the distant horizon. Three does and a spike had moved down a draw 150 yards away, heading for water, but that had been more than an hour ago. And suddenly there he was—not more than 250 yards away but moving purposefully through the mesquite. The brush was several feet higher than the tips of his antlers, and there was just a flash as he moved down from the slope of the ridge to the bottomland, following the general path of the does. The scope was set on 4X and it was necessary to take the moving shot before the buck hit the thick bottom brush. The Colt Sauer .270 finally steadied down, the scope picked up the tan and white of his coat as the buck passed through the series of openings. Over the pounding of the heart, the blast shattered the stillness and the "whack" of the 150-grain .270 slug echoed back before the muzzle of the rifle returned to level. The big buck collapsed in a cloud of red dust, kicked twice, and lay still. The scope remained on the still body for several moments more as the echoes of the shot wafted across the miles of brush country.

Just before darkness, with the western sky a profusion of red, yellow, and orange, the coyotes began their evening song. The thin, high-pitched yelps came from the black silhouetted ridge toward the west—as they had for the millions of years the coyote had owned this land.

And beyond that same ridge, and a dozen more like it, the hard land ran on to towns where the lights were being turned on against the darkness sliding over the big thicket ever so slowly from the east, towns like Eagle Pass and Uvalde—home of former Vice President of the United States John Nance Garner. "Cactus Jack," who grew up in the hard country, lived to his nineties, rocking on the front porch of his board house and spitting tobacco juice into the front yard. Some say the old man never gave a hoot what anybody thought of him and had a sneaking suspicion that everybody in Washington was a damned fool. It's probably no wonder. When you spend ninety years in the Big Thicket everything else seems kind of small and unimportant.

Tips on Hunting in Texas . . .

Separating Texas fact from Texas fiction is a task that has baffled non-Texans ever since Davy Crockett. But when a Texan tells you the hunting in Texas is prime, he is right.

It *is* prime. Not only is it prime, it is varied, offering everything from whitetail deer to bobwhite and blue quail. This broad and abundant range of game can be found in countryside that varies from outright lush to endless miles of what writer Larry King calls "hot empty."

Most hunting in Texas is done on private land, which means getting permission from a farmer or rancher. These landowners tend to be sympathetic to a hunter, but politeness and good hunting manners are an invariable prerequisite. Ignore the courtesies, or fail to get permission, and you'll find out just how swift and expensive Texas vengeance can be. If you would rather not deal with a private landowner, about the only sizeable public lands you will find are in the eastern part of the state, which means your choice of game will be somewhat restricted.

Little hunted, but rich in game—particularly waterfowl, which winter in many lakes that dot the region—is the famed Panhandle area. There you will find mallards, pintails, widgeons, greenwing teal, and Canada and snow geese, among others. The Panhandle also offers a good supply of bobwhite and blue quail.

Also good waterfowl country, but comparatively heavily hunted, is the Gulf Coast region. There, the hunting tends to be on the luxurious side—professional guides, highly-trained dogs, oil tycoons, and duck blinds stocked with bourbon—the works. Also along the Gulf Coast you will find pretty good pheasant hunting, the result of a recent and apparently successful stocking program.

Most whitetail deer taken in Texas come from the Edwards Plateau area; mule deer from the western part of the state. Here again, however, most deer hunting is done on private land, so practice your smile and your sincere handshake.

Turkey, once abundant along the Rio Grande, are fewer these days, and landowners are very protective of the remaining broodstock. An occasional bird can be taken, but chances are few and far between.

Javelina hunting is on the upswing, the doughty little porkers being deemed first-rate quarry. The population seems to be fairly stable, most of it concentrated in the western part of the state.

As in any other state, game seasons can vary from year to year. The usual quail season, for example, runs from about mid-November to mid-February. Exact dates, however, vary. The pheasant season is usually in December, whitetail deer from November to January. The season for mule deer usually starts around Thanksgiving and runs for about two weeks. Javelina season runs from October to January. Exact dates again vary, so check with the Texas Parks and Wildlife Department (see Appendix B) before you pack.

Speaking of packing, be sure you include long johns. Many a Yankee, thinking he was venturing forth to the Sunny South, has been sent home to thaw out. That "hot empty" countryside mentioned earlier can turn excruciatingly cold; no less empty (snow does not count), but cold, really cold.

Texans are used to hunters and tend to welcome them, meaning that anyone seeking appropriate accommodations will have no trouble finding a sympathetic ear. You can go the luxury route or you can opt for "just folks" friendliness. A good way to contact the folks is to sidle up to drivers of pickup trucks bearing gun racks. Just remember your manners; Texans, despite their informality, are as proper as deacons.

21.
Mexico
Sails

Sometimes it is difficult to remember one's first catch of a particular species of big-game fish. But there was one sailfish I took in the late 1950s off the west coast of Mexico that will remain etched in my memory for many years.

The station wagon hummed along U.S. 85 south to Hatch, New Mexico, then to Deming, then across the border of Arizona late in the afternoon, south of Tucson that night, and finally to the border of Mexico late in the evening. Art and Vince and I took turns driving. After passing through customs—a strictly routine matter which took only a few minutes—we headed south for Hermosillo. It was early in the morning when we passed through that Mexican town, and, spelling each other, we kept on. As the sun rose on July 6, we entered Guaymas, Mexico, perched on the sheer slopes of cholla cactus and rock-covered foothills at the edge of the Gulf of California. The water was as blue as the Mexico skies, and the surf looked like an oasis to three parched souls who felt as though they had been crawling across the Sahara for eight weeks on their hands and knees.

The first thing we did—after sixteen straight hours of driving—was to run down to the white curving beach and plunge into the almost lukewarm surf. I don't remember when anything ever felt as wonderful as that ocean after the 800 miles of New Mexico, Arizona, and Mexico desert.

We didn't go out for sails that first day. In the first place, we needed some sleep. So, later in the afternoon, we rented a 16-foot aluminum boat with a 40-hp outboard and went out to check the coastline and the general scenery. We took some light tackle and trolled off the jagged gull-and-pelican-covered islands offshore. We took several small grouper and a couple of bonito which fought well for their weight.

The next morning, we started out in all seriousness. Both Vince and I spoke Spanish, after a fashion. This did make things a little easier, but it certainly was not necessary. Almost all the boat owners and some boat captains spoke English. One was expected to do a little bargaining about the cost of a boat per day, depending on the number of avid fishermen about, the weather, the humor of the boat crew, the need of the boat owner, the preponderance of fish being caught, and the budget of the fisherman. The price of a good diesel or gasoline cabin cruiser will vary. A higher price means a new, fiberglass boat and a few more knots, and the cheaper price usually means a rather older boat—nevertheless, a seaworthy old job, and *quien sabe?* Maybe it has a smarter captain and first mate when it comes to stalking sails.

We decided to alternate in the fighting chairs and split the cost. That way nobody would get bored with the dull periods and everybody had about an equal chance to nail the big ones. Tossing for the first chance at the chairs and whether one wanted the right or left seat was our way of doing it. We did this every day for six days. That way nobody had any gripes when he missed his fish because of some arbitrary decision. We used a different boat and crew each day.

And miss fish we did. We had eight sails on and boated two the first day. The largest was a good one, 110 pounds. I still think that was an accident, but I'm not going to argue the point too much because I was the one who caught it.

Every boat captain and mate had his own system of fishing for the sails. Each rigged the mullet bait a different way—some running the hook down through the head of the bait and others burying the hook deep in the fish and sewing it up with twine.

Some skippers seemed to like the baits closer in than others, and even the angle of the outriggers changed with boats. The teaser plug ran fairly deep—several yards below the surface. The first day out, a wild sail flashed up from nowhere, took the teaser plug and a length of stout line, and went skipping across the surface of the ocean in a series of breathtaking leaps. Needless to say, both fishermen in the chairs thought they had the fish on and set hooks into thin air. We all saw sailfish before they struck the baits. They would come up behind the skipping mullet, the black dorsal fin would cut the surface first, and the fish would strike the bait. Naturally, this would trip the line from the outrigger, and the line would fall slack into the sea. At this moment, the skipper would throttle the engine down to idle, and we would wait. The sail would take the bait to a certain depth and then stop. The fisherman would put his thumb gently on the reel so he could tell when the big fish stopped. When it stopped, it was to turn the bait around in its mouth and begin to swallow it. If the big fish didn't feel the nip of the hook or the faint pull of the line, or become suspicious of some other aspect of the bait, the mullet would slide down its gullet, and the sail would begin to swim away. As to when to strike, it was all a matter of knowing sailfish. We depended entirely on the mates. They would stand over us and watch the reel—counting slowly to themselves in Spanish—then suddenly they would slap us on the shoulder and say, "Now!"

The reason we missed most of the sails was simply that we couldn't wait until the skipper said "Now!" It just seemed inconceivable that the big fish could take that long to be hooked. The first sail I lost, I counted to seven and threw on the brake and struck. The big fish came out of the ocean 100 yards astern with the hook stuck in the hard cartilage of its mouth. In two jumps, the hook came free, and I sat staring at the slack line like an idiot. The skipper shook his head sadly.

Vince lost one sail when it came up, took the bait, went down, started to swallow it, then changed its mind and spit it out just as he struck. Art lost one which grabbed the bait, let it go, and never did touch it again. He lost another which just wasn't hooked well and threw the hook after the third or fourth jump. I missed another which opened its mouth to take the bait, then changed its mind and disappeared—why, we will never know.

Vince set the season record for a pelican which grabbed his bait in spite of all the shouting and armwaving we did to frighten it away.

A dolphin caught by Art weighed 26 pounds, leaped all over the ocean, and put up one of the greatest fights I have ever seen. It came slashing in from an angle, took one of the baits, and went straight up in the air, beginning a series of jumps that left us all speechless. As far as Art was concerned, after a twenty-minute battle, a dolphin is a match for a sail anytime.

I got my biggest sail the fourth day out. It was the quietest angling day we had had all week. The sea was rough, and by late in the afternoon the man who was not in a fighting chair was napping between turns to fish. Art and I were in the chairs and it was about 3:30. I was in the right-hand chair and, weary from watching the skipping baits, I was watching another fishing boat several miles away. I never saw the sail take the bait. Art did. Later he said all he saw was a huge shape come up from the depths behind the bait, and suddenly the bait was gone.

Art yelled, "Sail!" and the line fell slack from the outrigger clip. At the yell, the skipper, Joe Morales, chopped the throttle back and jumped down behind me. The mate grabbed Art's rod and began hauling in his line. I sank the handle of the rod into the metal cup of the seat and braced myself.

I looked up at Joe. He shook his head slowly and put his thumb on the reel. It was turning slowly. Suddenly it stopped. Joe grunted to himself. The world seemed to have come to a stop. Each second seemed like hours. My mouth was dry and my hands wringing wet. Suddenly the reel spool began to turn, ever so slowly. Then it began to let out line, still slowly, but gradually gaining speed.

Joe began counting to himself under his breath, *"Uno, dos, tres . . ."* I reached for the brake. *". . . ocho, nueve . . ."* Never has time passed so slowly. Suddenly, when he reached the count of 13, he slapped me hard on the left shoulder and shouted. *"Ahora!* Hit him!" I flipped on the brake and struck.

The reel screamed, the rod went only about halfway back as the weight of the fish took up the slack and my arms straightened.

The surface of the ocean suddenly seemed to explode, and a great, unbelievable, silver, blue, purple, iridescent sailfish came hurtling straight up into the air. About 15 feet up it began a series of contortions—trying to throw the hook. Falling back with a tremendous splash, the huge fish shook its head wildly and leaped again. Later, the rest of them told me the sail leaped nine times before sounding. I

don't know. All I clearly remember is those first two. They will remain with me forever.

After the fish went for the depths, the work began. Vince grabbed a bucket and rope, dropped it over the side, filled it with water, and poured it over me every five minutes. He kept that up the whole hour and a half or so until the fish was boated. It probably saved my life.

When the fish finally tired, the mate reached down, took it by the bill, and tapped it once on the forehead. It always seems unbelievable that a fish which fights that long and so spectacularly can die so easily. But it simply quivered once and died. Another always astonishing thing to me is the way the blues, golds, purples, and silver colors fade to a solid black in a matter of seconds after the death of the fish. It weighed out at 138 pounds later.

Vince and his sailfish? It won't set any records, but then it didn't have to. It skittered across the surface of the sea just as though Zane Grey had ordered it for him, personally. It never quit fighting until its great heart stopped.

Tips on Fishing in Mexico . . .

One can easily overrate the fishing in Mexico, in part because of the country itself, in part because some of the Mexican people can be among the most delightful on earth, but mostly because it is so varied.

Mexican waters offer blue, striped, and black marlin, tarpon, snook, wahoo, yellowfin tuna, dolphin, roosterfish, weakfish (corvina and totoaba), sailfish, and many others. Inland, Mexico's mountain lakes and streams offer largemouth bass and rainbow trout. It would be hard to find fishing as diverse or as potentially interesting.

Superimposed on this incredible variety of game species is a culture that refuses to accommodate itself to whatever a Yankee sportsman might have in mind. At no point during a fishing adventure in Mexico will you get the feeling you are any place else. The skipper and crew of your charter boat, for example, will certainly be glad to have you aboard; they need the money. But at no point will their attitude be one of collective desperation; if you hadn't hired them, someone else would have. And if no one had, that would be all right, too; they would get by. Mexican stomachs have growled in hunger far too often for anyone to get terribly upset about a Yankee fisherman who, unless time and behavior indicate otherwise, has little to recommend him other than the probable money in his pocket.

If you can keep an open mind and accept that to a Mexican a nonexistent toilet, say, is not a major calamity, then you can have the time of your life. But

—cross the border snapping your fingers and demanding this and that, right and left, and you are going to be miserable.

While the fishing is pretty good up and down both coasts, the most fruitful and varied (as to species) is found off the Yucatán Peninsula and off Baja California, particularly in the Sea of Cortez (Golfo de California). Both areas have become significant sportfishing centers, and, as a result, you will be regarded as a resource, not a novelty.

Mexico's climate is more a matter of elevation above sea level than of proximity to the Equator. If you are below 2,500 feet, it is hot just about everywhere, so dress accordingly. It rains on and off from June through October, and every now and then a hurricane-like storm called a *chubasco* offers an eye-opening preview of Armageddon. Only rarely, however, are the charter boats confined to port because of high winds. If you have to pick an ideal season, it would be from November to June.

Available charter boats are, in general, not as modern nor as well equipped as Yankee fleets. The tackle on board most boats is strictly minimal, so visiting anglers are strongly advised to bring along their own gear. Line weights used in the area range from 20-pound-test for the smaller stuff to 50- or 80-pound-test for the big game. If you feel you might be lucky enough to tie into one of the occasional huge black marlin encountered in southern Baja waters, bring along a cable and a bazooka.

Although exact best times are open to debate, certain periods seem better than others for certain species. July to October, for example, is best for blue and black marlin. April to June is the peak time for sailfish and striped marlin. Spring is also best for yellowtail and yellowfin tuna. All fall is good for wahoo, but perhaps November is best. Roosterfish spend their summers in the northern half of the Sea of Cortez, their winters in the southern half.

In a country so big and varied in economic status, it is difficult to nail down the costs you can expect to encounter. A boat out of Acapulco, say, is going to be more expensive than a small, old (albeit adequate) boat out of some remote coastal village. Your best bet is to pick out where you want to go and start writing letters and making telephone calls. *Aero Mexico,* the Mexican national airline, and any one of the many offices of the Mexican tourist information agency in the U.S. (see Appendix C) can provide useful information. If all you have in mind is fishing, Adventures Unlimited can nail everything down for you.

22.
Florida: The Bull Dolphin

My oldest son, John, grabbed the spinning rod from the holder as the line dropped from the port outrigger and his reel began to sing.

Leaving the 85-hp outboard in slow forward speed, I swung the 17-foot boat to port to give him room to play his fish. I yelled, "Line down," and my thirteen-year-old son, Donald, popped out of the small cutty cabin where he had gone to get a cold drink. He usually acted as skipper when we were trolling and had been until just a moment before.

He jumped onto the console and grabbed the wheel as I reached out and took the other rod from the holder and began reeling in line as fast as I could, the rigged balao bait skipping across the tops of the Gulf Stream waves about fifteen miles off the Florida coast.

"Dolphin!" Johnnie yelled as a nice fish broke the surface about 50 yards back and sliced across the surface in a series of quick leaps.

"Keep your rod tip up," I cautioned as the speeding fish took out another 50 yards or so of his 17-pound-test monofilament line. It really wasn't necessary; the boy already had the tip high and was checking his drag with his left hand. Having caught saltwater game fish since he was a little boy in Cape May, New Jersey, he knew the ropes as well as I did.

I reeled the starboard balao bait until it was just below the outrigger and hung about a foot above the surface, then I jerked it from the clip on the outrigger line and reeled the bait aboard.

"Okay, John," I said, "the lines are in. This fish may go about fifteen pounds."

He nodded, grimly, playing the fighting fish.

I shoved the rod butt into the holder behind the console seat and took the wheel from Don.

"Buddy," I said, "hand me that light spinning outfit on the bunk, will you? You know how dolphin are. When Johnnie gets this one in close we can flip a lure out there and pick up another one. The school should stay around until he boats his. Put on a silver spoon or anything that flashes."

He nodded and ducked into the cabin again.

I turned to watch the water and slipped the throttle into neutral. The boy didn't need any help, and I glanced toward the distant shoreline of Fort Lauderdale, slightly hazy in the afternoon sunlight. The seas were running about 2 to 3 feet where we were, and the water of the stream was a deep, royal blue as it flowed northward about six miles per hour.

"I got him, Dad," John said, pumping his fish alongside where I could see the incredible gold, silver, green, and blue colors of the world's most beautiful game fish.

"He's not too big. I can gaff him by myself." He reached for the short gaff stored in the port gunwale. "There's a whole school of them down there, Dad."

I leaned over and peered into the cabin.

"You got the spinning rod, Don?" I asked.

The boy looked up from where he was sitting on the bunk, the tackle box between his feet.

"I'm putting a bigger swivel on the line," he answered. "Just a minute."

John reached over to gaff his fish and I knew it would be too late to take any of the others in a moment.

I knew I couldn't cast the bait with the larger boat rod that had the 4/0 reel on it, but I figured if I got a balao bait back there I might take another fish.

Slipping the throttle into forward, I reached out and took the rod from the holder and dropped the balao over the side. I flipped the lever and free-spooled the bait back behind the boat where it sank slowly in the clear water.

I engaged the drag lever and jerked the bait a couple of times. A streaking fish struck at it and the balao flew out of the water. Behind it was a small dolphin, apparently having just taken a small bite out of the bait. The balao fell back, and I let it sink, planning on jigging it a few more times.

Before I could do anything, though, I saw a flash as a fish took the bait and felt the line tighten. Thinking it was the same 8- or 10-pounder, I raised the rod tip a little and set the hook fairly easily, not wanting to pull the hook out of the small fish with 20-pound mono.

The strike almost tore the rod from my hands. I was sitting on the console seat and was holding the rod at an angle 90 degrees laterally from where the fish was. Don came up from the cabin at that very moment, the light spinning rod in his hand. John had just slid his small dolphin over the gunwale when the surface of the Gulf Stream 20 feet behind the boat burst open as though somebody had rolled a depth-charge can over the stern and it had exploded.

A great gold, silver, and green monster, with a head which looked as big as a whale's, thrashed up out of the water trying to rid itself of the No. 7 hook at the end of about 8 feet of stainless steel wire leader.

"Holy Cow!" Donnie shouted as the huge bull dolphin fell back to the surface, spraying water over the boat. "A fifty-pound dolphin!"

The boy didn't know how close he was to guessing the weight of that fish. He later said he just picked the largest round number he thought possible for a dolphin.

I was too busy to worry about the weight. A dolphin—pound for pound—is one of the toughest fish to boat. Its flat sides give it a tremendous advantage when it turns sidewise to the angler and either bores for depth or streaks for distance.

Fortunately I had the drag set light, having been trolling for sailfish, and I scrambled for the portable fighting chair. The reel screamed as 100 yards left the spool in a matter of seconds.

"Give me about a quarter speed," I shouted at Don, who stowed the spinning rod and leaped behind the wheel. "Watch my line and follow him."

I glanced down at the spool as the boy added power and the sleek boat picked up speed, a white wake boiling astern. John was stowing loose gear and sliding the top over the fish box. The night before I had wound 400 yards of new 20-pound line on the reel. I had about 200 yards out already and had no intention of increasing the drag much more with that giant of a fish on such light line.

I squinted to starboard where my line was cutting the surface 50 yards out and muttered something to myself as old as the contest between man and fish. I would need luck with this one.

We really hadn't been fishing for dolphin at all, although saltwater game fishermen expect to pick one up at any time and look forward to it. They are great fighters and my favorite eating fish.

The week before we had entered our boat in the annual billfish tourney at Fort Lauderdale—a tournament which attracts several hundred boats each year and which usually sees fine September weather.

This year a cold front had moved into the Middle Atlantic States and had pushed down to northern Florida. This, combined with a low pressure area in the Gulf of Mexico, had brought gale winds and driving rain to southeastern Florida and had cancelled the three-day tourney the previous weekend.

The wind had kept up most of the week and on Friday, the day before, the Coast Guard had not held out much hope for good weather. Most of the boats in the tournament were big sportfishermen in the 45- to 60-foot class and even they had no plans to tackle the sloppy seas of the stream.

Yet late Friday night the winds slacked off, and Saturday morning the seas were running 2 to 3 feet close to shore and 3 to 5 feet high in the Gulf Stream. The bad weather had pushed the clear blue water of the stream far from shore and it was more than ten miles out before we left the light green sandy water churned up by the violence of the past week and hit the beautiful blue of the stream.

We had left with the annual "Bimini Start"—all the contesting boats lined up along the beach heading for the Gulf Stream at the starting signal. With an 85-hp outboard on a 16-foot 8-inch double-hulled planing boat, we had the satisfaction of leaving practically every bigger and more luxurious sportfisherman far behind in the race for the fishing grounds.

Once there, however, we sacrificed air-conditioning and considerable space in the cockpit for the mobility of a small boat. But we were outrigged well—even carried kites for live bait fishing—had a good big bait box moulded into the hull, excellent tackle, and most important of all, we knew our boat and operated well as a crew. We had started training in the grim and cold seas years before with a 17-foot plywood, lapstrake-hulled outboard boat off the New Jersey coast, and the Florida Gulf Stream was heaven to us after the bitter winds and seas of early spring and late fall in the Atlantic to the north.

The boys know charts, weather, and navigation, and we carried every safety device required by the Coast Guard—plus a number we always added, such as a small auxiliary motor stowed in the bow, extra rations, fresh water, and foul-weather clothing.

Nevertheless, there had been some snickers when the boys and I checked in at the committee boat prior to the start of the tourney.

There were a few mentions of fishing from a dinghy and a couple of salty skippers and mates—probably many who had never seen a cold sullen rip off Cape Hatteras or Montauk in late fall—wondered aloud where we would put a billfish if we caught one.

The boys took it well—with grins—as we got the "go" sign for our boat, number 120. A lot of good fish have come aboard our small boats, and John, who is fifteen, has more saltwater game fish to his credit than most adult deep-sea anglers.

We trolled fruitlessly back and forth for hours, keeping just off the green water and blue water separation line and dragging one rigged balao bait and a small mullet—primarily fishing both for sailfish and white marlin. I was also prepared for a blue marlin at any time and hoped that if one did hit, it would be on the 20-pound rather than the 17-pound line on the spinning reel.

The last blue marlin I had on had battled me for $8\frac{1}{2}$ hours on 12-pound line, and I lost it to a shark just behind the transom by moonlight off North Key Largo. That heartbreaker had qualified me as a candidate for the Philip Wylie Hard Luck Trophy in the Greater Miami Tournament a few years back.

Shortly after noon I ran a fishing kite up and used it as an auxiliary outrigger—skipping a balao bait 50 yards out to starboard and about 50 yards astern. Even that didn't bring them up. We didn't know then that only four sails were to be taken that day by the almost 100 boats out. Apparently the bad weather had put them down and they had not begun to feed yet.

It was almost 2 o'clock when John took his small dolphin and suddenly all thoughts of billfish were put aside as I settled down to fight a giant dolphin I wasn't at all certain of landing. I wasn't concerned about the test strength of the line, as I usually fish with light tackle and have encouraged the boys to do the same. We find it much more fun than wearing down great fighting fish with 80- or 130-pound line. We lose a lot of fish but the ones we catch are fish of which we can be proud.

I was concerned about getting this monster aboard. Boating billfish, to my mind, is far easier than trying to land a dolphin—especially a big one. A billfish, when it finally tires, can be taken by grabbing the bill with gloved hands and whacking it between the eyes with a short bat. After that it is simply a matter of slipping a noose over its tail and then hauling it aboard by holding onto both ends. With a dolphin of this size, there was only one thing to do and that was to sink a gaff into it and hope it would hold long enough to get it over the side. John is big for his age, but he weighs only about 130 pounds. That is asking a lot from a boy.

Taking the wire leader in a gloved hand wouldn't do any good since this fish could easily break a leader, and we don't carry a flying gaff aboard.

"Slow it down, Don," I shouted over the engine noise, "I'm gaining line on him." The fish—not solving his problem by the several hundred yard run—decided to try depth.

Don swung the boat in a wide circle, watching the direction of my line, and eased back on the throttle as the angle of the line slanted down.

"That's the way, Skipper," I grunted as the big fish began shaking its head in the depths. I had shoved the rod butt into the gimbal of the folding fighting chair, and my arms were beginning to feel the battle. I weigh 175 pounds and keep in fair shape, but this fish was far more in his element than I was.

I always wear a leather Bimini Belt while fishing big-game fish and have found many times that it really pays—especially if one has to get up quickly and battle a fish which is in danger of passing under the boat or is coming in to the gaff.

"What time is it, John?" I asked, wiping the sweat from my eyes. "Two-thirty, Dad," John said from his position in the stern, where he stood holding the big gaff. "He's been on for more than forty-five minutes."

"Douse me, will you?" I said.

John slid the gaff inside the gunwale and dipped a small blue plastic bucket over the side. He poured the contents over my head and shoulders and grinned as I sputtered. It's a good trick and really feels welcome when a stubborn fish is not doing much.

"He's coming up," Donnie shouted from behind me. He was right. I started taking in line as fast as I could as the angle of the line slanted up.

Don eased the throttle open slightly to give me less slack and swung the bow away from the direction of the fish.

"There he is!" John yelled as the great fish burst from the water about 125 yards astern and shook its head violently in the bright sunlight.

The fish jumped twice more, each time shaking its head so violently I couldn't see how the hook stayed in. But after that the battle settled down to a brutal contest of gaining and losing line, while I watched the drag very carefully to see that the big fish didn't catch me off guard with a sudden run.

It was about 3:15 when the huge fish came alongside. It was getting tired but it wasn't licked. My arms felt like lead.

"Turn the motor off, Don," I said. "And, Johnnie, raise the engine. I don't want him lost in the prop if he makes a run under the boat. Besides we don't need the power any more."

John nodded, stowed the gaff, and heaved on the big motor until the lock snapped in place.

"Holy Cow," Don said again, staring down into the depths where the big fish was slowly circling. "What a fish! How we going to get him in, Dad?" he asked.

I looked at the leader. It was about 8 or 9 feet long. That, plus the length of the 6-foot 6-inch fiberglass rod, was as close as I was going to get to this fish. Either John was going to have to try and gaff it alone, or I was going to have to try it while holding the rod, because if I handed the rod to one of the boys while I gaffed the fish, I couldn't enter the dolphin in competition.

"I don't really know, Don," I said, bringing the fish to the surface where it lay on its side close to the starboard stern, weaving slowly.

"John?" I asked, looking at the boy. He stared at the fish, looked at me and at the gaff in his hands. He nodded slowly.

Then I made up my mind.

"Listen," I said quickly, "I think I can gaff him myself. It's not that you couldn't do it, John, but if you miss him and he gets away you are going to feel much worse about it than I am. If I miss, I'll have nobody to blame but me. O.K.?"

He stood quietly for a minute then silently nodded. I could see the relief on his face.

"O.K.," I said, "clear the cockpit."

I looped the leather thong of the long gaff around my right wrist and then reeled until the swivel connecting the line to the wire leader was right at the top guide of the rod. Then I slowly raised the rod with my left arm, the butt end stuck in the leather belt socket. The big fish swung in close to the boat and its dorsal fin broke the clear water.

Because it was vertical in the water I couldn't get a clear swipe at the underjaw or belly with the gaff and would have to settle for the hard head or back. I knew if I hit it too far back, it would have a lot of diving power once it got its head down, so I gambled on the top of the big forehead and, reaching far out, jerked down and toward me. The point struck hard gristle but held. The shock momentarily stunned the big fish, and for a second it did not thrash. I dropped the rod, propped my left foot on the gunwale, and hauled with all my strength.

The huge head slid over the white fiberglass gunwale, the gaff pulled out, and I fell backward across the boat. For what seemed an eternal second the fish teetered on the edge, then suddenly slithered forward and crashed to the floor of the cockpit.

A cheap styrofoam bait box—used to keep rigged balao and mullet on ice—was stowed in a corner. That was reduced to white powder in a matter of minutes as the fish pounded everything in sight with its tail.

I took a swipe across the right arm which stayed black and blue for two weeks. John, trying to locate our billfish club, almost suffered a broken ankle in the melee. I sank the gaff into the back of the dolphin and tried to yank him upright so we could clobber him with the club before he demolished the boat. I got his head up

and John—with all his might—smashed the 3-foot sawed off oar handle across the dolphin's forehead. That did it, but it broke the oar handle in half. The huge fish quivered and died, its fantasy of colors slowly fading.

I didn't realize I was so exhausted until I let go of the gaff handle and looked at my hands which were shaking from exertion. I sat down on the gunwale and hung on.

Donald, who had been shouting advice, warnings, and encouragement from the pilot's seat during the whole battle, climbed down in awe to touch the fish.

"Whew," said John and also found a seat. "Thanks for not letting me gaff him, Dad," he said. "I'd never have made it."

"Forget it," I laughed, shakily. "Nobody will ever come closer to losing a fish than I just did. Well," I got to my feet with an effort and grabbed the bucket. "Let's wash everything down and get this guy to shore before he dehydrates. We may have a world record here."

So that was it. We didn't have a world record, but we did have a dolphin weighing $47\frac{1}{2}$ pounds, and that is just a few pounds off the record—especially on 20-pound line.

The experts who joked about dinghies and where we would put a big fish were mysteriously absent at the weighing dock. But the dolphin took the biggest non-billfish prize of the tourney, and the four sailfish that came in that day weighed 44 pounds, 47 pounds, 42 pounds, and 39 pounds. The dolphin beat them all.

It confirmed what we already knew: It's not the size of the boat that matters. Even more important—to me, anyway—it proved that what really counts isn't the boat at all, but the way the crew acts as a team when a *big* big-game fish gets on the line.

[For further information, see Tips at the end of Chapter 9.]

23.
Botswana:
The Magnificent
Kudu

There is not a more majestic antelope in Africa, in my opinion, than the greater Kudu.

The roan and sable are regal and sporting game animals, and the gemsbok is a beautiful and nimble creature, as are most of the African antelope, but there is something special about the kudu which sets it apart from all the others. Perhaps it is because it is so incredibly wary and silent in its escape. It could be a ghost, the way it appears and suddenly fades from sight—its remarkable fawny gray and slightly violet coat, marked with white transverse stripes, making it, literally, invisible in the thickets.

Professional hunter Mike Bartlett and I had spent four days looking for a good kudu in the heavy cover along the Cuando River of Botswana. This is excellent kudu country although the hunting is very difficult. Not only is the cover of trees and shrubs very thick close to the big, meandering river, but less than a quarter of a mile back from the river thickets one hits soft sand and the almost impenetrable mass of thorn bush, acacia trees, and the light greenish-gray terminalia bush. And in this nightmare of heavy cover lurked the kudu—sometimes traveling in small herds but, in the month of June, often bulls alone. Travel was by Land-Rover, always four-wheeled drive and usually barely moving in the soft white sand. The Chobe hunting block was about 30 miles square so it was necessary to cover hundreds of square miles searching for the big bulls.

Mosquitoes were at a minimum, since this was late fall for this part of Africa. But the tsetse flies were abundant as soon as the sun began to warm up—from about 9 A.M. on— and they were their usual vicious selves; biting through shirts and trousers wherever one forgot to smear repellent. However, it was winter here and the temperature at dawn, when we left to hunt each morning, was close to freezing—cold enough to require gloves and down jackets. The temperature in the middle of the day shot, as the crosshairs moved back of the shoulder, when, with a flick of an ear, the kudu disappeared. It didn't leap, or run; it simply disappeared as though it had evaporated.

"Damn!" Mike said.

"Where the hell did it go?" I asked hoarsely.

Mike straightened up. July did the same, shaking his head slowly and holding both hands palms up.

"They just go," Mike said. "That's really all you can say about a bloody kudu. They are just like spirits. One second they are there and the next . . .? With that coloring, all they have to do is to take a few steps in either direction and the light values change, the heavy brush conceals them, and they are gone. He is probably a

Occasionally kudu are hunted from a tower built upon a raft powered by an outboard motor. The tower allows him to see by elevating the hunter above the miles of high swamp grass.

quarter of a mile away by now and running. He knows we are here and there's no use chasing him all day. Let's go back and hope for another." I shook my head in wonder and disappointment and flipped the shell from the chamber to the ground, where I retrieved it and put it back into the clip. Then I followed both men back to the car.

Harry was waiting for us, and listened to the account.

"Well," he said, "don't feel too badly about it. I know men who have hunted kudu for years and have never gotten a shot yet."

It was small consolation at that moment.

And that was only the beginning. The next stalk was even more frustrating. The following day July spotted several bulls in the same type of cover. We stalked them for more than an hour in some of the most impenetrable brush I have ever hunted. Just before we got within range, we came upon a small band of feeding impala. Mike thought the impala were going to spook, or bark and sound the alarm. We froze until they renewed their feeding and moved slowly past them. For some unknown reason, they never bothered to take much notice of us. It was not until we were almost upon the kudu, in gradually thinning brush, that we suddenly surprised a huge giraffe that had been standing off to our right. The tall, ungainly beast crashed off through the brush, sounding like a bulldozer, and off went our kudu without us ever having seen them clearly.

By the third day I was beginning to feel psyched-out by kudu. The final straw came as we ground to a stop in heavy sand, and Mike turned the motor off. George Coe had been riding with us all morning and was looking for a good buffalo. It was almost noon, and we stopped to eat a sandwich and drink a bottle of Castle Pilsner beer for lunch.

I got out of the Land-Rover and stretched.

"July," I asked, "where the hell are all the T'ndala?" He grinned and shook his head. Mike went around the back of the vehicle to open the lunch chest, and George leaned against the hood, eating an apple.

I heard July grunt suddenly. He pointed off to our right.

"You want T'ndala? I get you T'ndala," he said, grinning.

There were two young kudu bulls, not 50 yards away, standing behind a terminalia bush. Their horns were not more than 6 or 8 inches long and they stared at us curiously.

"Christ!" I said, and July grinned back. "Wouldn't you know?"

I reached into the Land-Rover and slid out the camera with the 300 mm telephoto lens. "I might as well get a shot of these two kids," I told George, "they may be the only kudu I see this trip!"

I was focusing the camera when I heard July shout. "T'ndala!" he yelled at the top of his voice, waving an arm past where the young bulls stood.

What must have been a herd of twenty-five animals suddenly appeared from nowhere in the terminalia brush and were streaking, single file, across in front of us.

"Damn it to hell!" was all Mike said, leaping on top of the Land-Rover. "Get that rifle and I'll try and call off the bulls as they leap the road."

It was a fiasco from the beginning. By the time I got around to the other side of the vehicle, worked a shell into the chamber of the gun, and looked ahead, half the herd had already jumped across the narrow opening of the dirt track. I raised the rifle and watched cows and small bulls flash over the narrow space like whitetail deer jumping a logging road in thick Maine woods.

"Bull coming up!" Mike shouted, and I looked through the scope. All I saw was a gray blur as the bull arched over the narrow track. There was no use even trying a snap shot.

"Another bull coming!" Mike yelled. "Big bastard."

I swung the rifle up again and almost fired as the huge bull soared across the opening, but it would have been a futile shot and I might have slightly wounded the animal.

All of us watched the dust settle as the herd streaked off through the bush to our left.

"Jesus!" George said. "What a damned shame. That last bull had some head!" I looked at Mike.

"I'd have given my left arm for a lever-action thirty-thirty with iron sights," I said.

"That's Africa for you," Mike said, shaking his head, "if you *had* been carrying one, the only shots you'd get would be three-hundred yard ones."

"I suppose so," I said. "Where the hell did they come from?"

Mike glanced at July, who looked a little sheepish. "They must have been lying down in the shade over in that thick cover. They do that in the middle of the day. That's probably why the two young bulls were just standing there. They were part of the herd. The kudu is a nocturnal animal mostly. They move from this stuff in the late afternoon to feed, and then lay up in it during the heat of the day. Sometimes they will move down to the river for a drink during the day if they get thirsty, but mostly they stay in this stuff. Old eagle eyes here," he looked at July, who suddenly pretended to find something interesting to study on the far horizon, "got too interested in the thought of lunch, I think. Usually he spots them well before they spook. Oh, well," he said. "What's done is done. Let's have a cool beer and count our sins."

I unloaded the rifle and slid it back into the car. I was beginning to think the gods of the hunt were trying to tell me something about my chances of getting a kudu.

The rest of that day saw us covering at least 30 miles of extremely rough terrain, getting one punctured tire from a thorn bush and having to change a fan belt which broke and caused the radiator to boil over. We saw one fair roan antelope, and George stalked a herd of buffalo with Mike, but there were no good bulls in it. I shot a nice impala for camp meat, but we saw no more kudu.

That night, after the sun had set in a panorama of red and orange sky across the great swamp to the north and west of us and we had gathered around the blazing fire of acacia tree logs, I released the kudu. It is something I find hard to explain to people, but—when I find myself hunting too hard or becoming tense at repeated failures at stalking or poor shooting—I release the game. I put it in other hands. Just before I had a final cold beer and headed away from the warmth of the fire to my tent, I took a deep breath and completely relaxed. If I were meant to get a kudu, I would get one. It is the hunt that counts. And so I went to bed.

We arose before dawn as usual and ate a big breakfast in the thatched-roofed mess hut. Guy Coleach wanted to photograph some buffalo that last morning before the plane picked us up around noon at the landing strip to fly us back to Victoria Falls. George was going to try one more time for his sitatunga antelope in the swamps, and Ed Zern had saved the last day to pick out a good zebra.

Mike, a cup of hot coffee in one hand, moved over to me. "Well, old boy," he said, "shall we have another go at it?"

"Why not," I said and smiled. It had been a marvelous safari—the last two weeks some of the best in my life. I had shot just well enough to make it a fine hunt. The kudu really didn't matter. Mike did not know that, and there was really no way I could tell him. He knew how hard we had been trying.

I was very cold as we left camp and headed north up the border of the swamp. The brush was even thicker here than back away from the river.

"I just have an idea," Mike said, "that we might pick up a herd leaving river after watering and heading back into the sandy area." The sun was not completely above the horizon as we inched through the cover—branches constantly slapping back at us through the open windows of the Land-Rover and causing us to duck constantly as we zigzagged in first gear on the narrow, rutted track. We had not gone more than two miles from camp when July reached down with one hand and solidly thumped Mike on top of the head. The vehicle jolted to a stop. "T'ndala!" July grunted

hoarsely, and there was no mistaking the excitement in his voice. Mike looked up through the open roof of the car. July was immobile—his face contorted. He didn't dare move his head, but pointed slowly with his left finger held just in front of his face.

Mike leaned slowly forward and twisted his head to look to his right. "Christ!" he whispered, turning slowly to me. "There's a kudu bull standing broadside not thirty yards from us in thick brush. Just step out and take him . . . and for God's sake move slowly!"

I couldn't believe it. The first thing I did wrong was to forget where the door handle was. I had been opening the damned door for weeks and suddenly the handle was no longer there.

"Move, move!" Mike said. "He's not going to stay there all day!"

I finally found the handle, swung the door open slowly, and stepped out. The door sounded like the door of a bus as it swung on its hinges. The crash of the bolt as I worked a shell into the chamber echoed through the stillness like a gunshot. My heart beat in my chest and temples and felt like someone was beating on me with a club. I slowly stepped to one side and looked up. The most beautiful kudu I have ever seen was standing broadside in sparse brush about 30 yards away—its magnificent horns spiraling upward as it gazed quietly at me.

I will never know what I did with that shot. I might as well have been shooting at a climbing woodcock with a .20 gauge shotgun. I just snapped a shot at the kudu. The slug must have gone 4 feet above its shoulders because I never really looked through the scope at all. The animal spun around and disappeared into the brush. Mike stepped out of the car and looked at me. I shall never forget the look on his face. He had seen me shooting at running game and killing animals at 300 yards or more for weeks.

I jerked another shell into the chamber and ran for an anthill not more than a dozen yards away. Scrambling up its hard, cementlike side, I managed to reach the top of it, about 8 feet high. Looking out into the brush I saw the kudu still running, head up, in heavy cover about 250 yards away. I raised the rifle, picked it up as it suddenly slid to a stop in a clearing and looked back at us over its shoulder. I held the crosshairs on what I thought was its shoulder, held my breath, and slowly squeezed the trigger. At the crash of the shot and the recoil the kudu disappeared. At the same time July and Sam both let out whoops and jumped from the back of the Land-Rover and came running toward me. Mike, who could see nothing from where he stood, yelled something at July, got an answer, then broke into a grin.

I stood staring at the spot where the kudu had disappeared. I don't think I have ever felt more disappointed while hunting.

And suddenly both black men grabbed me and were pulling me off the anthill. July grasped my hand and pumped it violently while Sam pounded me on the back and both men began spinning me about in a frenzy of shouts and laughter.

Mike's face suddenly appeared in the middle of the rest—a grin from ear to ear.

"You bastard!" he shouted, shaking my hand. "If you had missed that shot, I would have killed you!"

I couldn't say anything. It was probably a good thing I didn't because all three, I found out later, were convinced I had intentionally made one of the best neck shots they had ever seen. That was the reason the kudu disappeared at the shot. It had dropped like a stone, its spine broken, and had not struggled nor moved a bit. By the time we reached it, it was dead—only a few convulsive muscle twitches remaining. The early morning sunlight, filtering through the tree limbs, played on the magnificent gray and purple hide, laced with wide, white vertical markings. The spiral of the horns seemed never to stop.

The kudu I released had returned.

Tips on the African Short Hunt . . .

Something new, comparatively so anyway, has been added to professionally-guided hunting in Africa: the African Short Hunt. Designed for sportsmen who find it impossible to be away from their offices for more than ten days or so, a Short Hunt can take you to two of the most productive hunting areas in southern Africa, areas offering a great variety of species. What's more, the cost of a Short Hunt is comparable to a North American hunt of similar length.

Conducted mostly throughout a vast area of 2.3 million square miles of unspoiled and unexploited countryside, an African Short Hunt is quality all the way. The main differences between it and a full-bore safari are the amount of time spent in the field and the cost. For Short Hunts, costs are held down, in part because the trips are organized so that two sportsmen can utilize the services of one professional hunter.

Accommodations are usually mobile tent camps and are far from Spartan. Sleeper tents, for example, have attached "bathrooms." Each camp also includes a dining tent in which are served meals of top quality, often centered around freshly-taken wild game.

Most Short Hunts are conducted during Africa's winter, a dry season that finds game concentrated around waterholes. In Botswana, for example, thirsty winter game includes the highly prized greater kudu, the Cape buffalo, the impala, and other species. In southwest Africa, you will get a crack at giant gemsbok, mountain zebra, and so on.

Don't pack a lot of clothes for a Short Hunt, because laundry is done in camp almost every day. Permanent press suntans, both shirts and pants, simplify things considerably. Be sure to bring along a sweater or two, even a lightweight down jacket; despite any impressions you might have of African heat, it can get cold from May through August—especially in the early mornings. Also bring along a good hat, a pair or two of sunglasses, and at least one good pair of shooting glasses. Ankle-high desert boots or lightweight birdshooting boots are recommended.

Although firearms can be rented for a Short Hunt (some base prices include gun rental), sportsmen are advised to bring along their own, plus appropriate ammunition. Include a shotgun, too; you may be able to get in a little wingshooting. You're on your own as to calibers, but a .270, .300, or 7mm magnum should handle most situations. If heavier stuff is likely, bring along a .375.

With the exceptions of airfare, trophy fees, tips, booze, firearms rental, and any personal items you might have to order, a Short Hunt will cost in the neighborhood of $3,000, entitling you to the services of one professional hunter and all amenities.

If you'd like to know more, contact Adventures Unlimited or write to Hunter's Africa (P.O. Box 11, Kasane, Botswana).

24.

Brown Trout of New Zealand

It could have been the Wind River in Wyoming, the Snake in Idaho, or even stretches of the Madison—particularly in May or early June. The country was rugged and spectacular, the sky clear, and the slopes strewn with the first bloom of spring wild flowers. And the wide river was as clear as any I had ever seen—running smoothly over a pebbled bottom and sweeping under steep banks to form magnificent runs and pools.

But it was November, we were about halfway between the Equator and the South Pole, and the magnificent river was the Matuara in what Ian Cameron, my friend and fellow angler, referred to as "the southland" of New Zealand's South Island.

"She's bloody beautiful, isn't she?" Ian asked quietly as we stood on the bank after walking a few hundred yards from the road where an "Anglers Access" sign had indicated we could fish.

"My God," I said. "You promised she would be, but I didn't think it would be anything like this. You say they will hit all day?"

"Not all day," he said, sliding a section of his 10-foot double-handed rod from its cloth case. "Oh, you can take trout all day if you walk the banks and cast to the single fish, but," he glanced at his wristwatch, "it's almost two P.M. and they really start hitting well from now on until dark." He eased himself to a sitting position and reached for his pipe and tobacco pouch. "I really think this and the Oreti, a few miles to the west, are the best brown trout streams in the world—and you know I have fished a lot of them—from yours in the States to those on the North Island."

Ian was a native New Zealander, born and raised in Wellington to the north. I had met him a few years before when he flew for Civil Air Transport (CAT), a Nationalist Chinese and U.S.-CIA owned airline operating out of Taiwan. I had been based in Tokyo with United Press. We had fished Sun Moon Lake on Taiwan and had caught some good trout in the mountains of Japan in those years before he left CAT and had come home to fly for a charter air company.

I had kept in touch with him, and he had extended an open invitation to come to New Zealand. When I finally got the chance to go to Australia to fish for

black marlin on the Great Barrier Reef off Cairns, I had cabled him, since it was so close by. Ian had met me with a car at the Invercargill Airport when I got off the Air New Zealand flight. We had driven about 20 miles from there to the town of Gore and had stopped for lunch at the Croydon Lodge before continuing on. The plain Scottish food—mutton, boiled potatoes, and cabbage—reminded me of my own childhood food in Rhode Island and my Glasgow-born mother's penchant for non-spiced cooking. The light New Zealand beer was excellent, and we finished off several bottles of that before Ian stopped at a sporting goods store to pick up some flies.

Our destination was the Te Anau Hotel, some 80 miles to the west on huge Te Anau Lake. We intended to spend three days fishing for rainbows, browns, and salmon on the lake, but Ian said we should spend the first of our four-day holiday fishing the Matuara just for browns. I could see why—looking at the magnificent river. As I watched, a trout that must have been at least 3 or 4 pounds slowly rose to the surface and took a tiny insect not 30 feet upstream from us.

"Good Lord!" I said, "did you see that monster!"

Ian laughed. "That wee fish?" he said. "Wait until you see some of the big ones."

My fingers began fumbling with the straps that held my gear together. That same fever I have had since I was a small boy comes over to me at such times, and I hope it always will. I can recall running from a car to a stream, as a teenager, in my eagerness to start fishing. I must admit I do not run any more, but there is still that same love of the sport.

I was carrying my bulging fishing vest—its zippered pockets loaded down with fly boxes, insect repellent, reels, leaders, extra spools of line, and the myriad things that a trout fisherman manages to acquire to burden himself down. Each time I look at that vest I am reminded of my friend Ed Zern's unforgettable late wife, Evelyn. Once, while Ed was staring hopelessly at a car trunk full of assorted fishing gear, preparing himself for a morning's fishing, she had said to him: "The trouble with you, Ed, is that you are tackle-bound!"

I slid the sections of my Hardy break-down rod from its case. The four-piece rod makes up into a fine, sturdy 8-foot rod and, of all the rods I own, I prefer it for traveling. Its $27\frac{1}{2}$-inch aluminum case can fit into any large suitcase—along with waders and the fishing vest—and one is ready for either trout or salmon. If I don't have to fly, I prefer my bamboo rods—the light 7-footer and the large 9-foot salmon rod, but I won't ship them on jet airlines any more. Between the thievery that goes on and the rough handling by baggage loaders, a man is foolish to put an expensive or fragile rod aboard a plane as cargo these days.

I watched Ian put together the sections of his 10-foot rod. "You are worse than the English," I laughed. "You remind me of an English friend I fish the Spey with for salmon. He uses one of those damn telephone poles, too."

"Does he catch fish?" Ian asked.

"He catches fish," I said, "he and his blasted Spey roll cast. But what kind of sport do you call that, when you haul the poor fish out of the river with something resembling a tree trunk?"

"A fat lot you know, laddie," Ian grunted. "You are going to wish to hell you had brought along something else besides that toothpick before this day is over!" I smiled and finished putting the rod together. I fitted the Hardy reel on and threaded the line through the guides. I was using a No. 8 weight forward floating line with 200 yards of linen backing. It was one of my Atlantic salmon reels, but I thought it might be sensible to use it on this big river—at least if Ian's predictions were to come true.

"Think we will need the waders?" I asked.

Ian nodded. "You can walk the banks and catch good fish," he said, "but they can see you far too easily in this clear water. It's better to get down to their level and cast upstream to them. I've taken a lot here on streamer flies and wet flies fishing downstream, but all in all I think it's not only better fishing upstream with dry flies at this time of the year but more fun. Besides," he added, "if you hook into one of these big browns, you are going to need all the room you can get to play him, and it's easier done from the river."

I nodded and slipped off the loafers and slid them into the back pocket of the fishing vest. After donning the waders, I slid the fly box from one zippered pocket. "What fly would you suggest?" I asked.

He snapped open his own fly box and poked a finger around at an assortment of flies before coming up with one. "This is called Dad's Favourite," he said, "and it's mine, too, on this stream. Lots of these others will do," he added, "but if you've got something in there that looks like this fellow, it should work."

"It looks like a Quill Gordon," I said, flipping open several compartments before finding the one I wanted and holding it up. "Fine, fine," Ian said. "That should do nicely. A size twelve or fourteen will be about right. These are big fish with big appetites."

I tied the Quill Gordon on to a 9-foot knotless leader—tapered down to 2-pound test, and looked at the river. "How do you want to fish it?" I asked.

"Go ahead and work your way up," Ian said. "I'll walk down several hundred yards and work back up to here, then I'll join you in about an hour and see how you are coming along. Fish it the way you would any trout stream," he said. "There's no secret to it. There should be several hatches this afternoon and just play it by ear, as you blokes say. But," he added, "don't get careless. What you think might be a normal strike can be a bloody great brown, and he will break you off before you know what's happening."

I nodded, smiled, and eased slowly down the bank into the clear water. The air temperature was almost 70 degrees and felt like a warm spring day in the Rockies. The water felt cold through the waders, however, and reminded me that the New Zealand winter had not been too long past.

I eased my way upstream, thigh-deep in the strong current, to where the trout had taken the insect some time before. I dropped the Quill Gordon over the spot several times and caught nothing. The sun was warm on my shoulders and flocks of gulls circled over the river and stood stoically on the gravel and sandbars. Near a pocket under a cut bank a trout flashed out of the shadows and savagely struck the fly. Caught by surprise, I reacted too late and tried to set the hook after the fish had felt the steel and spit out the fly.

"Damn!" I said to the sea gulls in general and the trout in particular. There was a long, quiet run just short of the next bend, and I made three casts to it from the near center of the stream with no results. On the fourth cast, the fly rode high and dry on the surface—the Mucilin keeping it buoyant—when a dark shape rose from the bottom and the fly disappeared in a swirl on the surface. I set the hook, and a trout of what must have been 4 pounds came thrashing out of the water, made two arm-wrenching jumps, and parted the leader as though it were spider web.

"Holy Christ!" was all I said—staring at the spot where the fish had jumped and disappeared.

I slowly reeled in the line and ran my fingers down the leader. It had parted a good foot above the fly. I took off what was left of the 9-foot leader and replaced it with a 7-foot knotless leader tapering down to 4-pound test. I had just been convinced. It was going to be salmon tackle from now on. I was not fishing any normal Stateside trout stream!

I took a 2-pound brown at the head of the long pool and missed another one I never saw. The 2-pounder fought like a 5-pounder and jumped like a rainbow—not like the stubborn, rolling, and twisting underwater fight that most browns usually put up on the streams where I was used to fishing for them. I released the brown and continued on.

In a beautiful, deep pool 20 yards upstream, a dark shape, which looked like a sunken log, glided up from the bottom, smashed the fly, took it down and—when it felt the pressure of the strike—ran straight up the center of the pool for at least 50 yards and never broke water. I tried to cup the spinning reel handle with my left hand as the fish took line quickly into the backing, but it was just too fast and too powerful. The leader parted—leaving me with a startled look on my face and a heart beating loud in my chest. It was incredible! In all my years of trout and salmon fishing I had never seen fish hit as hard or move so fast.

I reeled in and looked at the leader. It had broken at the knot—an improved clinch—and that made me feel a bit better. Perhaps I had tied it carelessly. I very carefully tied on another Quill Gordon and moved upstream.

I caught two browns in the next pool—both in the 2- to $2^1/_2$-pound category—and could have sworn they would have weighed 4 to 5 pounds by the fight they put up. At the head of a riffle in the next stretch, a trout hit the dry fly in no more than a foot of water, yet I never saw the fish before it struck, in spite of my polarized glasses. It took the fly from an angle, slashed across the stream, broke water twice in a headlong rush to get around me, and headed downstream. To my credit this time, I held the rod tip high and cupped the reel just lightly enough to keep some pressure on the streaking fish but not enough to cause the leader to break. Most trout fishermen like to mount their reel so that they can retrieve the line with their left hand—most times not winding at all but simply letting line run through the left hand and bringing it in the same way.

The big trout fought its way downstream into the next pool before turning under an undercut bank and shaking its head. I moved cautiously downstream—keeping the rod high—and got some line back until the fly line was partly back on the reel. The trout suddenly burst out, made two unbelievable jumps in the middle of the river, and headed back upstream—taking all the line I had gained and then some. I was suddenly very thankful for the 200 yards of backing! I ploughed my way back upstream—knee-deep in the cold current—as the big fish stubbornly fought its way up the river, acting like a big permit or tarpon after it had settled down to an underwater battle on a fly rod. I finally battled the fish to a standstill but not until after twenty minutes of the most anxious and cautious trout fighting I have ever done. When the big brown finally came to shallow water on a sandbar—exhausted and with gills slowly opening and closing—I slid the net under it and thrashed through water and gravel to the bank where I lunged up and collapsed to the grass with my fish. Finally getting it untangled from the net and slipping the hook of the small scales into a gill slit, I held it up. It weighed 7$\frac{1}{2}$ pounds and gleamed in the bright sunlight—the most beautiful brown trout I had ever caught or seen, before or since.

I kept that fish, and we ate it later that night after bribing the cook at the Te Anau Hotel to keep the kitchen open for a couple of starving and tired trout fishermen. It was a steep bribe, too, I might add!

And the rest of the day faded into an unbelievable mosaic of sunlight, huge river, grassy banks, wheeling sea gulls, and leaping, smashing, battling brown trout. There were several hatches of small gray mayflies, but the Quill Gordon kept attracting fish as it did from the first strike.

Ian joined me at about 4 P.M., and we continued to fish upstream—alternating pools and joining each other whenever one of us hooked into a big brown, whooping with joy and excitement at each new fish. Ian lost two fish which we know would have weighed more than mine and one of them—which he fought almost to a standstill before it made one last run and broke off—would easily have weighed 10 to 12 pounds!

He released all his fish and his biggest weighed just over 6 pounds. We both caught and released several dozen fish each. At close to 5:30 we quit—literally arm-weary and satiated with catching big browns.

Stripping off the waders and tossing fishing vests into the trunk of the car, we continued to talk of the fish caught and the fish lost, like two schoolboys chattering happily away.

I have never returned to that great land and that marvelous river. But there is no reason to believe it has changed. And, in a way, I really don't want to return. It might not be quite as incredible as it was that first time—and that would make it less than the perfect experience it had been.

Tips on Fishing in New Zealand . . .

Serious trout fishermen (as if there were any other kind), weary of the elbow-to-elbow flogging of North American trout waters, will find themselves in a trout fisherman's heaven if they can spend two weeks in New Zealand. There, in lakes, rivers, and gravel-bottomed streams, they will find not only the aesthetics that seem to go hand-in-hand with this most rewarding of fishing activities, but also browns and rainbows of sufficient size and number to make a trip halfway around the world more than worthwhile.

New Zealand consists of two islands, North Island and South Island. North Island is smaller and less mountainous than South Island and also, possibly, offers somewhat better fishing for rainbows. In any event, it's a bit warmer on North Island, something that can, on a chilly morning streamside, provide a bit of consolation. ("If you think it's cold 'ere, mate, you should be down on the big island.")

The big lakes of central North Island—Rotorua, Taupo—and the Tongariro River are first-rate rainbow waters, with fish averaging 3 to 4 pounds. You will find brown trout, too, but rainbows are the resident lords, many of the biggest being taken once the sun goes down.

Keep in mind that our winter is New Zealand's summer, so December, January, and February are best, particularly for fly fishing in and around the mouths of the rivers and streams that feed the lakes. Experience has indicated that streamers can be dynamite, fished shallow or deep.

South Island is brown trout country. There are also landlocked Atlantic salmon (in the Waiau River system and its lakes) and Chinook salmon (called Quinnant salmon locally, and found in the rivers of the island's east coast), but browns averaging 2 or 3 pounds are the most sought-after and commonly taken fish. Incredible as it may seem, South Island also offers excellent rainbow fishing, some getting up in the neighborhood of 5 and 6 pounds.

The dry fly holds sway on South Island (in fact, some waters are restricted to dry fly fishing), but spin fishing is gaining in popularity. Determining the most effective fly pattern calls for a bit of on-the-job experimentation on any given day, but once you've settled on what appears to be a producer, hold onto your hat, because the action can be fast and furious. If you want to try spinning gear, the smaller spoons and spinners—the brighter the better—can send you back to your hotel or lodge in a wonderful frame of mind.

No matter which island you choose, remember that peak seasons will vary. The northern parts of North Island are almost semi-tropical, whereas the southern parts of South Island can be decidedly cool. Ideally, if you have the time and the means, you should spend a couple of weeks working each island; there are places on both that are good throughout the year.

Barring a mass exodus of the world's trout fishermen to New Zealand, it would be hard to imagine a more satisfying or productive spot to stalk and take trout. All the ingredients are here: good-sized fighting fish, spectacular scenery, clear, roaring streams, serene lakes—the works.

The New Zealand Government Travel Commissioner (630 Fifth Avenue, New York, New York 10020) is an old hand when it comes to dealing with trout fishermen and can provide all data regarding dates, travel, accommodations, and so on.

25.
The Trout
of Nikko

On such a morning a man sometimes wonders whether he is really there at all. It has happened to me often and always at such times—as in the half-light before dawn in a duck blind on some lonely marsh, with the wind moaning through marsh grass.

I have had the same feeling on stormy days high in the mountains where deer trails cross on a craggy ridge and the winds whistle through twisted pines and a man's normal world is far away and feels far in his past.

I was wading a twisting, black-water river a few miles above Lake Chuzenji in Japan. A light rain was falling steadily, making the cool June morning appear like the Japanese paintings on the long scrolls I had seen for years. Ferns overhung the banks, and the rocks, a pale green covering of moss and lichens making them slippery to the touch, picked up little light filtering down to the stream through the matted boughs of hemlock overhead.

Adding to the otherworldly feeling was the stillness. No bird chirped in the dense growth on either side of the stream, and my world was reduced to a narrow tunnel with gray mist at both ends.

I was standing at the tail of a short pool. The water appeared deep and the current, after dropping around a large boulder upstream about a dozen yards, swirled close to the bank at my left. The butt end of a hemlock limb jutted from the bank, creating a slight riffle and a small eddy immediately behind it.

I shifted the 7-foot, two-piece bamboo rod in my right hand. It was impregnated and weighed only $3^3/_8$ ounces—an American fly rod, rather than a Japanese one, and one I carry all over the world. The Japanese make rather good fly rods for the money, but I find them somewhat heavy.

It had not proven to be much of a morning so far for dry flies. Because of the lack of sunlight there had not been any hatch of flies. I had only been fishing about twenty minutes and had not had a strike on anything. I stripped in the No. 7 weight-forward floating line and slid my hand down the 9 feet of tapered 3X leader until I came to the tiny dry fly. I clipped it off and replaced it with a No. 16 Black Ant. Then I stripped the line out from the battered old reel I have carried around for twenty-five years and dropped the tiny wet fly a few feet above the eddy. Moving it in short jerks toward me as the slight current carried it downstream, I almost missed the strike completely as the fish took the little ant about a foot below the surface.

It made three slashing jumps in a row as it tore the surface of the pool into a confusion of waves. I kept the rod tip as high as I could and tried to keep the fish away from the limb. It headed directly upstream and apparently wanted to climb the current into the next pool, but the little rod is far stronger than it looks and the fish decided that was too much punishment. It jumped again and came downstream as I took in slack line with my left hand. The fish swirled at my feet, jumped twice more, then bored for the bottom of the black pool, where it shook its head a number of times. I thought I had seen a flash of orange when the fish struck but I couldn't be sure.

Ten minutes later I was sure—as the fish tired and slowly turned on its side and slid into the net. I hefted a 16-inch rainbow and guessed his weight at about 2 pounds. And in the solitude of that misty morning on an isolated stream in the highlands about 100 miles north of Tokyo in Japan, I smiled and released a familiar old friend, and my real world suddenly was back with me.

The rainbow trout is found all over the globe wherever trout fishermen seek it, and Japan is no exception. Japan, with its unbelievable beauty of mountains and rivers, can lay claim to being one of the best trout-fishing areas in the world. Why more people do not know this is a mystery to me.

I suppose we tend to associate trout fishing with cold climates and cold water, and to many Americans who have never been in Japan, the country is thought of as warm and subtropical. It is anything but that—especially in the northern half of its biggest island, Honshu, and its northernmost island, Hokkaido.

There are mountain ranges in central Honshu that rival the Alps in Europe. Hokkaido has mountains that remind one of the Scandinavian countries, and not only is the trout fishing magnificent but so is the fresh-run salmon fishing in Hokkaido.

The pressure of business in Japan had kept me from trout fishing until this trip, however. I knew there were trout in Japan, because I had been told so by friends. The friend I was fishing with on this trip, Kei Hagewara, had long urged me to try it. I also knew it because once, back in about 1951 during the United States occupation of Japan, I had gone to Nikko National Park to visit the great shrine of Toshogu—dedicated to Tokugawa Ieyasu (1542–1616). This beautiful combination of Buddhist and Shinto architecture, topped by a five-story pagoda, was completed in 1636 and is breathtaking to see.

While there I had been idly leaning on the red wooden railing of the Skinkyo, or Sacred Bridge, over the Daiya River near the shrine, when I glanced down and saw a number of long shapes in a deep pool. They looked to me like trout that must have averaged about 5 pounds each. Asking a guide what they were, I was told *Iwana.* I later found out from Japanese fishing friends that these were Japanese brook trout, very much like ours. I was also told they were considered sacred, too—as everything in the Nikko National Shrine is—and that if I had gone and gotten a fishing outfit the way I started to do, there would have been hell to pay—occupation or not.

I was sitting on the bank recalling this when I heard a light cough and looked up to see Kei moving down the bank toward me—his wicker fishing creel banging against his leg. He sighed and sat down, leaning his long rod against a tree and taking out an insulated container from a leather case slung around his shoulder. He unscrewed the cap, filled one of the cups and handed me a cup of tea.

"How goes the fishing?" he asked in English.

"Fine," I said, sipping the tea. "I just ran into an old friend. A rainbow trout."

"Ah!" Kei said and grinned. "Fine! You are satisfied that we have good fishing now?"

"I'm satisfied," I said. "I never doubted your word. I just wasn't certain whether I could catch one using my own system."

"Do you have him?"

"I caught him," I said, "But I let him go."

"So," Kei nodded and sipped his tea. "I do the same thing many times."

He was silent for a few moments. The sun began to filter through the haze above us and the steady rain had let up.

"Catch any?" I asked casually.

Kei put his plastic teacup down and unlatched the cover of his creel. He reached in and took out several 8- to 9-inch rainbows, which he placed on a bed of ferns.

"They are not very big," he said with a smile. "I released one larger, but these will make a fine meal."

"What did you take him on?" I asked, running a finger down the side of a chunky rainbow.

Kei reached back into his creel and took out a small, round wicker basket in which he kept his live bait. He reached down and stirred up some moss until he came up with a small, black insect that could only be a member of the stonefly larva family. He told me what its name was in Japanese but I have forgotten it. Besides, most larvae, like our hellgrammites, look very much the same to me.

Kei had examined my tackle earlier in the morning before we had left our lodgings at the Lakeside Hotel on the eastern end of Lake Chuzenji. He had nodded carefully over each piece of tackle, then had taken a canvas case out of the back of the car and had put together his trout rod. It was four sections of bamboo; the butt section was about an inch and a half thick and tapered to about a quarter-inch thick at the tip. The entire rod must have been about 12 feet long. To the end of it—he did not use a reel—Kei fastened about 12 to 15 feet of very filmy monofilament line. I would estimate the breaking strength to have been at about that of a 2-pound-test line. To this he tied a tiny hook—about a No. 18.

The night before he had a local guide catch him his live bait from the shallow water of the lake shore by using a square box with a glass bottom.

"I am an old-fashioned trout fisherman," Kei said now, holding his live bait in the palm of his hand. "Many Japanese trout fishermen today use modern tackle much like yours—though not so well made," he hastened to say politely. "They catch trout also." He paused and smiled quietly at the slowly moving stream. A warbler-like bird began its song in the bushes behind us. "But my father was a fine trout fisherman. He used to come here for Yamame, you would call them native trout, and he taught me how to fish. He, like Japanese trout fishermen for thousands of years, fished as I do. I think," he paused to look down at the small insect in his palm, "I like the old ways better in some things—like this," he added softly.

I finished the cup of tea and screwed the top back on the container before handing it to Kei.

Kei and I were both about the same age and at one time were on different sides in a long-ago war in China.

"Many American trout fishermen today use fiberglass rods and automatic reels. They also catch a lot of trout," I said. But touching my light bamboo rod softly, I added, "I also like some old ways better."

"Let's go," I said, getting to my feet. "Show me how you catch Yamame. Do you think they will take an artificial fly like the rainbow did?"

"I do not know," he said, "but every trout fisherman must know there are no rules a trout has not broken." He turned and started upstream, jumping from hummocks to slippery rocks with his rope wading sandals. I took it a little slower because my felt-soled wading shoes didn't hold that well on the moss-covered rocks.

The sun came out and the weather—at more than 4,000 feet above sea level—was wonderfully cool. Glancing at my watch, I noticed it was only 7:20 A.M. Kei stopped at a large pool and walked into the bushes to keep himself hidden while he made his way to the head of the pool, where the water tumbled in from a fall a few feet high. I sat down and watched him stoop and move behind a large boulder. He reached into his creel and took out a larva and put it on the hook, then carefully eased the long rod out over the waterfall where he slowly dunked the bait and let the rod tip sink about 5 feet lower. Nothing happened. He repeated this, moving slowly down the bank to where I was seated.

About two-thirds of the way down the pool he suddenly jerked the rod tip slightly, after floating the larva on the bottom close to a small rock. A trout broke the surface and began a tail-dance across the surface of the pool. Kei's face was set in a happy smile as he carefully maneuvered the battling trout away from sharp rocks, sunken logs, and fast water. The long rod appeared beautifully built for this, and I could see why there was no need for a reel.

When the fish was tired, Kei merely lifted the long rod until the trout slid on its side across the surface and onto the shallow gravel of a bar—where he reached down and picked it up with two fingers behind the trout's head.

It was a 10-inch rainbow, and we both admired it, glinting in the morning sunlight, before Kei carefully released it to swim slowly upstream in the shallow water.

He explained that rainbow trout, which were raised at a commercial hatchery close to us at the northwestern end of the lake, were the most plentiful trout in the Daiya River. Also there were some brook trout *(Iwana)* and a very few native Yamame. The native trout were the result of natural propagation, he said, and therefore much harder to catch.

We alternated pools for another hour and a half. I caught four more rainbows—keeping only one nice one for lunch. I took no brook trout, nor did Kei, though he caught three more rainbows—one an 18-inch beauty that put up a spectacular battle on his light line.

Shortly after 9 o'clock, we took a breakfast break of more tea and some good cakes Kei had brought along, and later began to fish the last stretch of the river—about a mile and a half from where we had parked the car we had driven up from Tokyo the day before.

I was casting a small nymph across the stream and letting it float down and across the current when I heard a shout. Kei was playing a fish in the pool above me, and occasionally he let go of the rod to wave his left arm at me without looking up. I waded ashore and hurried up to find him sliding a small trout into the shallows. He stepped carefully to the graveled edge of the stream and gently picked up a 6-inch trout. Smiling widely he walked up to me, holding the fragile fish.

"Yamame," he said simply, turning the trout slowly in the bright sunlight.

As near as I could tell, it looked like a cross between a rainbow and the native cutthroat trout caught in the Rockies—without the bright red slash beneath the jaw on the dentary bone. Its general color was a soft, silvery purple with vertical bars of a shade of dark gray barely visible through the speckles customarily found on the rainbow.

I mentioned to Kei that the rainbow and the native American cutthroat trout oftentimes hybridize. He admitted this was possible but seemed to think the Yamame was a separate strain of native trout rather than a cross. At any rate I have seldom seen a more beautiful trout and really was sorry I did not have color film in my camera. I did take a black-and-white picture of it before we released it and started back to the hotel for lunch.

We saw a number of other trout fishermen on the stream as we drove slowly along until we came to the lake and drove beneath beautiful Mt. Nantai, an 8,148-foot-high volcanic mountain, which at one time erupted and blocked the Daiya River, forming Lake Chuzenji and also creating Kegon Falls at the eastern end of the lake. Kegon Falls is a spectacular long plume of waterfall that drops from the lake level about 30 feet wide and 316 feet straight down into a pool of the Daiya River below. It brings visitors from all over the world. I have been at the lake in October when Mt.

Nantai and the surrounding landscape turns scarlet, yellow, and orange from the autumn foliage. There are few spots in the world more beautiful.

The Japanese are ardent freshwater fishermen. Most Western cultures think of the Japanese as a seagoing commercial fisherman, but he is extremely fond of freshwater fishing on light tackle, and he has several species of fish to seek. *Ayu,* a small trout-like fish, is sought in many streams in central and northern Japan. Rainbow trout and largemouth black bass are caught in many lakes. I have seen Japanese ice fishermen on the surface of Hakone Lake, south of Tokyo, when the cold was enough to chill an Eskimo, catching Wakasagi—which I guessed to be a species of smelt.

Mountain fishing resorts are plentiful and usually are incorporated into spas so that the angler can take hot sulphur baths after a long day on the stream. The hotels are spotlessly clean and the rates—if one prefers the Japanese-style accommodations as I do—are very reasonable. For the fisherman who prefers Western-style hotels (with tables, chairs, beds, etc.) the rates are still very reasonable—averaging about $4 to $9 per night for a single with bath to from $8 to $16 per night for doubles with bath.

Excellent train and bus service is available to most mountain areas. At one time driving was a problem, but today anyone with an international driver's license can obtain an American rent-a-car from airports and hotels as well as from a half a dozen Japanese rent-a-car companies.

Fishing licenses are required for freshwater but almost any hotel can arrange for one. Any Japanese city has fishing-tackle stores galore. I spent as much time in the fascinating tackle shops of Tokyo as I do in the better sporting-goods stores of New York. If it has anything to do with fish, the Japanese make it. The fishing season lasts from March until September.

The better known streams of Japan are filled with trout fishermen equipped with the same gear to be found on the Neversink and Battenkill in America's East and the Gunnison and Snake rivers of the West.

Kei and I had lunch in the screened-in dining room of the hotel overlooking the lake. The hotel chef had prepared our trout and served it broiled. We ate the fish with fresh lemon and butter and a pinch of *wasabi,* or green horseradish mixed with soy sauce—slightly hot to the tongue and tasting great with beer.

After an early afternoon nap, we drove the car back up the Daiya River a few miles above where we fished in the morning. We fished below Ryuzu Falls, and, while I caught no native Yamame or brook trout, I did catch and release half a dozen fine rainbows.

I was resting on the bank, chewing on a long stem of grass and watching the late afternoon sun filter through the pine boughs overhead, when I heard footsteps.

Kei unslung his gear and dropped beside me, propping himself against a tree and lighting a cigarette. He sighed and blew smoke at a limb.

"How did it go?" I asked, propping myself up on one elbow.

"Very well," Kei said. "I took one more Yamame and missed a large trout. It might have been an Iwana, but perhaps a big rainbow. It broke the line when I struck."

"Too bad," I said, "I would like to have seen the brookies here."

"Yes," he said, "they are beautiful fish." He was silent for a while. "But then I know what pool he lives in and perhaps another time . . ."

"The everlasting optimist," I said, and settled back.

"It must be the same in your country," Kei replied. "In Japan there are trout fishermen who—though they catch no fish—are content to fish such a stream and to breathe the air. On such a day as this," he said, "it is enough to be alive."

Tips on Fishing in Japan . . .

A trout by any other name is still a trout, even in Japan, which offers some of the world's best fishing for rainbows and brookies. The countryside of Japan is dotted with lakes and laced by streams that abound in trout. Most pleasingly, the majority of Japan's trout waters are in truly picture postcard settings, the sort of which exotic Oriental dreams are made.

Perhaps the best spots in which to try your hand at taking Japan's trout are the lakes. Usually clear and cold, the lakes offer not only rainbows and brookies, but also unusually scrappy black bass. Lake Ashi (also known as Lake Hakone) in Hakone is such a spot, as are Lake Saiko and Lake Motosu, both of which are dominated by the incredible sight of Mt. Fuji. Lake Haruna, near Ikao Spa in Gumma Prefecture, is yet another haven for trout fishermen. You will find good to outstanding hotel accommodations at or near just about all the most productive trout waters.

The seasons for different fish vary from locale to locale (and should be determined for the waters you have in mind before you venture forth), but in general the trout season runs from March through September. You will find that hotels and various tourist agencies are aware of possible fishing dates, so speak up (a truly amazing number of Japanese—particularly those in the tourist/travel business—speak English).

Keep in mind that trout and bass aren't the only game fish at which you can try your hand. Both inland and offshore waters offer a wide range of fish, including sea bream (*tai*), yellowtail (*buri*), Spanish mackerel (*sawara*), sea bass (*suzuki*), gray mullet (*bora*), flounder (*hirame*), and many others.

Although a spin rod fan is assured of action (small spinners and spoons, bright and flashy, can work wonders), a fly fisherman will find himself right at home in Japan. However, pay attention to localized techniques and patterns; the Japanese have been stalking trout for a long time, and they have learned a thing or two in the process.

A populous, tightly-knit country, Japan offers a wealth of accommodations for visitors. The key to a rewarding trip is to place yourself in the right hands. A good place to start is the Japan National Tourist Organization, which maintains offices in New York (45 Rockefeller Plaza, 10020), Chicago (333 North Michigan Avenue, 60601), Dallas (1420 Commerce Street, 75201), Los Angeles (530 West Sixth Street, 90014), and San Francisco (651 Market Street, 94105).

26.
U.S. Southwest: Javelina—the Desert Ghost

There used to be a lot of native javelina in New Mexico, but they almost became extinct, and some years ago the state decided to reintroduce them in the southwestern corner of the state. These little wild animals did well, and restricted hunting began in the early 1960s. Having hunted wild boar in many parts of the world, from Florida to Taiwan, I was curious about this pig-like creature, and over the years I made several applications for a lottery permit, but my name was not chosen in the annual drawings for 100 permits.

Then my luck changed. Not only was my name drawn, but I got a party permit for my friends Harry Norvell and Bob Clyde and myself. New Mexico and some other states are farsighted enough to issue a number of party permits, knowing that a man will frequently not want to go hunting alone or with a stranger but with friends.

We were to hunt in the rough desert-and-canyon country of New Mexico just east of Arizona and north of Mexico. Gusts of cold March wind were blowing when we checked into a motel in Lordsburg before reporting to the trailer which housed officials of the Department of Game and Fish. By the time our permits had been checked it was dark night, so we returned to the motel. The hunt would begin a half hour before sunrise the following day.

I had never hunted javelina in New Mexico before, or elsewhere for that matter. They had the reputation of being fast, tough, and smart, but I'd become conditioned to hunting big wild boars in such dissimilar places as the Southeast and Asia and wasn't inclined to be nervous about a little wild pig running from 30 to 50 pounds. I was in for a few surprises.

The javelina, or peccary, is not a true pig, wild or otherwise. It's a member of another family, but it does look like a pig and its odor, produced by a musk gland on its back, is distinctive. Levon Lee, of the game-management team, dropped in on us at the motel and gave us a briefing on the local animals. Moreover, he offered to show our party areas where the hunting might be good when we set out in the morning.

Up well before dawn, Harry, Bob, and I breakfasted at a cafe, then reported to the game department trailer. Lee guided our car down a narrow, rutted ranch road bordered by a barbed wire fence. We went about ten miles, still in the dark and opening and closing a half dozen gates in the process, before we arrived at the area Lee had chosen. By now the eastern horizon was bright with the desert dawn and the weather was bitterly cold.

Hidalgo County in southwestern New Mexico has a lot of flat desert land, but it also has some of the roughest foothills and mountains I've ever seen. We were in an area of header canyons at an elevation of about 4,000 feet by the time it was light enough for us to see. The landscape was mostly straight up and down, and the hillsides were a jumbled mass of rocks, talus slopes, scattered mesquite clumps, beds of prickly pear and yucca, and rimrock-covered high ridges.

Lee waved an arm in the general direction of west and said, "That's where you'll find them. We've spotted some scattered bands in here but you never know where they'll show up next."

Harry slung his .30–06 over his shoulder and asked, "Do we just keep walking west? I don't have an Arizona hunting license."

"Don't worry," said Lee. "Arizona isn't far but it would take you a month to reach it through that country."

We agreed to rendezvous at the car for lunch, then headed in the same general direction but working outward on several ridges. All of us had binoculars and canteens, and I—following an old habit—had stowed several small cans of stewed tomatoes in my pockets. I've found the tomatoes useful in restoring energy after hours of sliding, stumbling, and climbing in rough country. Levon Lee accompanied me, though he carried no rifle. Born in Las Cruces, some miles to the east in the Rio Grande Valley, he knows New Mexico. He's a fine naturalist, too, and as we walked along he pointed out species of desert cactus, unusual rock formations, and an occasional small animal or bird. From time to time we heard the soft cooing of mourning doves.

But we didn't see a javelina all morning long, though we hiked for miles. We did find some sign, once, where a small band had crossed an arroyo the day before, again where another band had rooted up some yucca plants. Then we started back for the car, and Lee talked about New Mexico javelina.

"They probably know more about them in Arizona than we do," he said. "Ours were extinct for many years. From observing our herds, we've found they seem to travel in small packs, called sounders. They don't see too well but they have a darn good sense of smell and they can hear a long way off."

The peccary's favorite food seems to be prickly pear cactus, the yucca plant, and mesquite beans. Apparently the little pig doesn't require much water; some have been known to go as long as three months without visiting a waterhole. Lee believes they live on the water in the cactus. The females weigh about 30 pounds on the average, and the boars somewhat more—a big one reaching about 50 to 60 pounds.

Bob and Harry were cooking lunch when we arrived at the car. Bob had seen no pigs but Harry had spotted two crossing a ridge about 600 yards away. He didn't see much sense in trying a snap shot at that distance. "Besides," he said ruefully, "they were going faster than desert mule deer."

I decided to hunt alone in the afternoon. The sun was high and there was no longer any need for a jacket. I began working the side of a canyon, stopping now and then to sweep the canyon bottom and walls with my glasses. It was hot work, and the footing was tricky. Once I heard several shots in the distance, and later others from over the ridge in the next canyon.

It must have been about 2:30 or so—with the sun dipping slowly into the western half of the sky—when I heard a burst of shots just over the ridge across the canyon. I slipped behind a large boulder and watched the ridge. After a few minutes I saw three pigs come across the top and start down the canyon slope opposite me. They were moving at a gallop and there was little use in trying a shot at them as they slipped and slid down the slope at full speed, about 400 yards away.

Since they were heading for the bottom of the canyon, I thought they might come up on my side, giving me a halfway-decent shot. When they reached the bottom I eased out from behind the big rock and looked down to see if I could catch sight of them. There was nothing.

Muttering in disappointment, I began to move along the base of the rimrock, about 300 yards above the canyon floor. Then, having played a waiting game with mule deer and antelope in this same type of terrain, I decided to sit them out. Moving slowly, I headed for a large boulder about 30 yards away.

I had gone about five steps—always watching the canyon floor—when I passed the mouth of a deep cut in the rimrock on my left. The interior was in shade. I stepped into the mouth of the cut, unslung the .270, and took a look at the dry arroyo bed at the bottom of the canyon.

Then I heard a sudden noise behind me—as if someone were pounding a stick on a rock. Glancing around, I saw a javelina coming straight up the cut at me. The pig made loud clicking and chopping noises with its tusks as it scrambled for the opening in which I was standing. It was not charging me; I had appeared out of nowhere and blocked its escape route, and it wanted out. But my reaction was the same as if it had been a 400-pound Romanian boar—I made that big flat rock in three leaps. The little boar went hurtling past me and headed down the slope.

The one shot I got off was not bad. In fact, I have been doing a lot of bragging about it ever since—knowing full well it was one of the luckiest I've ever made. I flipped off the safety, swung the .270 to my shoulder, and fired. The bullet caught the little boar right between the ears as he was going away. He was stone dead before his hoofs hit the ground again, but his momentum carried him at least 100 yards down the slope before he wound up at the base of a mesquite bush.

I was staring at the still figure—the rifle at my shoulder—when the base of the rimrock started erupting javelina in all directions. They had been taking a siesta in the small, shady pockets and crevasses at the base of the rock wall far up the slope. Some rushed to the bottom of the canyon, others crossed the ridge. There were scattered shots from both the other canyons, and I hoped someone had got a good shot.

Small animal or not, by the time I had field-dressed my boar and slung him across one shoulder—with all four hoofs tied together with a leather thong—I found him hard to carry. Peccary are compact creatures. And with the footing as uncertain as it was in that country, it took me more than two hours to get him back to a place a vehicle could reach. Darkness was setting in as I hung the boar on a juniper limb in the bottom of a large wash just down the canyon from the camp. But before I could start for camp, I heard sounds below me and saw Harry coming up the arroyo. He was dragging a sow—one of the pigs I had sent scampering over the ridge.

Harry said he had been crouched under a mesquite when half a dozen javelina came over the ridge and down into his small header canyon. His third shot killed the sow.

It was dark by the time we got to camp and returned to our trophies with Lee in his game department pickup truck.

"That's a good boar," he said, pointing at mine as we hoisted both animals into the truck. "He'll go well over fifty pounds."

Bob was at the car when we got back. He'd had one long shot at a javelina, he said, but missed it and got only fleeting glimpses of two more later in the day. He was not too upset. We'd figured on spending two days on the hunt, and Bob was sure he'd get his pig next day.

Back at the check station, game department men were operating a scale while biologists recorded data of the pigs being brought in. About twenty animals had been taken that first day, and mine was the largest. Jim McClellan—another veteran Department of Game and Fish field man—weighed the boar and estimated it would have gone 55 pounds before being field-dressed.

Next day, McClellan (one of the few game department men lucky enough to draw a permit) went out with us. Harry stayed in the motel to catch up on his sleep, but I went with Bob and Jim, carrying only my binoculars. Since we planned to leave for home that night, I wanted to give Bob an assist if I could.

We saw pigs almost from the first, but at considerable distances. They had been scattered by yesterday's shooting and most were in groups of three to five animals. Almost all were high on the slopes at the base of rimrock, making hunting very difficult. Bob got several extremely long shots, but he'd have been very lucky if he connected. Once we walked past two pigs in thick brush—only to have them break out behind us and quickly disappear down a small draw before anyone could get a shot.

There were tracks everywhere. We found clusters of chewed yucca plants and areas where herds of pigs had rooted up the hillsides getting at prickly pear cactus.

Harry had joined us by then, and we figured out some strategy. He and I would take a car and drive to the bottom of one of the valleys, then walk up the canyon while Bob and Jim started high up and worked down. Harry and I hoped to drive the pigs in front of us, giving the two others a chance to shoot from high on the slopes.

We did not see any pig sign at all at the mouth of the canyon nor for a mile up it. With the sun high over us in the early afternoon, and the land sloping steeply in front, we stopped climbing after the first hour and walked back to the car. There we sat in the shade and glassed the two sides of the canyon. We finally spotted Bob on one rim and Jim on the other.

We watched them move to the end of the rimrock, then ease off the ridgetops and begin climbing down the canyon slopes toward us. They were still several miles up the canyon when we saw the first of the pigs moving half a mile ahead of them. The wary little animals were slinking through the dense cover, moving in short bursts. When the two men moved, so did the pigs. When either man stopped, the pigs froze.

How could we get the message to the stalkers?

We tried standing on top of the car, waving our hats, blowing the car horn, and yelling. Nothing seemed to work.

"Only one thing we can do," Harry said. "Let's get in there as fast as we can and try to turn the pigs back up the canyon."

We set off at a fast jog up the dry wash. About ten minutes of that, in the heat and high altitude, slowed us to a walk. My heart was pounding in my ears.

We were about half a mile from the hunters when we saw the first of the pigs through the glasses. We were not able to tell how many there were in the bunch; they were moving too rapidly. Climbing on top of a mound of sand we began shouting and waving. Finally I saw Jim McClellan stop, raise his glasses, and look at us. I waved frantically and pointed up the canyon. He shifted his glasses and for a long time scanned the valley floor. Finally he lowered the glasses and set off down the slope with long strides that caused miniature landslides. Bob finally realized what was going on and began hurrying down his slope.

The pigs suddenly appeared ahead of us and slid to a halt about 50 yards up the canyon. There were about fifteen javelina in the herd, and they stood there, first looking back at the two hunters bearing down the slopes above them, and then at us.

What made them decide we were the lesser of two evils, I will never know. Harry claims they could tell who was carrying guns. He may be right. At any rate, they suddenly came right at us. We picked up rocks and threw them at the pigs as they scooted through the dense mesquite clumps, but they ducked the stones and kept on coming. Harry tried waving his white sombrero and shouting, but that didn't stop them. The entire herd went right past us, one boar not ten feet away from me. Harry let out a whoop and threw his hat at it. The pig never changed direction.

We were sitting on the mound of sand—still breathing hard and watching the last of the herd disappear on the mesquite flats below the canyon mouth—when the two hunters puffed to a stop behind us. Neither had gotten a shot.

"Well," McClellan finally drawled, "personally I think both of you are sorta long in the tooth for bird-doggin'." He looked at the wisps of dust out on the flat where the pigs were still running. "Also, you sure don't hold a point at all."

Out on the flats we tried to find the pigs. We finally jumped one—a small sow, and Jim made a nice running shot at about 200 yards. He estimated the weight of the little pig at about 30 pounds. Bob never got another shot, though we covered what seemed like hundreds of square miles before dark.

Driving the long trip to Albuquerque that night—I had to catch a flight the next morning—we did work up a sort of "do and don't" bit of advice for the sportsman who is going on his first javelina hunt.

In the *Do* column: Stay *high* and use binoculars more than half the time. The little pigs are smart and will move ahead of a hunter. Use a flat-shooting, medium-caliber rifle. Our .270 and two .30–06's were fine. Jim McClellan used a .250–3000. Do more glassing and listening than walking. Some game men told us the javelina's eyesight is poor, but I'm not entirely convinced of that. I do know his hearing is acute and his sense of smell is excellent.

Hunt around areas where the pigs have been feeding—such as the prickly pear and yucca clumps on sunny hillsides. Either hunt very slowly or find a good spot where ridges cross and wait. Expect to find a javelina anywhere. Like us, you may walk right over a couple in dense cover.

Wear rugged but light boots for climbing, carry water and some light rations, and wear tough but light clothing and a wide hat to keep off the sun. Carry a knife for field skinning and some thongs to lash the feet together for carrying. Work the base of the rimrock and investigate the caves; the little pigs like to hole up in the heat of the day. Wear tough trousers; mesquite thorns and desert brush can tear ordinary clothing to shreds.

In the *Don't* column: Don't go stumbling around making noise. The pigs apparently have lookouts with darn good hearing. Don't smoke unless you have to; the odor carries much farther than you realize on the clear desert air. Don't try to climb to the top of each ridge for a look at the country; you will just tire yourself out early. Don't snap-shoot at a running herd; pick an individual javelina—much the same as in antelope hunting or, for that matter, in a flushing covey of birds. The javelina is a small target, but under 150 yards he shouldn't be too hard to hit on level ground. On the rocky slopes and at the base of rimrock, try to work up for a closer shot. Once the pigs start to run they can move as fast as a horse.

Don't remove the musk sac just because somebody told you to. It will come off naturally when you skin the animal. Some people think that javelina meat is dry, but Jim McClellan's wife cooked his pig and everyone agreed they'd never tasted better barbecued wild game. If you intend to eat your javelina, skin it completely before taking it home. If you intend to have the head mounted, cape it out as you would any other trophy.

Don't chase a herd if it starts to run; it may stop and give you a shot. You don't have a chance of catching them afoot anyway. Take the advice of the game department men running a hunt. They know where the herds live. A javelina will spend its entire life in an area of about five square miles.

Javelina hunting is a sporty business and a lot of fun. The country the desert pigs live in is beautiful but very rugged, and it pays to go prepared. Here's to a pig in your sights!

[For further information, see Tips at the end of Chapter 20.]

27.
Iceland:
Land of the
Salmon

A warm and moist wind, carrying the lung-soothing freshness of the North Atlantic Drift, bathes the green island in August. And in the clear rivers with almost unpronounceable names—the Laxa Adaldal, the Nordhura, the Grimsa, and the Haffjardhara—the great Atlantic salmon leap and churn their way inland to spawn.

Gleaming silver, and fresh from the depths of the sea, the fish gradually change to bronze-purple as they move irresistibly through historic pools with names known for centuries to salmon fishermen long passed on to greater pools and fish which never die.

On pools named The Grastraumur, and runs called the Stekkur, guides like Jonnas Halldorsson, Heimir Sigurdsson, and Thor Thors—many of them owners of the land through which the rivers twist—point out the traditional spots where salmon rest briefly before fighting their way up the next twisting current or plunging waterfall. And for the angler who stands thigh-deep in the cold and clear water while the salmon leap clear and fall back to the surface on their age-old journey, as inflexible as the rise and fall of the ocean tide, it is not difficult to see what brought European fly fishermen, centuries ago and in wooden ships, to fish Iceland.

For in a world where man has poisoned, polluted, dammed, channelized, diverted, and filled his once-magnificent salmon rivers with nets, the streams of Iceland represent the last great unspoiled and well regulated paradise for the salmon angler. Here the fly fisherman may cast in solitude on a river as pristine today as when Norse settlers drank from them in the 9th century. The fish leap as spectacularly now as they did when the beautiful island passed under the sovereignty of the Danish Crown in 1380. And while astronauts photographed the 40,000 square-mile island on their orbits about the earth in 1973, the salmon rose to a double-hooked No. 8 Blue Charm as readily as they did to an English angler who cast the same fly in the days when the only things that flew over the solitary fisherman were gulls from the nearby sea.

And a gull watched me from above as I cast repeatedly to a smooth run on a beat of the Haffjardhara, where my host, guide, and friend Thor Thors had assured me several salmon held at all times during the spawning run. The water was running swiftly over a boulder-strewn bottom and footing was difficult even with felt-soled waders. The bottom was not slippery, as on many salmon streams—such as Scotland's River Spey—but the surging current made shifting position without carefully testing the next foothold a risky move.

The midmorning sun was a pleasant warmth on my shoulders, helping to counteract the chill of legs subjected for the past half-hour to the penetrating cold of water only slightly warmed from its origin in the glaciers not far to the north. There had been a flash beneath the fly about ten minutes before, but it seemed to be a halfhearted rise and the fish had only come up a foot or so from where it was holding.

It was resting close to the bottom, in about 4 feet of water and slightly to my side of a rock jutting from the current about 30 feet downstream and to my left. I had glanced up the green slope to where Thor was sprawled out in the sunlight—hoping he had seen the rise and could spot the fish's position better from his vantage point about 50 yards from me. But he was apparently asleep, lying on his back with one forearm across his eyes. I had gone back to my casting.

Far downstream I could just see Lee Wulff, who had come down from the Laxa the day before to fish with me at the invitation of Thor. Lee's trademark, snow-white hair, was visible for miles in the clear air.

My heart pounded suddenly as a salmon leaped several feet into the air and slapped back to the surface not more than a dozen feet from me. The unexpected jump of a salmon—whether on Quebec's mighty George River or Scotland's Tay—has never ceased to startle me. I doubt if it ever will. It is difficult to disassociate the jump of a spawning-run salmon from the jump of a feeding trout when a person first begins to angle for these fish. The leap has nothing to do with hunger, as salmon heading upstream for the gravel spawning beds are not interested in food. The jump, sometimes, is to rid itself of tiny sea lice, parasitic copepods that are distant cousins of the shrimp and lobster. At other times it simply leaps—for reasons its ancestors millions of years ago also leaped and perhaps puzzled some primitive, fur-clad man, much as it puzzled me. Much of the mystique of the Atlantic salmon that has driven anglers for centuries to search out this great fish stems from the reason it does take an artificial fly. Scientists and expert salmon anglers are generally agreed that it is a reflex action, stemming from the days when it fed on insects and tiny fish in the same stream as a small fry, before making the long journey down to its three- or four-year life in the sea.

As any Atlantic salmon angler will tell you, it is not unusual to cast to the same fish for hours—and have it clearly in sight—without getting it to show any interest in a fly. Yet suddenly, many times after hundreds of casts to the same spot, the fish will inexplicably rise and take the fly.

The fly came up on the backcast as my heart slowed down after the salmon leap, and I dropped the No. 6 Black Doctor a bit farther upstream. The movement of the strong current was transmitted through the 6-pound-test leader tippet, up the floating fly line, and through the 7 feet of light ($3^3/_8$ ounce) split-cane rod. The wet fly made the same swing across the current—no movement other than that normally

caused by the moving water imparted to it—and curved over the spot where the flash had occurred earlier. The big, gray herring gull wheeled slowly above as the fly came up again, and again, and again, landing gently each time within a few feet of the same spot. The lush, rolling, and treeless expanse of the land stretched to the horizon, tilting gradually upstream to the heights of an icefield far to the northeast. To the left it sloped gently away until, lost from sight in the clear air, it met the cool waters of the Denmark Strait and the Irminger Current to the southwest.

The rod tip began to lift gently as the fly reached the beginning of its swing close to the rock. The line was coiled in my left hand, and I took up the slack there as the tip rose slightly for the backcast. Suddenly the fly stopped moving. Instinctively the wrist snapped back slightly to set the hook. There had been no flash of a strike, and I assumed the fly had hung up on a bit of weed or stick. The fly was imbedded in something solid, but there was no give or movement for a moment. Then suddenly there was the slightest motion away from the rock and toward the center of the river. My heart sped up as I felt the familiar beginning of the power the great salmon possesses.

The fish picked up speed, and the line tore from the reel as the salmon reached the depths of the main current in the midstream and headed upriver. The rod tip was high overhead as the butt end of the fly line left the whirling reel and the fish was 30 yards into the backing before it became annoyed at the pressure and hurled itself into the air. I heard myself shout as the beautiful fish climbed several feet into the air and twisted itself into bows of coiled power several times before falling back to the surface of the current.

It has always been very difficult to explain what it is that makes the fight of a salmon different from that of a trout. A trout is a magnificent fighter—leaping, slashing across the surface at high speed and making fast, strong subsurface runs until it is finally whipped. It then comes to the net, or hand, defeated, after putting up a great battle. An Atlantic salmon does not fight like a trout, in my opinion at least, in this respect: The salmon seems to start from a somewhat lethargic, almost indifferent, take of a fly, as opposed to the vicious, slashing strike of a trout. And from that initial take, when the salmon suddenly realizes it has something annoying stuck in its jaw, its power builds up, like the climbing line on a graph, to a steady peak.

A trout will sometimes rest between leaps and rushes. The salmon I have caught have all had one thing in common—whether they were great jumpers or powerful underwater battlers—and that is that they never seemed to rest or stop fighting the rod during the entire battle. A trout which is released has a reserve of energy left and can make a quick dart for final freedom. When a salmon finally gives up, it is because it is nearly dead, literally. It fights until it has nothing left. Atlantic salmon fishermen will testify to this. If one wishes to release a salmon after catching it, the fish has to be revived first, by moving it slowly back and forth in the water until enough oxygen passes through the gills to allow it to swim upright.

Upstream, the salmon went into its third leap and about half the backing was now gone as I raised the reel at arm's length above my head to give the tiny rod more altitude and to take as much pressure from its arc as possible. The fish apparently chose to utilize the power of the current to its own advantage about then, angling slightly across it and heading for the far bank more than 100 yards upstream. I began cautiously backing out of the stream, slipping and sliding into pockets between the rocks, as I realized this fish would take some following along the bank.

"That's quite a fish," a voice said from behind me, "on that toothpick which you insist on using."

I was too busy to answer Thor. The shortest rod I had seen an Icelander with in the last day must have been a 9-footer. Several British anglers I had seen at the lodge carried 10-foot rods with huge reels. I finally managed to back up onto the grass as the fish, fortunately, took up a head-shaking position behind a large boulder. The shocks bowed the rod tip each time the fish thrashed its head from side to side.

"What woke you?" I grunted, stumbling up the slippery grass bank and trying to hold the rod tip up at the same time.

"Wasn't asleep," said Thor. "Just resting. Never sleep when guiding. Too many bloody amateurs lose fish."

I began to get some line back on the reel as I walked upstream, Thor following me. The salmon made another leap when the headshaking failed to dislodge the hook, then turned and headed down the main current—taking me several hundred yards downstream in a stumbling run that lasted at least twenty minutes. It almost resulted in the fish getting away, too, the leader passing within inches of several sharp rocks. Only a last-second raising of the rod tip as high as I could reach prevented it from parting.

After that it was a few more jumps, fully as strong as the first three, and back upstream to the same spot where it had been hooked. Sometimes a salmon will return to the spot where it was holding when hooked. Perhaps it is seeking familiar surroundings in an attempt to regain some sense of normality in a situation it has never encountered before. Even there, however, it did not come to a complete stop. Also, it began to shake its head again, as violently as before.

"Damn strong fish," said Thor.

My right arm was beginning to feel the strain. With the tiny rod just held in the hand and no butt extension such as used on the bigger rods to shove into a stomach to relieve the strain, the forearm was becoming numb.

As if the fish sensed this, it started up the main current again, acting as though it had just been hooked, and took off another 75 yards of backing in a streaking run.

It was necessary to cup the reel with the palm of the left hand—allowing the reel handle to barely touch the palm as it whirled—slowing it just enough to prevent a highspeed backlash, which would cause the light leader to part instantly.

"It's incredible," I said, as much to take my mind from the aching forearm as to express my disbelief, "that these fish have so much power for their size!"

"Well," Thor said, gazing upstream at the fish boring up the current, "think of it this way. These fish are fresh from the depths of the cold ocean where they have spent three or four years feeding on herring. They have traveled God knows how far to get back to the very same stream in which they were hatched. They are in awfully good shape."

I nodded, thinking of the schools of salmon plunging through the ocean for months seeking to locate, fisheries biologists say by a sense of smell (or taste of the water), a tiny river mouth from which they emerged years ago.

"How far do you think they come, Thor?"

"We really don't know here in Iceland," he said. "The commercial high-seas fishermen have found where the Greenland salmon feed beneath the polar ice cap. Damn near wiped them out, too, before we got them to agree to limit the catch. But nobody knows where the Icelandic salmon winter. I hope they never find out. But I do know salmon go a hell of a way sometimes. One Atlantic salmon was tagged at a lake in Scotland, Lochna Croic it was, and caught in the Eqaluk Fjord in Greenland—more than eighteen hundred miles away!"

I whistled as my own salmon jumped again and swapped ends in midair. Thor laughed with pleasure.

"I love these fish," he said. "I have loved them since I was a small child. I enjoy watching another angler catch one almost as much as I do catching them myself. I will fish for them until I can no longer stand in the river." There was a silence as I tried not to put too much pressure on the fish.

"Perhaps I will even fish for them from a chair," Thor mused, as if to himself, "when I can no longer walk."

"Thor," I asked, "how do you think the fish finds its way back to the same stream?"

"I have talked to many scientists about that," he said. "Our scientists here say that every river, and for that matter every tributary of every river, has a different-tasting water to the salmon. The different taste is caused by dissolved organic matter, such as plants. Even though by the time it gets to the estuary at the sea it is reduced to extremely low concentrations, the fish can pick it up. I read in a scientific journal that a salmon can perceive dilutions of one part in a billion. Can you imagine that!"

My fish turned and started down the current again. But I was able to sense a slight difference in the strength of his pull. The light limber rod was beginning to take its toll.

"I think he is tiring," I said. Thor looked at his watch.

"He should be," he said. "It's been fifty minutes."

As usual I was surprised. It had felt more like fifteen.

The great fish was indeed tired. Four more runs saw it close to me in the shallow water. Thor waded in to tail it with his hand, but when the fish saw his legs it took off on a last, long, desperate run—taking me well into the backing again. But this time, when I slowly worked it in again, I knew it was finally finished. Thor grasped it firmly behind the tail and lifted it gently high in the air as he climbed the bank. The deep, steely blue and silver of the salmon's sides and back glistened in the bright sunlight.

"A beautiful fish, your first Icelandic salmon," he said. "Here, hold it, and I will get the camera. You will want the picture of the first."

I held the inert fish while he snapped the photograph, then we gently removed the hook from its jaw and placed the salmon in the shallows. I watched as Thor, holding it by the base of the tail and maintaining it upright in the water, moved it slowly backward and forward. Gradually its gills began to work slowly.

"It's good they don't die after spawning once," I said.

"Yes, isn't it," Thor said. "Some do, however, but many do not. When I was young I thought they all died, and I used to be sad at the end of each spawning season. But our scientists say that perhaps as much as twenty percent of the females spawn more than once, unlike your Pacific salmon where both males and females die at the first spawn. They say that a number even survive to make as many as four spawning runs. I am always sad at the end of a spawning season," he added, "for many must die each year, but," he smiled, "I am not as sad as when I was a boy. Death must occur that life go on."

He gently released the fish and we watched it slowly swim into the current—sinking gradually as it reached greater depth.

"Well," Thor laughed, shaking my hand with a wet and slippery one, "the first fish is always the best. Come," he said, "we will catch some more."

And during the next four days we caught more. We caught more on the Haffjardhara, below the huge waterfall on the Nordhura, and from the steep rocky pools near the farmhouse on the Grimsa. We caught them on Blue Charms, Hairy Marys, Irish Shrimp, and Black Doctors. We caught several on the Nordhura, on a fly a guide's brother tied, called "the secret weapon."

We caught beautiful fish, and we talked of the salmon, of flies, reels, and fine fly rods, and of the men who used and loved them. And I released all the fish I caught—simply because I like to see them swim away. They were wonderful days, and I intend to go back. But the high point of the trip was when Thor and I walked upstream together after catching my first Icelandic salmon.

"You know," Thor said, an arm across my shoulders as we slogged up the bank toward the car and a waiting lunch, "the English, years ago, taught us how to catch the salmon with the rods. But," he stopped and looked at his river, "you Americans taught us the sport of it."

Tips on Salmon Fishing in Iceland . . .

It's no secret that fishing for Atlantic salmon is at its best in Iceland, in part because of an abundant natural supply and in part as a result of enlightened fishery management. What *is* a secret known only to the fish themselves is the location of their feeding grounds, a happy mystery that has kept them from being subjected to the indiscriminate netting that has so drastically reduced the numbers of salmon on this side of the Atlantic. Iceland's salmon are alive and well and flourishing, and sparse indeed is the imagination of a fisherman who hasn't dreamed of one day taking a crack at them.

If you're thinking about such a trip, remember that the season opens June 15 and closes September 15. What's more, fishing each day during this season is restricted to twelve hours, usually two sessions of six hours each. The first session begins at 7 A.M. and ends at 1 P.M. The next starts at 4 P.M. and ends at 10 P.M. (the days, remember, are long). Fishing times may vary from water to water, but a total of twelve hours is all the time you're going to get.

Influenced by an offshoot of the Gulf Stream, Iceland's climate is relatively mild, particularly along the coast where most Icelanders live. Summer

temperatures will average in the high 50s and low 60s, but even then the weather is quite variable, a change often taking place in what seems like minutes. Regardless of what is indicated on the calendar, be prepared for numbing winds, biting cold, and chilling rain. You can, for example, start off a day's fishing in shirtsleeves or in a light sweater and finish it bundled up like a polar explorer. In addition to sweaters and a windbreaker, bring a down jacket, a rainsuit, and long johns.

Although spin fishing, even bait fishing, is permitted on certain waters, the whole idea of fishing for Atlantic salmon cries out for a fly rod. On most rivers, a fly rod is all you will be allowed to use. And because you will be fishing under varied conditions—even on a given day along a single beat—it's wise to bring along two or more rods, at least one of which should be rigged to enable you to cast into what at times can be fierce winds. It's all personal, of course, but if you've ever wondered where you will need a 9-footer packing as much as a 10-WF line, this is the place.

Reels should be big enough to hold a line and at least 150 yards of backing, and spools should be interchangeable. Figure on bringing along at least three lines of varying weights, both floaters and sinkers in each weight.

Fly patterns are up to you, but you'll find the usual salmon patterns to be effective—Silver Gray, Jock Scott, Silver Doctor, Black Doctor, Blue Charm, etc. Although you'll want a few tied on both larger and smaller hooks, the most popular sizes are 4, 6, and 8.

And don't be chauvinistic when it comes to fly patterns; some of the Icelandic designs can outperform anything you will have in your kit.

Pack at least one pair, preferably two, of felt-soled waders and a wading staff. You can forget the idea of picking up a handy streamside stick; Iceland is virtually treeless.

Note details regarding every fish you catch, even those you release; just about all the fishing lodges at which you'll be staying have log books into which every catch must be recorded, the idea being to provide the Icelandic Institute of Fresh Water Fisheries with vital statistical data.

The fishing lodges are just that—fishing lodges. Many of them are rustic, but all are comfortable and every provision is made to assure you of the experience of a lifetime. Although their purpose—that is, fishing—is serious, their atmosphere is informal, the dress casual/comfortable. Meals are served before you go out and when you come in.

Just about the finest salmon beats in Iceland are along the Laxa Adaldal on the northwestern shore. You can wade, fish from the bank, or, in two pools, from a boat. Only seven fishermen are allowed to work this stretch of the river each day, so any arrangements should be made well in advance. There's a lodge right on the river and the per rod charge for a week comes to about $2,000, which includes transportation from and to the airport at Reykjavik.

Light tackle devotees will find the Grimsa to their liking. The bottom in most spots is unobstructed (by lava outcroppings) gravel, so wading is easy and pleasant. The Grimsa features a new lodge designed by Ernest Schwiebert, a man who has fished a few streams in his day. Here, too, the weekly charge is about $2,000 per rod, including the three-hour trip from and to Reykjavik.

On the north coast of Iceland is the Midfjardara, a river that in the past has given up salmon weighing 20 pounds or more. It's a four-and-one-half-hour drive from Reykjavik (forty-five minutes by air), but worth the trip. The Midfjardara offers visiting fishermen about 80 pools, all of which hold salmon during the run. Again, there is a lodge right on the river, and prices are similar to those quoted above.

Finally, on the west coast, there's the Laxa, about a three-hour drive from Reykjavik. It's a small river, easy to fish, and its salmon average in the 10- to 15-pound range. There is a correspondingly small lodge situated on the river, so get your bid in early if somewhat less rugged fishing is what you want.

All fishing rights on Icelandic rivers are auctioned off annually, so last year's leasee isn't necessarily this year's leasee. To find out what the current situation is, contact Adventures Unlimited or write to Ideal Fishing (Austurstraeti 6, Reykjavik, Iceland); either outfit will make all arrangements or will advise you of your next step.

28.
Key Largo:
The Special World
of the Blue Marlin

We were kite fishing with Captain Allen Self out of North Key Largo aboard the 31-foot *Sea Elf,* and it was a perfect spring day for blue-water fishing—the hot sun pouring down on the dazzling white gunwales and cockpit of the idling, compact sportfisherman.

I had fished with Allen a number of times. I consider him one of the true pioneers in the kite-fishing field. While it is true that Tommy Gifford, Johnnie Harms, and Bob Lewis, among others, did much to promote the sport of kite fishing in America, Allen Self—more than any other skipper I know—sticks to this type of big-game fishing almost exclusively. Allen has refined kite fishing to the point of using helium-filled balloons to keep his kites aloft when the winds die down and the sea becomes calm. He averages 100 billfish a year off his home port.

He was using a balloon today, a large orange one he had filled from his compressed-helium cylinder. He had run out two lines—both 20-pound mono on 9/0 reels, one at 100 feet out and the other fastened to a second clip at 50 feet out. The slight breeze blew from the southeast, and the two lines dropped to the surface of the royal-blue Gulf Stream water as we drifted northward toward Biscayne Bay. The more distant line was baited with a blue runner, hooked lightly through the flesh of the back with a No. 7 hook. The inboard bait was a pilchard, hooked the same way and on the same-size hook. Allen stood by the port gunwale, where he could work his remote controls to the twin engines and also keep a hand on the kite reel, keeping the swimming baits just below the surface.

We had taken a double on dolphin just before noon, Larry and I—one 26 pounds and the other close to 30—lines crossing and fish slicing across the surface behind the boat. We boated both. Then his wife Claudia, a fine fisherman, brought in a 61-pound sail after thirty minutes. When the mate took it by the bill she leaned over the side. "Let it go," she said.

"It's bleeding," the mate said. "It probably wouldn't get far—the sharks . . ." She thought a moment, then nodded. The sail came aboard, glistening in the bright sunlight. We went back to fishing, and had beer and sandwiches.

It was 1:25 in the afternoon when the marlin showed close to the bait.

"Billfish!" was all the captain shouted from above. I reached out and took the rod and fitted the rod handle into the leather belt socket.

"Line down!" the captain shouted. The fish had struck, and the line had been plucked from the clip of the outrigger line. When the fish had had enough time, having taken up the slack, I struck it. Nothing happened. I raised the rod tip higher and began to pump the rod slowly, reeling steadily. There was pressure on the line.

The first leap caught me by surprise. Fortunately I kept the tip on the fiberglass rod high as the fish went up about 10 feet and fell back with a tremendous splash. I backed into the chair and jammed the rod handle into the seat socket as the fish came out again 50 feet or so out from the boat and headed toward shore 10 miles away.

"Yeoowwww!" the mate screamed. "Marlin! Jesus, look at him go!"

The golden reel on the throbbing rod whined as the light line was stripped from it. The fish began a series of straight jumps—none of them high—and headed for the big red buoy about a quarter of a mile off our starboard bow, crashing through the low chop each time it came down.

I don't know how many times the fish jumped. Later they told me perhaps as many as twenty.

I had 600 yards of line, and the fish had run about 400, leaving precious little on the spool. Suddenly the fish came out of the water and fell back to the surface in a shower of white spray. Claudia gasped. "My God," she said, "how beautiful."

"I don't think it's a white," Larry said. "I think it's a blue." Whites this size broke records; among blues my fish would not be unusual.

But the mate said, "I think it's a big white. No blues taken off Largo this season so far."

"I don't know," Larry said. "It sure looked like a blue when it jumped the first time."

I settled down to my business. The line had been pretested at 20 pounds, but it had been on the reel for more than three weeks, during which time it had taken a number of sails and little white marlin. All this meant that the wet breaking test now was probably around 14 pounds. I would have to be very careful not to increase the drag too much. From what I had seen of the fish on its first jump up close, the marlin might weigh 200 pounds. It appeared to be about 8 feet long, and it looked like a blue. I had to be careful on the jumps—not to let the fish have enough slack while in the air to shake out the hook, and not to let it gain too much slack by coming at the boat. I eased back in the chair.

"What kind of a marlin do you think it is, Skipper?" Larry asked.

Allen—nearing sixty years, forty of them in charterboat fishing—shook his head slowly. His weathered forehead creased as he frowned. "I really don't know. It could be a white. I was pretty busy with the boat. It looked more like a small blue to me."

I nodded. "What time is it, Captain?" I asked. "Two-nineteen," he said.

That had been a fast half-hour. I slowly took the cork grip in my right hand, and let go with my left hand for the first time. I flexed the fingers of my left hand. I had trouble straightening them out.

"Damn!" the mate said. He was about twenty-five, with blond hair bleached white from the Florida sun. "If this really is a white it will be something."

The captain grunted. "Better boat it first," he said.

Twenty minutes passed; I raised the rod tip and began reeling slightly faster.

"He's coming in," I said. "He couldn't be tired yet." I glanced at the captain.

The fish came up rapidly behind the stern—not too deep—and I took up the line until I could feel the slight vibration of the current. The fish was just back of the stern on the starboard side. I had seen marlin quit after thirty minutes for no apparent reason. Maybe he was hooked in the throat and the bleeding had tired him.

The mate reached out slowly. He grasped the leader and led the fish closer to the boat. He looked down into the prismatic sea and slowly waved his free left hand behind him.

"A little forward, Skipper," he shouted. "Keep him away from the screws." I felt the boat surge forward a little as the captain added power. The line began to slip slowly through the gloved fingers and suddenly the mate let go and nodded at me.

"Take him again," he said. "It's a blue." I kept the tip up, and suddenly the marlin began another series of jumps, thrashing its head and bill as it churned across the choppy surface. The reel shrieked as the line stripped off. "I think he just came in to look at us."

"The fish is foul-hooked," the mate said, his tone sympathetic. "I guess when it took a swipe at the bait the hook caught in the leading edge of the dorsal fin. That's a solid hooking spot. I could see it real clear in the water. So you're not hurting him with a hook in the mouth or throat, not at all."

I reeled slowly, not gaining on the diving fish. It might not even feel the steady pressure of the rod and the resistance of the line. The marlin was slowly pumping downward.

"It's a fine fish," Claudia said.

Larry said nothing.

I swung the chair around and looked at the captain. "What about a flying gaff?"

"Don't have one aboard," he said.

There was no reason he should. Most of the whites taken off the Keys were in the 50- to 70-pound class. An ordinary gaff would do on them.

"Any boat close by carry one?"

The captain nodded. "The *Semper Fi* has one. She's a few miles off. Let's raise her and see if they won't come by and drop one off."

The mate climbed the ladder to the bridge and headed for the radio. I went back to concentrating on the fish. By the time I got it close—or the time after that—they might have a flying gaff ready. The hook and line of a flying gaff disengage from the pole after the barb is set. With it the mate can handle the fish with greater control and land it sooner.

The marlin was still going down.

This was no classic *Old Man and the Sea* battle. I was not miles at sea in a dory, nor was I using a hand line. I was just a man who loved to fish, and who was getting a lot of it.

After a while the mate climbed back down the ladder. He moved up to the captain.

"The radio cuts in and out," he said. "Can't carry on a conversation."

"Check the battery-terminal connection?"

The mate removed the engine hatch and climbed down. He climbed out a moment later.

"Seems O.K."

"Damn," the captain said. "What a time for it to act up. Must be a tube."

The mate nodded and moved over to the gunwale and sat down. I shifted my right hand to the rod again and looked at Larry leaning against the ladder.

"Anything against drinking a beer?"

He smiled and opened the ice chest. He popped the top of the can and placed it close to me on the gunwale.

"Looks like I'm going to spoil your afternoon's fishing," I said.

"Maybe it will be worth it," he said quietly, keeping my beer can from sliding as the boat rolled with a swell.

There was nothing to do now except apply enough pressure to make it as difficult as possible for the marlin to dive and yet not break the line. I shifted in the seat and then stood up. "I'm tired of the chair." I stuck the rod handle into the leather belt socket and braced myself against the transom. "I'm going to try to work him up," I said. Allen nodded.

Claudia had gone up forward and was sitting in a chair in the cabin. She had picked up a magazine. Larry had lowered himself into a folding chair, with a beer, and was staring out at the faint outline of the Keys on the horizon to the west. It was 3:55. The wind was clean and sweet over the Gulf Stream. There was the steady pressure of the marlin, fathoms below, pumping for the bottom—fighting something it did not understand. There was the tilting horizon, the slow passage of a freighter, hull down, with a plume of smoke blowing back from one stack. There was the warmth of the sun on my back, shoulders, and the back of my thighs. My arm muscles had long ceased to ache.

My attention would be preoccupied for minutes by a bit of seaweed drifting, the yellow of the weed against the blue depths. There was a man-o'-war bird overhead, circling. Gradually everything was reduced to the basics: There was the fish on one side, I on the other, and the great, clean sea lay between. I was faced with the utter simplicity of a fish I could not control.

At 4:38 I brought the fish alongside. The mate grasped the leader, could not maneuver the weight, and had to let go. The fish jumped three times and sounded.

At 5:20 I brought the fish alongside again—under the stern at the starboard side. The mate again grasped the leader, brought the fish up to within two feet of the surface, and then, feeling it turn its side toward the current, let go of the leader again.

About 6:00 P.M. the captain, after a long discussion with me, advised that I might increase the drag some—not enough to break the line but perhaps enough to make a slight difference in tiring the fish.

I advanced the drag and was able to bring the fish alongside twice more in the next half-hour, but always on the starboard stern—the wrong angle for the mate to try to grasp the bill and allow me to turn it over to him. Each time the fish was able to move away.

It was between 6:00 and 6:30, I believe, when the captain stood beside me watching the line slanting back 200 yards to where the marlin had just wallowed on the surface for a few moments—appearing as fresh as five hours earlier. He coughed and looked at me carefully. "You say what you want. It's a good fish. I'll stay as long as you want."

The sun was low on the horizon, and the seas were up a little. The wind had freshened and, with no shirt on, I was feeling the chill. I looked at him and then went back to the fish.

"I'll stay," I said.

"Good," he said gruffly, and went back to his throttles. The sun dropped. Then the full moon came up out of the sea. There were times when I thought the fish was weakening and brought it close to the boat, only to have it move out and down again. I really believe it was weakening—thinking back on it now—but it was difficult to tell at the time.

By 7:30 the darkness had begun to set in, and the mate brought out a flashlight. He held it so that I could see the line and could judge the direction of the fish.

The sandwiches were gone, the beer had been disposed of hours before, the wind was whipping, and the seas were higher. The captain estimated that we had drifted more than 20 miles north of North Key Largo on the Gulf Stream. The climbing moon made a silver path on the irregular surface of the sea behind the boat, and occasionally the marlin would surface and break the silver band with a black, jagged tear of energy.

It was probably about 7:45 when I sensed the fish was defeated. Closer and closer it came and this time I began to believe that I was going to be able to bring it along the port side at the stern, giving the mate a good chance to grasp the bill.

Larry moved up close to me as I began to talk to the mate. He had another flashlight and played it on the black water. The line came in slowly, until I suddenly saw the brass swivel again. The mate leaned over the side, grasped the leader, and nodded his head when Larry switched the light over to the other side of the stern.

"My God," he said. "Look at the size of that shark!"

We saw the huge, tan-colored fish as it passed below the stern, and suddenly there was a sharp jolt on the line and it went slack.

The mate flipped the leader into the boat and ran the line up through his glove. The stainless-steel hook lay in the palm of his hand. On the tip of the hook was a chunk of white flesh with a fleck of gray skin.

"What happened?" Larry asked.

"I don't know," I said numbly. "There was a jolt and then the hook came free."

"The shark took him," the mate said, shaking his head and fingering the bright hook. He took off the small piece of meat and flipped it over the side.

The four of us stood looking at the black water boiling beneath the stern.

I glanced at the captain's watch close to my right hand. It was 8:05 P.M. I shoved the rod in the holder of the gunwale and rubbed my mouth with the back of one hand.

"I wish it hadn't been a shark," I said. "That was too good a fish."

Nobody said anything. Claudia was standing a few feet behind us.

"Well," Allen said, "we had better get started back. It's going to be a rough ride over the reef." I nodded and moved toward the cabin to get a sweatshirt.

"It was a . . ." Allen paused. "It was a damn good fight."

The mate nodded. "The hook just finally pulled out," he said. "Maybe the shark didn't even touch him. He couldn't have been bleeding, hooked in the dorsal the way he was."

The captain smiled and nodded. He began to climb the ladder to the bridge. The mate followed him, and I felt the engines speed up as we began the long run for the marina.

Larry dug out a bottle of scotch he kept in a camera case, handed Claudia and me glasses and took one himself, and we all settled in chairs as the cruiser slammed into the seas on its way in.

We seemed to be running up a long runway of silver, the ribbon of moonlight stretched behind us to the horizon.

Claudia was silent, lost in thought. Larry, balancing his glass in the lurching cabin, stared at the silver sea behind us.

And in my mind, I could see the marlin, miles away, swimming slowly, tiredly toward the depths of the Gulf Stream.

[For further information, see Tips at the end of Chapter 9.]

Epilogue

My three sons and I were crouched low in the pit blind on Barnegat Bay as the day began to wane. The cold wind bobbed the several dozen assorted decoys which were spread on the gray and ruffled surface of the water in front of us.

I shifted my position a bit and tried to get some feeling into my numbed feet by rapidly clenching and unclenching my aching toes inside the rubber feet of the chest waders. We were standing in about 2 inches of slush—water we had not been able to pump out of the wooden blind and additional ice and snow that kept crumbling from the ice cakes we were using to camouflage the jumbled black rocks that protected the blind from the waves.

"Dad," whispered my oldest son John, "a big flock. Way out. Two o'clock." At eye level with the rocks, the houses and cottages half-a-dozen miles away, located at the edge of the ocean, resembled a child's drawings done in black ink on dark-gray paper. Just above a drawbridge, opening to let a commercial clam boat pass through, the strung-out, ragged line of broadbills angled toward us.

"I see them. Keep down now. Don't make any sudden moves."

My worn side-by-side rested against the blind as I cupped my hands to try calling them in.

"Wow!" breathed Jimmie, my twelve-year-old, as he slowly slid the muzzle of his new .20-gauge automatic over the edge of the blind. "There must be fifty of them!"

"Easy, Jimbo."

It was easy to remember the agonizing, breathless feeling at his age when waterfowl began to come in toward decoys. The boy nodded and kept his head down.

Chuuuhhh, chhuuuhhh, chhuuhh. The sound floated from between gloved hands and rode the steady wind across the white chop of the bay and over the brown marsh grass and black mud flats. The flock was angling slightly northwest and would pass a quarter of a mile or so to our left—unless they sighted the decoys soon.

Chhuuhhh, chuuhhh, chuuhhhh. More effort went into the explosive burst of air needed to produce the sure call that would catch the attention of scaup. Two ducks on our side of the streaking flock slowly began to peel off and swing more toward the west and toward us.

"They're starting to turn," Donald whispered hoarsely from where he was stationed between his older and younger brothers. He was flicking the safety on and off his .12-gauge automatic.

"Don!" He glanced quickly at me. "The safety."

He flushed slightly and, leaning forward tensely, dropped his hand to his lap. Of the three, he is the most intense about hunting, the most liable to shoot when the birds are just a little too far out or too high.

At age fourteen, Don realizes an almost unbearable ache while waiting to fire. And that sensation won't necessarily dim with the years. It's similar to the way you feel walking up behind a pointing bird dog, watching Canada geese suddenly swinging in toward a set of decoys in a cornfield, or catching the first glimpse of that dorsal fin or the sickle tail of a blue marlin surfacing behind a trolled outrigger bait. Time tempers our physical reactions, not our inner excitement.

"They're all starting to turn!" John said.

John always shoots at the left side of blinds because he's a left-handed shooter. Also, the spent shells from his left-handed .12-gauge automatic are ejected to his left, not in Donald's direction. At sixteen John, having been raised shooting trap and skeet as well as wild birds, has a smooth, effortless swing on waterfowl.

The lead ducks had definitely spotted the decoys now and commenced their descent into the wind while the rest of the flock banked and flared a little to get into position for landing. There was no need to call again. The sound might do more harm than good at this point. I slid the old .12-gauge double over until the tip of the barrels rested just below the ledge. The worn, almost silver color of the barrels reflected the late-afternoon sunlight as did the grained walnut stock.

"Man!" Don breathed. "Here they come, here they come."

"Easy now, let some of them get their legs down and wings set. Then we can take them."

The sound of my heart pounding seemed to echo in the blind. I could imagine what the boys' hearts were doing. Two bluebills suddenly flared up and off to our left, but the rest of the flock was committed, dropping rapidly now to the surface. My numbed feet came together under the seat as I raised the double and shouted, "Take 'em!"

I held off a few seconds, hoping to give the two younger boys a chance at the closer ducks. The blast of Donald's gun preceded that of Jimmie's by a fraction of a second, and one big scaup folded a foot above the water and sent spray several yards in the air. A big, climbing drake broadbill to my right suddenly fell to the modified-barrel load of the old double.

Donald's triumphant yell rang out as another duck, almost directly above us and about 30 yards up, spun out of the climbing flock.

"I got him, I got him!" Jimmie shouted. "I got him!" he yelled again with sheer joy.

A straggler whipped in from the right, and I tried to get on it by coming up from behind and swinging through and ahead of the bird, but after I fired the full-choked barrel it was obvious that I didn't get quite far enough ahead. It didn't matter much though, because an instant afterward, the scaup pinwheeled out of the sky as John nailed it cleanly.

"I got him!" Jim yelled again, pointing to the water where a big bluebill flapped its wings—its head under water. Laughing, I opened the double to reload.

"Heard you the first, second, and third times. How many times did you shoot?"

The boy looked at me, his eyes still wide and astonished at his shot. "Times?" he asked.

"Times. You have three shells in that Christmas present of yours, Jimbo. How many ducks did you get?"

"Darn!" he looked flustered. "When he came down, I was so surprised I forgot to shoot again."

Jim, like the other two boys, had been taught to shoot with a single-barrel .410 shotgun that had to be cocked with a hammer. He had owned the new .20-gauge automatic only four days, and he hadn't gotten used to the reserve shells. I had started the boys with the .410 for a couple of reasons: I wanted to be able to see whether they had the safety on or off at all times; and, perhaps even more important, I wanted them to learn the value of making that first shot count. It is too easy for a youngster just beginning to hunt to count on those two other shells in an automatic or that extra one in a double-barreled gun.

This was the first season that none of the boys was shooting the old, battered, hammer .410. John had suggested we have it bronzed and retired to the wall of the den. It has a 30-inch barrel, full-choked and capable of firing 3-inch shells. The stock is short enough for a ten-year-old to fire without too much trouble, and yet an adult can swing it with ease—in spite of the short stock. There is almost no drop to the stock, which is one of the reasons that all three boys have no trouble getting their cheek down easily on their own shotguns. All their shotguns were ordered with about the same straight stock as the old gun.

"I'll get the ducks," John said, climbing out of the blind. We had not needed a dog at all. The wind had been blowing out of the north at a steady twelve to fifteen miles per hour since before dawn, so every duck knocked down had blown ashore close to us.

"I'll help," said Don. "Besides, my feet are freezing." He jumped out of the blind and lurched across the rough rocks toward a scaup that was bobbing just a foot or so offshore to our right. Jim dug a hand warmer out of his jacket pocket and rubbed it against his cheek. His cheeks were rosy from the cold—the steady wind having added a chill factor to the mid-40s of the flats.

"How much time do we have left, Dad?" the boy asked.

"About forty-five minutes until official sundown," I grunted and looked eastward.

"Darn!" he said. "Duck hunting days sure go fast."

Duck hunting days go fast, young man. The hours on the marshes will always be too few. And if you think time on the marshes goes fast now, Boy, wait until you watch your sons grow from awkward children trying to hold up a .410 too heavy for them to sons entering the last years of high school who won't be accompanying you to the marshes and the woodcock coverts in a few more years.

"They sure do, Jimmie. But we have next weekend, don't forget that."

"Yeah," he grinned and stood up. "Com'on!" he shouted to his brothers. "You're scaring away all the ducks."

Both the boys were back in the pit blind a few minutes later with several broadbills in each hand. They stashed them away on the shelf in front of us. The birds would hang against the north wall of the house for the next four or five days and then the boys would clean them. They would be soaked in a marinade for two days, then a few would be eaten. We would put the others, packed in paper milk cartons filled with water, in the freezer, until we were ready to eat them with a special recipe we use for broadbills: wild rice, oranges, cognac, ginger, and dry mustard. A lot of water-fowlers don't think scaup make good eating, but we know better. Years ago, when we first began to hunt the New Jersey marshes, a number of city-bred hunters told us brant were not good to eat. We found out from Cape May waterfowlers that if we got the birds before they fed too heavily on the sea lettuce, the breasts would make some of the best waterfowl meals we'd ever tasted.

The wind was picking up, and the spray from the chop of the bay was beginning to come over the edge of the rocks in front of us. The salt tasted fine on the lips, and the smell of the huge marsh was clean and invigorating.

"Little ducks!" said Don. "Three o'clock."

It was a pair of buffleheads, skimming across the water and heading right for the decoys. Though not the smartest waterfowl in the world, they are nevertheless fast and a difficult target.

"Easy," I said. "They will probably land quite a way out and then swim in."

They came in a lot farther than expected and landed just on the fringe of the decoy set—about 50 yards out.

"I'll see if I can't talk them in," John said, digging out the duck call and starting a series of feeding calls. The pair of small ducks immediately began swimming toward the blind.

"When they get in range," I said, "let's let Jimbo try the first shot. Maybe he can remember how many shells he has. As soon as he fires, you guys take a crack at them. They will probably flare right or left to get into the wind."

John kept up a constant burbling, chittering, and gurgling on the call.

"I'm starving," Jim said.

"Me too," said Don, ejecting the shells from his gun to the floor of the blind. The other two boys did the same thing. I broke open the old double and pocketed the shells.

"Grab the ducks, and we might as well start walking across the marsh," I said.

"I'm going to run," Jim said, "to get my feet warm. Com'on, Don," he said. "I'll race you."

"Easy, boys," I said, "Don't trip carrying those guns.

"Carry them empty and with the action open," I said. "Hold a shell in your right hand, but don't leave it in the chamber."

They both nodded and trotted off toward the east where the weatherbeaten shack stood—barely visible against the horizon.

The exercise felt good as my frigid feet began to stop aching.

"Marsh hawk," John said, pointing to a low-flying brown hawk with a white-rump patch that quartered across the tops of the marsh grass.

"Heading south," I said. "Not much for it to eat this time of the year—an occasional rat, mouse, or muskrat." John nodded. We walked in silence for awhile.

"This was a good day, Dad," John said. "Hope the weather gets bad tomorrow. It will be even better." I nodded. The only noises were the sighing of the wind in the marsh grass and the sloshing of our boots.

"Jimbo's going to be a good shot," John said. "Did you see the way he got off that second shot at that bufflehead?"

I laughed, remembering the shot.

"I've been thinking about something," John said. "You know that old four-ten I said we should have bronzed and put on the den wall?"

"Yup."

"I have a better idea. Why don't we get a metal plate—brass or something—and put everybody's name on it?"

"Saying what?"

"Well," the boy said, "not really saying anything. Just like maybe the dates I started shooting it and the date I got my own shotgun. The same with Don and Jim."

I looked at the darkening horizon and breathed deeply of the rich, earthy marsh air.

"Good idea," I said. "I'll go you one better."

"What?"

"Why don't you guys make it a big plate and keep it going. The oldest kids of the family each learn how to shoot it and pass it along to the next oldest—girls or boys."

John walked for a moment and then shifted his automatic to the crook of his arm.

"That's cool," he finally said. "It could last forever that way."

I moved the old double to a shoulder and looked ahead to where the other two boys were halfway to the gray-shingled duck shack.

"Maybe not forever, Johnnie," I said. "But as long as people love this kind of life."

"That ought to be a long time," he said.

"Let's hope so, Son," I said, as the salt-marsh wind whipped my parka. "Let's hope so."

Appendices

A. General Tips

Traveling with Firearms

It is, as any newspaper will tell you, becoming increasingly more complicated to transport firearms. Hijackings, explosive political situations, fanatics, and just plain crackpots have subjected the sportsman traveling with his own guns and ammunition to closer and closer scrutiny.

Therefore, it is best to transport a rifle or a shotgun in specially-designed, rigid, foam-lined cases. A good one will cost anywhere from $50 to $100, but will be worth every penny in terms of safety, damage prevention, and the avoidance of suspicious glances, even—sad to say—uncalled for insults.

Remember that your firearm will—in all likelihood—be piled in with a lot of other luggage, particularly on an airplane. Some of it will be heavy enough to damage a rifle or its scope, or a delicate shotgun, unless you pack it in an impact-resistant case. Lock the case, but don't seal it; chances are it will be subject to inspection, if only to make certain it is not loaded.

A good idea, and one that will be appreciated by the carrier, is packing the bolt of your rifle separately, preferably with your personal luggage. That way, there will be no question whether or not your firearm is "safe" for transport.

Carry ammunition in its original boxes. There are laws against carrying loose ammunition—laws specifying that ammunition must be in boxes with dividers between each round, or in a box within a box. In other countries, regulations regarding the transport both of ammunition and firearms vary widely, so if you're traveling outside the United States, be sure you check beforehand.

Once you arrive at your destination, unpack and check your firearm as soon as possible, and report any damage to the carrier immediately. Keep in mind that guns are insured by the carrier the same as other baggage, with a liability limit of about $500 in the United States, about $9 a pound in international travel. If your gun is worth more than that to you, buy additional insurance before you depart. While in transit carry a record of the gun's manufacturer, model designation, caliber, serial number, and other pertinent and/or distinguishing characteristics. Also, make certain your name and address appear prominently on the outside of the case in which your gun is packed.

. . . a *clear* plastic bag. Rain and spray (particularly saltwater spray) can ruin a camera and its film. You can protect both with a plastic bag. Cut a hole in the bag big enough to accommodate your lens and secure the bag with a rubber band, making certain you don't foul the shutter-snapping or film-wind mechanisms.

Anticipation is the key to good action photography. Determine approximately where and roughly how the action will take place, and plan accordingly: get in position, set your focus and exposure, compose the picture in your mind, and snap away when the action takes place.

If you are taking photos of animals, focus on their eyes. If the eyes are in focus, the picture will work, even if, say, the hindquarters are a little fuzzy. Also, as a rule of thumb, if an animal you are photographing in bright daylight suddenly darts into shade, open your lens two stops.

Finally, unless you are superbly equipped with a variety of cameras and lenses, accept the fact that satisfactory pictures of leaping fish have to be taken close-up.

B. Fish and Game Departments of the United States and Canada

When writing for information, address queries to Director, Information and Education.

UNITED STATES

Alabama Department of Conservation and
   Natural Resources
64 North Union Street
Montgomery 36104 (205–269–7221)

Alaska Department of Fish and Game
Subport Building
Juneau 99801 (907–586–3392)

Arizona Game and Fish Department
2222 West Greenway Road
Phoenix 85023 (602–942–3000)

Arkansas Game and Fish Commission
Game and Fish Building
Little Rock 72201 (501–371–1145)

California Department of Fish and Game
The Resources Agency
1416 9th Street
Sacramento 95814 (916–445–3531)

Colorado Department of Natural Resources
Division of Wildlife
6060 Broadway
Denver 80216 (303–825–1192)

Connecticut Department of Environmental
   Protection
State Office Building
Hartford 06115 (203–566–5460)

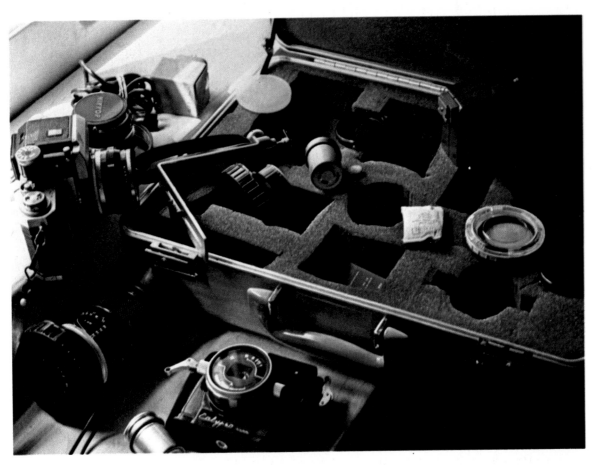

Suggested method of carrying camera gear in lightweight and waterproof cases

Fly rod, reel, and streamer flies

Mississippi Game and Fish Commission
Robert E. Lee Office Building
239 North Lamar Street
P.O. Box 451
Jackson 39205 (601–354–7333)

Missouri Department of Conservation
P.O. Box 180
Jefferson City 65101 (314–751–4115)

Montana Fish and Game Department
Helena 59601 (406–449–3186)

Nebraska Game and Parks Commission
P.O. Box 30370
2200 North 33rd
Lincoln 68503 (402–434–0641)

Nevada Department of Fish and Game
Box 10678
Reno 89510 (702–784–6214)

New Hampshire Fish and Game Department
34 Bridge Street
Concord 03301 (603–271–3421)

New Jersey Department of Environmental
　Protection
Division of Fish, Game, and Shellfisheries
Box 1390
Trenton 08625 (609–292–2965)

New Mexico Department of Game and Fish
State Capitol
Santa Fe 87501 (505–827–2143)

New York Department of Environmental
　Conservation
Fish and Wildlife Division
50 Wolf Road
Albany 12201 (518–457–5690)

North Carolina Wildlife Resources Commission
325 North Salisbury Street
Raleigh 27611 (919–829–3391)

North Dakota State Game and Fish Department
2121 Lovett Avenue
Bismarck 58501 (701–224–2180)

Ohio Department of Natural Resources
Division of Wildlife
Fountain Square
Columbus 43224 (614–466–4603)

Oklahoma Department of Wildlife Conservation
1801 North Lincoln
P.O. Box 53465
Oklahoma City 73105 (405–521–3851)

Oregon Fish Commission
307 State Office Building
Portland 97201 (503–229–5671)

Oregon State Wildlife Commission
Box 3503
Portland 97208 (503–229–5551)

Pennsylvania Fish Commission
P.O. Box 1673
Harrisburg 17120 (717–787–6593)

Pennsylvania Game Commission
P.O. Box 1567
Harrisburg 17120 (717–787–3633)

Puerto Rico Department of Natural Resources
P.O. Box 11488
San Juan 00910

Rhode Island Department of Natural Resources
Division of Fish and Wildlife
83 Park Street
Providence 02903 (401–277–2784)

South Carolina Wildlife Resources Department
Box 167
1015 Main Street
Columbia 29202 (803–758–2561)

South Dakota Department of Game, Fish and
   Parks
State Office Building
Pierre 57501 (605–224–3381)

Tennessee Wildlife Resources Agency
Box 40747
Ellington Agricultural Center
Nashville 37220 (615–741–1431)

Texas Parks and Wildlife Department
John H. Reagan Building
Austin 78701 (512–475–2087)

Utah State Department of Natural Resources
Division of Wildlife Resources
1596 W.N. Temple
Salt Lake City 84116 (801–328–5081)

Vermont Agency of Environmental Conservation
Fish and Game Department
Montpelier 05602 (802–828–3371)

Virginia Commission of Game and Inland
   Fisheries
4010 West Broad Street
Box 11104
Richmond 23230 (804–770–4974)

Washington Department of Fisheries
115 General Administration Building
Olympia 98504 (206–753–6623)

Washington Department of Game
600 North Capitol Way
Olympia 98504 (206–753–5700)

West Virginia Department of Natural Resources
1800 Washington Street
East Charleston 25305 (304–348–2754)

Wisconsin Department of Natural Resources
Box 450
Madison 53701 (608–266–2243)

Wyoming Game and Fish Department
Box 1589
Cheyenne 82001 (307–777–7631)

CANADA

Alberta Department of Lands and Forests
Natural Resources Building
Edmonton T5K 2E1 (403–229–4461)

British Columbia Department of Recreation and
   Conservation
Fish and Wildlife Branch
Parliament Buildings
Victoria (604–387–6409)

Manitoba Department of Mines
Resources and Environmental Management
Box 18
139 Tuxedo Boulevard
Winnipeg R3M 0H6 (204–786–7931)

New Brunswick Department of Natural
   Resources
Fish and Wildlife Branch
Fredericton (506–453–2433)

Newfoundland Department of Tourism
Wildlife Division
Confederation Building
St. John's (709–722–0711, Ext. 327)

Nova Scotia Department of Lands and Forests
Wildlife Division
Box 516
Kentville (902–678–4198)

Ontario Ministry of Natural Resources
Division of Fish and Wildlife
Parliament Building
Toronto M7A 1W3 (416–965–4704)

Prince Edward Island Environmental Control
    Commission
P.O. Box 2000
Charlottetown (902–892–3561, Ext. 34)

Quebec Department of Tourism, Fish and Game
Parliament Buildings
Complex "G"
Quebec City (418–643–8452)

Saskatchewan Department of Tourism and
    Renewable Resources
Government Administration Building
Regina S4S 0B1 (306–522–1691)

Yellowknife Department of Industry &
    Development
Yellowknife, N.W.T. (403–873–7411)

Yukon Game Department
Box 2703
Whitehorse, Yukon Territory (403–667–5228)

C. Foreign Hunting and Fishing Information*

Country	In the United States	Abroad
Austria	Austrian National Tourist Office 545 Fifth Avenue New York, New York 10017	Isterreichische Fischereigesellschaft A-1010 Wien 1, Elisabethstrasse 22
Bahamas	Adventures Unlimited also, Bahama Tourist Office 30 Rockefeller Plaza New York, New York 10020	see "Tips on Going for Bonefish or Barracuda in the Bahamas," page 122.
Belgium	Belgian National Tourist Office 750 Fifth Avenue New York, New York 10019	Confederation des Pecheurs a la Linge Place Jean Jacob, 1, 1000 Brussels
Botswana	Adventures Unlimited	Hunter's Africa P. O. Box 11, Kasane

*Information about many countries is available from Adventures Unlimited, Abercrombie & Fitch, 19 East 45th Street, New York, New York 10017; telephone 212–682–3600.

Bulgaria	Bulgarian Tourist Office 50 East 42nd Street New York, New York 10017	Balkantourist 1 Lenin Square Sofia Att: Overseas Dept.
Canada (For salmon)	Adventures Unlimited Mr. Bill Littleford Nemacolin Inn Farmington, Pennsylvania 15473	Quebec Ministry of Tourism Fish and Game 12 St. Anne's Street Quebec
Czechoslovakia	"Cedok" Czechoslovak Travel Bureau 10 East 40th Street New York, New York 10017	Cedok, Dept. of Fishing, Panska 5, 11135, Prague
Denmark	Danish National Tourist Office 505 Fifth Avenue New York, New York 10017	Fiskeriinspektoren, Borgergade 16, 1300 Copenhagen K Denmark's Sports Fishing Assoc.—Denmark Sportsfiskerforbunds Sekretariat, Sydkajen P.O. Box 194, Vejle
East Africa	Adventures Unlimited	Ker, Downey & Selby Safaris Ltd. P.O. Box 41822 Nairobi, Kenya
England	British Tourist Authority 680 Fifth Avenue New York, New York 10019	British Tourist Authority 64 St. James' Street London SW1A 1NF
Ecuador	Adventure Associates 150 S.E. Second Avenue Miami, Florida 33131	Hotel Punta Carnero P.O. Box 5589 Guayaquil
Finland	Finnish National Tourist Office 505 Fifth Avenue New York, New York 10017	Finnish Tourist Board, Kluuvikatu 10, Helsinki 10 Real Estate Office of the National Board of Forestry Uudenmaankatu 4-6. F, SF-00120, Helsinki 12

France	French Government Tourist Office 610 Fifth Avenue New York, New York 10020	Provincial Tourist Information/ or town halls ("mairie")
Germany	German National Tourist Office 630 Fifth Avenue New York, New York 10020	Verband Deutscher Sportfischer, D. 605 Offenbach, Waldstrasse 6
Iceland	Icelandic Airlines Tourist Information 610 Fifth Avenue New York, New York 10020	Icelandic Airlines Vesturgata 2 Rekjavik 20200 Ideal Fishing Austurstraeti 6 Reykjavik
Ireland	Irish Tourist Board 590 Fifth Avenue New York, New York 10036	Irish Tourist Board Angling Information Service Baggot Street Bridge Dublin 2
Italy	Italian Advisory Tourist Office Scandinavia House 505 Fifth Avenue New York, New York 10017	Federazione Italiana della Pesca Sportiva, Viale Tiziano 70 Rome
Japan	Japan National Tourist Organization 45 Rockefeller Plaza New York, New York 10020	Japan National Tourist Organization Head Office 2-13, Yurakcho Tokyo
Mexico	Adventures Unlimited Mexican Government Ministry of Tourism 630 Fifth Avenue New York, New York 10020 Wide World Sportsman Inc. P.O. Box 787 Islamorada, Florida 33036	

Netherlands	Netherlands National Tourist Office 505 Fifth Avenue New York, New York 10017	General Angler's Association Weyeringschaus 106 Amsterdam
New Zealand	Adventures Unlimited New Zealand Government Travel Commission 630 Fifth Avenue New York, New York 10020	
Norway	Norwegian National Tourist Office 505 Fifth Avenue New York, New York 10017	Norway Travel Association H Heyerdahlsgathe 1 Oslo, 1 Norway
Poland	"Orbis" Polish Travel Office Information Bureau 500 Fifth Avenue New York, New York 10036	"Orbis" Polish Travel Office Warszawa, U1, Bracka 16
Rhodesia	Adventures Unlimited	Rhodesian Safaris, Ltd. P.O. Box 191 Salisbury
Rumania	"Carpati" Rumanian National Tourist Office 500 Fifth Avenue, Room 328 New York, New York 10036	"Carpati" National Tourist Office Bucuresti Hunting Dept. 7, Maghern
Scotland	Adventures Unlimited British Tourist Board 680 Fifth Avenue New York, New York 10019	Scottish Tourist Board 2 Rutland Place Edinburgh EH12YU Arthur Oglesby European Editor *Field & Stream* 9 Oatlands Drive Harrogate, England